P9-DJV-843

THE NEW FOLGER LIBRARY SHAKESPEARE

Designed to make Shakespeare's great plays available to all readers, the New Folger Library edition of Shakespeare's plays provides accurate texts in modern spelling and punctuation, as well as scene-by-scene action summaries, full explanatory notes, many pictures clarifying Shakespeare's language, and notes recording all significant departures from the early printed versions. Each play is prefaced by a brief introduction, by a guide to reading Shakespeare's language, and by accounts of his life and theater. Each play is followed by an annotated list of further readings and by a "Modern Perspective" written by an expert on that particular play.

Barbara A. Mowat is Director of Research *emerita* at the Folger Shakespeare Library, Consulting Editor of *Shakespeare Quarterly*, and author of *The Dramaturgy of Shakespeare's Romances* and of essays on Shakespeare's plays and their editing.

Paul Werstine is Professor of English in the Graduate School and at King's University College at Western University. He is a general editor of the New Variorum Shakespeare and author of *Early Modern Playhouse Manuscripts and the Editing of Shakespeare,* as well as many papers and essays on the printing and editing of Shakespeare's plays.

The Folger Shakespeare Library

The Folger Shakespeare Library in Washington, D.C., a privately funded research library dedicated to Shakespeare and the civilization of early modern Europe, was founded in 1932 by Henry Clay and Emily Jordan Folger. In addition to its role as the world's preeminent Shakespeare collection and its emergence as a leading center for Renaissance studies, the Folger Library offers a wide array of cultural and educational programs and services for the general public.

EDITORS

BARBARA A. MOWAT
Director of Academic Programs
Folger Shakespeare Library

PAUL WERSTINE
Professor of English
King's University College at the University of Western Ontario, Canada

FOLGER SHAKESPEARE LIBRARY

The Tragedy of

Othello

The Moor of Venice

By

WILLIAM SHAKESPEARE

EDITED BY BARBARA A. MOWAT
AND PAUL WERSTINE

Simon & Schuster Paperbacks
NEW YORK   LONDON   TORONTO   SYDNEY

Simon & Schuster Paperbacks
A Division of Simon & Schuster, Inc.
1230 Avenue of the Americas
New York, NY 10020

Copyright © 1993 by The Folger Shakespeare Library

All rights reserved, including the right to reproduce this book or portions thereof in any form whatsoever. For information address Simon & Schuster Paperbacks Subsidiary Rights Department, 1230 Avenue of the Americas, New York, NY 10020.

First Washington Square Press New Folger Library Trade Paperback Edition November 1999
This Simon & Schuster paperback edition January 2009

SIMON & SCHUSTER PAPERBACKS and colophon are registered trademarks of Simon & Schuster, Inc.

For information regarding special discounts for bulk purchases, please contact Simon & Schuster Special Sales at 1-800-456-6798 or business@simonandschuster.com.

The Simon & Schuster Speakers Bureau can bring authors to your live event. For more information or to book an event, contact the Simon & Schuster Speakers Bureau at 866-248-3049 or visit our website at www.simonspeakers.com.

Manufactured in the United States of America

20

ISBN-13: 978-0-7434-8282-0
ISBN-10:   0-7434-8282-4

From the Director of the Folger Shakespeare Library

It is hard to imagine a world without Shakespeare. Since their composition four hundred years ago, Shakespeare's plays and poems have traveled the globe, inviting those who see and read his works to make them their own.

Readers of the New Folger Editions are part of this ongoing process of "taking up Shakespeare," finding our own thoughts and feelings in language that strikes us as old or unusual and, for that very reason, new. We still struggle to keep up with a writer who could think a mile a minute, whose words paint pictures that shift like clouds. These expertly edited texts, presented here with accompanying explanatory notes and up-to-date critical essays, are distinctive because of what they do: they allow readers not simply to keep up, but to engage deeply with a writer whose works invite us to think, and think again.

These New Folger Editions of Shakespeare's plays are also special because of where they come from. The Folger Shakespeare Library in Washington, DC, where the Editions are produced, is the single greatest documentary source of Shakespeare's works. An unparalleled collection of early modern books, manuscripts, and artwork connected to Shakespeare, the Folger's holdings have been consulted extensively in the preparation of these texts. The Editions also reflect the expertise gained through the regular performance of Shakespeare's works in the Folger's Elizabethan Theater.

I want to express my deep thanks to editors Barbara Mowat and Paul Werstine for creating these indispensable editions of Shakespeare's works, which incorporate the best of textual scholarship with a richness of commentary that is both inspired and engaging. Readers who want to know more about Shakespeare and his plays can follow the paths these distinguished scholars have tread by visiting the Folger itself, where a range of physical and digital resources (available online) exist to supplement the material in these texts. I commend to you these words, and hope that they inspire.

Michael Witmore
Director, Folger Shakespeare Library

Contents

Editors' Preface

In recent years, ways of dealing with Shakespeare's texts and with the interpretation of his plays have been undergoing significant change. This edition, while retaining many of the features that have always made the Folger Shakespeare so attractive to the general reader, at the same time reflects these current ways of thinking about Shakespeare. For example, modern readers, actors, and teachers have become interested in the differences between, on the one hand, the early forms in which Shakespeare's plays were first published and, on the other hand, the forms in which editors through the centuries have presented them. In response to this interest, we have based our edition on what we consider the best early printed version of a particular play (explaining our rationale in a section called "An Introduction to This Text") and have marked our changes in the text—unobtrusively, we hope, but in such a way that the curious reader can be aware that a change has been made and can consult the "Textual Notes" to discover what appeared in the early printed version.

Current ways of looking at the plays are reflected in our brief introductions, in many of the commentary notes, in the annotated lists of "Further Reading," and especially in each play's "Modern Perspective," an essay written by an outstanding scholar who brings to the reader his or her fresh assessment of the play in the light of today's interests and concerns.

As in the Folger Library General Reader's Shakespeare, which this edition replaces, we include explanatory notes designed to help make Shakespeare's language clearer to a modern reader, and we place the

ix

notes on the page facing the text that they explain. We also follow the earlier edition in including illustrations —of objects, of clothing, of mythological figures—from books and manuscripts in the Folger Library collection. We provide fresh accounts of the life of Shakespeare, of the publishing of his plays, and of the theaters in which his plays were performed, as well as an introduction to the text itself. We also include a section called "Reading Shakespeare's Language," in which we try to help readers learn to "break the code" of Elizabethan poetic language.

For each section of each volume, we are indebted to a host of generous experts and fellow scholars. The "Reading Shakespeare's Language" sections, for example, could not have been written had not Arthur King, of Brigham Young University, and Randal Robinson, author of *Unlocking Shakespeare's Language,* led the way in untangling Shakespearean language puzzles and shared their insights and methodologies generously with us. "Shakespeare's Life" profited by the careful reading given it by S. Schoenbaum, "Shakespeare's Theater" was read and strengthened by Andrew Gurr and John Astington, and "The Publication of Shakespeare's Plays" is indebted to the comments of Peter W. M. Blayney. We, as editors, take sole responsibility for any errors in our editions.

We are grateful to the authors of the "Modern Perspectives," to Leeds Barroll and David Bevington for their generous encouragement, to the Huntington and Newberry Libraries for fellowship support, to King's College for the grants it has provided to Paul Werstine, to the Social Sciences and Humanities Research Council of Canada, which provided him with a Research Time Stipend for 1990–91, and to the Folger Institute's Center for Shakespeare Studies for its fortuitous sponsorship of a workshop on "Shakespeare's Texts for Students and

Teachers" (funded by the National Endowment for the Humanities and led by Richard Knowles of the University of Wisconsin), a workshop from which we learned an enormous amount about what is wanted by college and high-school teachers of Shakespeare today.

Our biggest debt is to the Folger Shakespeare Library: to Werner Gundersheimer, Director of the Library, who has made possible our edition; to Jean Miller, the Library's Art Curator, who combed the Library holdings for illustrations, and to Julie Ainsworth, Head of the Photography Department, who carefully photographed them; to Peggy O'Brien, Director of Education, who gave us expert advice about the needs being expressed by Shakespeare teachers and students (and to Martha Christian and other "master teachers" who used our texts in manuscript in their classrooms); to the staff of the Academic Programs Division, especially Paul Menzer (who drafted "Further Reading" material), Mary Tonkinson, Lena Cowen Orlin, Molly Haws, and Jessica Hymowitz; and, finally, to the staff of the Library Reading Room, whose patience and support have been invaluable.

Barbara A. Mowat and Paul Werstine

Shakespeare's *Othello*

In *Othello*, Shakespeare creates a powerful drama of a marriage that begins with fascination (between the exotic Moor Othello and the Venetian lady Desdemona), with elopement, and with intense mutual devotion and that ends precipitately with jealous rage and violent deaths. He sets this story in the romantic world of the Mediterranean, moving the action from Venice to the island of Cyprus and giving it an even more exotic coloring with stories of Othello's African past. Shakespeare builds so many differences into his hero and heroine—differences of race, of age, of cultural background—that one should not, perhaps, be surprised that the marriage ends disastrously. But most people who see or read the play feel that the love that the play presents between Othello and Desdemona is so strong that it would have overcome all these differences were it not for the words and actions of Othello's standard-bearer, Iago, who hates Othello and sets out to destroy him by destroying his love for Desdemona.

As Othello succumbs to Iago's insinuations that Desdemona is unfaithful, fascination—which dominates the early acts of the play—turns to horror, especially for the audience. We are confronted by spectacles of a generous and trusting Othello in the grip of Iago's schemes; of an innocent Desdemona, who has given herself up entirely to her love for Othello only to be subjected to his horrifying verbal and physical assaults, the outcome of Othello's mistaken convictions about her faithlessness.

At this point in our civilization the play's fascination and its horror may be greater than ever before because we have been made so very sensitive to the issues of race, class, and gender that are woven into the texture of *Othello*. Desdemona is white, Othello black. Their interracial marriage is a source of a stream of slurs from Iago that runs throughout the play. Class is emphasized when Iago is presented as someone bitterly resentful of his social inferiority (surely a factor in his initial failure to be named Othello's second-in-command) and so knowledgeable about the workings of prejudice and self-doubt that he can easily twist others' feelings and actions to serve his own mysterious ends. The issue of gender is especially noticeable in the final scenes of the play—with the attacks on Bianca, Emilia, and Desdemona—which are vivid reminders of how terrible the power traditionally exerted by men over women can be.

After you have read the play, we invite you to turn to "*Othello:* A Modern Perspective," written by Professor Susan Snyder of Swarthmore College, printed at the back of the book.

Reading Shakespeare's Language

For many people today, reading Shakespeare's language can be a problem—but it is a problem that can be solved. Those who have studied Latin (or even French or German or Spanish) and those who are used to reading poetry will have little difficulty understanding the language of Shakespeare's poetic drama. Others, however, need to develop the skills of untangling unusual sentence structures and of recognizing and understanding poetic compressions, omissions, and wordplay. And even those skilled in reading unusual sentence structures may have occasional trouble with Shakespeare's words. Four hundred years of "static"—caused by changes in language and in life—intervene between his speaking and our hearing. Most of his immense vocabulary is still in use, but a few of his words are not, and, worse, some of his words now have meanings quite different from those they had in the sixteenth and seventeenth centuries. In the theater, most of these difficulties are solved for us by actors who study the language and articulate it so that the essential meaning is heard—or, when combined with stage action, is at least *felt*. When reading on one's own, one must do what each actor does: go over the lines (often with a dictionary close at hand) until the puzzles are solved and the lines yield up their poetry and the characters speak in words and phrases that are, suddenly, rewarding and wonderfully memorable.

Shakespeare's Words

As you begin to read the opening scenes of a play by Shakespeare, you may notice occasional unfamiliar words. Some are unfamiliar simply because we no longer use them. In the opening scene of *Othello*, for example, you will find the words *certes* (i.e., certainly), *affined* (i.e., bound, obliged), *producted* (i.e., produced), as well as expressions like *forsooth, God bless the mark,* and *Zounds* (i.e., by Christ's wounds). Words and expressions of this kind are explained in notes to the text and will become familiar the more of Shakespeare's plays you read.

In *Othello*, as in all of Shakespeare's writing, the most problematic words are those that we still use but that we use with different meanings. In the first scene of *Othello* we find, for example, the words *circumstance* (meaning "ceremonious talk"), *spinster* (meaning "one who spins"), *propose* (meaning "converse"), *peculiar* (meaning "personal"), *owe* (meaning "own"), and *bravery* (meaning "impertinence, defiance"). Again, such words will be explained in the notes to this text, but they, too, will become familiar as you continue to read Shakespeare's language.

Finally, some words are strange not because of the "static" introduced by changes in language over the past centuries but because these are words that Shakespeare is using to build a dramatic world that has its own geography and history and background mythology. In *Othello*, three such worlds are built. First is the world of Venice and its surrounding territory, created through references to gondoliers and "togèd consuls," to "the magnifico," to Florentines, to Janus, to the Venetian signiory, to "carracks" and "prizes." These "local" references build the Venice that Othello and Desdemona, Iago, Cassio, and Brabantio inhabit for the first act of the play. Second is the world from which Othello has come, a world of "antres vast and deserts idle," of Anthropophogi, of the tented field and the imminent deadly breach. In the opening scenes of Act 2, the language that has built the worlds of Venice and of Othello's "extravagant" past is replaced with language that creates the Mediterranean island of Cyprus, to which the action moves—references to "high wrought floods," to "barks" (i.e., ships), to "shots of courtesy," to the "guttered rocks" and "congregated sands" of the ocean, to "the citadel" and the "court of guard." Where necessary, such local references will be explained in notes to the text, and will soon become a familiar part of your reading of the play.

Shakespeare's Sentences

In an English sentence, meaning is quite dependent on the place given each word. "The dog bit the boy" and "The boy bit the dog" mean very different things, even though the individual words are the same. Because English places such importance on the positions of words in sentences, on the way words are arranged, unusual arrangements can puzzle a reader. Shakespeare frequently shifts his sentences away from "normal" English arrangements—often in order to create the rhythm he seeks, sometimes in order to use a line's poetic rhythm to emphasize a particular word, sometimes to give a character his or her own speech patterns or to allow the character to speak in a special way. Again, when we attend a good performance of the play, the actors will have worked out the sentence structures and will articulate the sentences so that the meaning is clear. In reading for yourself, do as the actor does. That is, when you become puzzled by a character's speech, check to see if words are being presented in an unusual sequence.

Look first for the placement of subject and verb. Shakespeare often places the verb before the subject or places the subject between the two parts of a verb (e.g., instead of "He goes," we find "Goes he," and instead of "He does go," we find "Does he go"). In the opening scenes of *Othello*, when Iago says (1.1.61) "such a one do I profess myself" and when Brabantio says (1.1.178) "Gone she is," they are using constructions that place the subject and verb in unusual positions. Such inversions rarely cause much confusion. More problematic is Shakespeare's frequent placing of the object before the subject and verb (e.g., instead of "I hit him," we might find "Him I hit"). Brabantio's statement to Roderigo at 1.1.134, "This thou shalt answer," is an example of such an inversion. (The normal order would be "Thou shalt answer this.") Othello uses an inverted structure when he says, at 1.2.29–31, "I would not my unhousèd free condition / Put into circumscription and confine / For the sea's worth" (where the "normal" structure would be "I would not put my unhousèd free condition into circumscription . . .").

In some plays Shakespeare makes systematic use of inversions (*Julius Caesar* is one such play). In *Othello*, he more often uses sentence structures that involve instead the separation of words that would normally appear together. (Again, this is often done to create a particular rhythm or to stress a particular word.) Roderigo, when he says "I take it much unkindly / That thou, Iago, who hast had my purse / As if the strings were thine, shouldst know of this" (1.1.1–3), separates subject and verb ("thou shouldst know"). Iago also separates subject and verb when he says "Three *great ones* of the city, / In personal suit to make me his lieutenant, / *Off-capped* to him" (1.1.9–11) and again when he says (1.1.13–14) "But *he*, as loving his own pride and purposes, / *Evades* them with a bombast circumstance." In order to create for yourself sentences that seem more like the English of everyday speech, you may wish to rearrange the words, putting together the word clusters and placing the remaining words in their more normal order. You will usually find that the sentence will gain in clarity but will lose its rhythm or shift its emphasis. You can then see for yourself why Shakespeare chose his own unusual arrangement.

Locating and, if necessary, rearranging words that "belong together" is especially necessary in passages that separate subjects from verbs and verbs from objects by long delaying or expanding interruptions. For example, when Iago tells Roderigo about having been passed

over for the lieutenancy, he uses such an interrupted
structure:

And *I*, of whom his eyes had seen the proof
At Rhodes, at Cyprus, and on other grounds
Christened and heathen, *must be beleed and calmed*
By debitor and creditor.   (1.1.29–33)

Brabantio, accusing Othello of having used witchcraft
on Desdemona, also uses an interrupted construction:

For I'll refer me to all things of sense,
If she in chains of magic were not bound,
Whether a maid so tender, fair, and happy,
So opposite to marriage that she shunned
The wealthy curlèd darlings of our nation,
Would ever have, t' incur a general mock,
Run from her guardage to the sooty bosom
Of such a thing as thou—to fear, not to delight!
                                             (1.2.83–90)

In both of these cases, the interruptions provide details
that catch the audience up in the speeches. The separation of the basic sentence elements "I must be beleed
and calmed" forces the audience to attend to supporting
details (of Iago's military experience, of the geographic
regions where he had served Othello) while waiting for
the basic sentence elements to come together; a similar
effect is created when "Whether a maid would ever have
run" is interrupted by details about Desdemona's character (as perceived by her father) and by descriptions of
moments from her past.

   Occasionally, rather than separating basic sentence
elements, Shakespeare simply holds them back, delaying them until much subordinate material has already
been given. At the council of the Venetian senators, for

instance, the First Senator uses a delayed construction—

> When we consider
> Th' importancy of Cyprus to the Turk,
> And let ourselves again but understand
> That, as it more concerns the Turk than Rhodes,
> So may he with more facile question bear it,
> For that it stands not in such warlike brace,
> But altogether lacks th' abilities
> That Rhodes is dressed in—if we make thought of
>   this,
> *We must not think the Turk is so unskillful*
> *To leave that latest which concerns him first*
>   (1.3.24–34)

—delaying the basic sentence elements ("We must not think the Turk is so unskillful") to the end of this very long sentence, thus holding audience attention as the relationship of Cyprus, Rhodes, and the Turks is explained.

Shakespeare's sentences are sometimes complicated not because of unusual structures or interruptions or delays but because he omits words and parts of words that English sentences normally require. (In conversation, we, too, often omit words. We say "Heard from him yet?" and our hearer supplies the missing "Have you." Frequent reading of Shakespeare—and of other poets—trains us to supply such missing words.) In some plays (*Macbeth*, for example) Shakespeare uses omissions to great dramatic effect, omitting words and parts of words to build compression and speed in the language of the play. In *Othello* this device is more rarely used, occurring primarily in such constructions as Brabantio's "But if you know not this" (1.1.144), where the omission of the word "do" and the placing of "not" after "know" creates a regular iambic rhythm.

Shakespearean Wordplay

Shakespeare plays with language so routinely and so variously that books are written on the topic. Here we will mention only two kinds of wordplay, puns and metaphors. A pun is a play on words that sound the same but that have different meanings. In many plays (*Romeo and Juliet* is a good example) Shakespeare uses puns frequently. In *Othello* they are found less often; when they are used (except in Iago's "comic" verses in Act 2, scene 1), they carry meaningful ambiguity or complexity. When Brabantio accuses Desdemona of "treason of the blood" (1.1.191), for instance, his pun on *blood* allows the phrase to mean both "betrayal of her father and family" and "rebellion of the passions"; when the word *abused* appears (it occurs eight times in this play), it often means both "deluded, deceived" and "violated, injured"; the word *erring* means both "wandering" and "sinning"; *complexion* means both "temperament" and "skin color"; and *period*, in Lodovico's "O bloody period!" (5.2.418), signifies (powerfully) the end of Othello's speech (a rhetorical term) and the final point or limit of his life. In this play that focuses so relentlessly on sexuality, many of the puns are on words like *play* (meaning "wager," but carrying a secondary meaning of "engage in sexual sport"), *cope* (meaning "meet, encounter," with a secondary meaning of "copulate"), and *sport* (meaning "fun," but also "amorous play").

It is possible to argue that, in the largest sense, puns are extremely important to *Othello*. The visual contrast of black Othello and white Desdemona, for example, is echoed and complicated in punlike wordplay, as Desdemona becomes seen by Othello as morally "black" and as Othello, who has been called "far more fair than black," later talks about the "blackness" of his own face. A second set of punlike expressions turn on the word *honest,* whose various meanings play against each other throughout the play. *Honest* occurs more than forty times in *Othello,* almost always in reference to Iago—where it is both an indicator of his supposed truthfulness and a condescending term for a social inferior—and in reference to Desdemona, where, as is standard when it refers to a woman, it always means "chaste."

A metaphor is a play on words in which one object or idea is expressed as if it were something else, something with which it shares common features. For instance, when Iago says (1.1.31–32) that he has been "beleed and calmed" by Cassio, he is using metaphoric language: as a way of saying that Cassio has interfered with his military career, he uses nautical terms, picturing himself and Cassio as sailing ships, with Cassio coming between Iago and the wind, putting Iago in the lee and thereby stopping his progress. In many of his more inflammatory metaphors, Iago pictures lovers as mating animals (as in the famous statement to Brabantio about Othello and Desdemona: "An old black ram is tupping [mating with] your white ewe"). And, after working out the details of his entrapment of Desdemona, Cassio, and Othello (2.3.373–82), Iago sums up his plot in graphical metaphorical language: "So will I turn her virtue into pitch, / And out of her own goodness make the net / That shall enmesh them all"—where the qualities of pitch (a substance that is black, malodorous, and extremely sticky) make it the perfect substance for Iago to picture as helping him "enmesh" his victims.

Implied Stage Action

Finally, in reading Shakespeare's plays we should always remember that what we are reading is a performance script. The dialogue is written to be spoken by actors who, at the same time, are moving, gesturing, picking up objects, weeping, shaking their fists. Some stage action is described in what are called "stage directions"; some is suggested within the dialogue itself. We need to learn to be alert to such signals as we stage the play in our imaginations. In the second scene of *Othello*, for example, Brabantio says "Down with him, thief!" Iago answers "You, Roderigo! Come, sir, I am for you," and Othello says "Keep up your bright swords, for the dew will rust them" (73–77). In this passage, the stage action is obvious: i.e., several of the characters must draw their swords. Again, when, at 3.3.358–65, Emilia shows Iago a handkerchief, saying "Look, here 'tis," and a few lines later, after his order to "Give it me," she says "If it be not for some purpose of import, / Give 't me again," the stage action is fairly clear: Iago has snatched the handkerchief from her (or, less likely, she has handed it to him and then changed her mind). However, a bit earlier in that scene, at the crucial moment when the handkerchief is dropped, the action is not so clear. Othello complains of a headache, Desdemona offers to bind his head with her handkerchief, and Othello says "Your napkin [i.e., handkerchief] is too little. / Let it alone. Come, I'll go in with you," and he and Desdemona exit. Emilia, alone onstage, then says "I am glad I have found this napkin." It is almost certain that Emilia picks the handkerchief up, but just how it fell and why neither Othello nor Desdemona saw it fall is a matter that the director and the actors (and the reader, in imagination) must address. Learning to read the language of stage action repays one many times over when one reaches a crucial scene like that in Act 4 in which Othello sees the gestures made by Cassio but cannot hear his words, or when one reads the play's final scene with its complicated murders and attempted murders; in both of these scenes, implied stage action vitally affects our response to the play.

It is immensely rewarding to work carefully with Shakespeare's language so that the words, the sentences, the wordplay, and the implied stage action all become clear—as readers for the past four centuries have discovered. It may be more pleasurable to attend a good performance of a play—though not everyone has thought so. But the joy of being able to stage one of Shakespeare's plays in one's imagination, to return to passages that continue to yield further meanings (or further questions) the more one reads them—these are pleasures that, for many, rival (or at least augment) those of the performed text, and certainly make it worth considerable effort to "break the code" of Elizabethan poetic drama and let free the remarkable language that makes up a Shakespeare text.

Shakespeare's Life

Surviving documents that give us glimpses into the life of William Shakespeare show us a playwright, poet, and actor who grew up in the market town of Stratford-upon-Avon, spent his professional life in London, and returned to Stratford a wealthy landowner. He was born in April 1564, died in April 1616, and is buried inside the chancel of Holy Trinity Church in Stratford.

We wish we could know more about the life of the world's greatest dramatist. His plays and poems are testaments to his wide reading—especially to his knowledge of Virgil, Ovid, Plutarch, Holinshed's *Chronicles*, and the Bible—and to his mastery of the English language, but we can only speculate about his education. We know that the King's New School in Stratford-upon-Avon was considered excellent. The school was one of the English "grammar schools" established to educate young men, primarily in Latin grammar and literature. As in other schools of the time, students began their studies at the age of four or five in the attached "petty school," and there learned to read and write in English, studying primarily the catechism from the Book of Common Prayer. After two years in the petty school, students entered the lower form (grade) of the grammar school, where they began the serious study of Latin grammar and Latin texts that would occupy most of the remainder of their school days. (Several Latin texts that Shakespeare used repeatedly in writing his plays and poems were texts that schoolboys memorized and recited.) Latin comedies were introduced early in the lower form; in the upper form, which the boys entered at age ten or eleven, students wrote their own Latin orations and declamations, studied Latin historians and rhetoricians, and began the study of Greek using the Greek New Testament.

Since the records of the Stratford "grammar school" do not survive, we cannot prove that William Shakespeare attended the school; however, every indication (his father's position as an alderman and bailiff of Stratford, the playwright's own knowledge of the Latin classics, scenes in the plays that recall grammar-school experiences—for example, *The Merry Wives of Windsor,* 4.1) suggests that he did. We also lack generally accepted documentation about Shakespeare's life after his schooling ended and his professional life in London began. His marriage in 1582 (at age eighteen) to Anne Hathaway and the subsequent births of his daughter Susanna (1583) and the twins Judith and Hamnet (1585) are recorded, but how he supported himself and where he lived are not known. Nor do we know when and why he left Stratford for the London theatrical world, nor how he rose to be the important figure in that world that he had become by the early 1590s.

We do know that by 1592 he had achieved some prominence in London as both an actor and a playwright. In that year was published a book by the playwright Robert Greene attacking an actor who had the audacity to write blank-verse drama and who was "in his own conceit [i.e., opinion] the only Shake-scene in a country." Since Greene's attack includes a parody of a line from one of Shakespeare's early plays, there is little doubt that it is Shakespeare to whom he refers, a "Shake-scene" who had aroused Greene's fury by successfully competing with university-educated dramatists like Greene himself. It was in 1593 that Shakespeare became a published poet. In that year he published his long narrative poem *Venus and Adonis;* in 1594, he followed it with *The Rape of Lucrece.* Both poems were dedicated to the young earl of Southampton (Henry Wriothesley), who may have become Shakespeare's patron.

It seems no coincidence that Shakespeare wrote these narrative poems at a time when the theaters were closed because of the plague, a contagious epidemic disease that devastated the population of London. When the theaters reopened in 1594, Shakespeare apparently resumed his double career of actor and playwright and began his long (and seemingly profitable) service as an acting-company shareholder. Records for December of 1594 show him to be a leading member of the Lord Chamberlain's Men. It was this company of actors, later named the King's Men, for whom he would be a principal actor, dramatist, and shareholder for the rest of his career.

So far as we can tell, that career spanned about twenty years. In the 1590s, he wrote his plays on English history as well as several comedies and at least two tragedies (*Titus Andronicus* and *Romeo and Juliet*). These histories, comedies, and tragedies are the plays credited to him in 1598 in a work, *Palladis Tamia*, that in one chapter compares English writers with "Greek, Latin, and Italian Poets." There the author, Francis Meres, claims that Shakespeare is comparable to the Latin dramatists Seneca for tragedy and Plautus for comedy, and calls him "the most excellent in both kinds for the stage." He also names him "mellifluous and honey-tongued Shakespeare": "I say," writes Meres, "that the Muses would speak with Shakespeare's fine filed phrase, if they would speak English." Since Meres also mentions Shakespeare's "sugared sonnets among his private friends," it is assumed that many of Shakespeare's sonnets (not published until 1609) were also written in the 1590s.

In 1599, Shakespeare's company built a theater for themselves across the river from London, naming it the Globe. The plays that are considered by many to be Shakespeare's major tragedies (*Hamlet, Othello, King Lear,* and *Macbeth*) were written while the company was resident in this theater, as were such comedies as *Twelfth Night* and *Measure for Measure.* Many of Shakespeare's plays were performed at court (both for Queen Elizabeth I and, after her death in 1603, for King James I), some were presented at the Inns of Court (the residences of London's legal societies), and some were doubtless performed in other towns, at the universities, and at great houses when the King's Men went on tour; otherwise, his plays from 1599 to 1608 were, so far as we know, performed only at the Globe. Between 1608 and 1612, Shakespeare wrote several plays—among them *The Winter's Tale* and *The Tempest*—presumably for the company's new indoor Blackfriars theater, though the plays seem to have been performed also at the Globe and at court. Surviving documents describe a performance of *The Winter's Tale* in 1611 at the Globe, for example, and performances of *The Tempest* in 1611 and 1613 at the royal palace of Whitehall.

Shakespeare wrote very little after 1612, the year in which he probably wrote *King Henry VIII*. (It was at a performance of *Henry VIII* in 1613 that the Globe caught fire and burned to the ground.) Sometime between 1610 and 1613 he seems to have returned to live in Stratford-upon-Avon, where he owned a large house and considerable property, and where his wife and his two daughters and their husbands lived. (His son Hamnet had died in 1596.) During his professional years in London, Shakespeare had presumably derived income from the acting company's profits as well as from his own career as an actor, from the sale of his play manuscripts to the acting company, and, after 1599, from his shares as an owner of the Globe. It was presumably that income, carefully invested in land and other property, that made him the wealthy man that surviving documents show him to have become. It is also assumed that William Shakespeare's growing wealth and reputation played some part in inclining the crown, in 1596, to grant John Shakespeare, William's father, the coat of arms that he had so long sought. William Shakespeare died in Stratford on April 23, 1616 (according to the epitaph carved under his bust in Holy Trinity Church) and was buried on April 25. Seven years after his death, his collected plays were published as *Mr. William Shakespeares Comedies, Histories, & Tragedies* (the work now known as the First Folio).

The years in which Shakespeare wrote were among the most exciting in English history. Intellectually, the discovery, translation, and printing of Greek and Roman classics were making available a set of works and worldviews that interacted complexly with Christian texts and beliefs. The result was a questioning, a vital intellectual ferment, that provided energy for the period's amazing dramatic and literary output and that fed directly into Shakespeare's plays. The Ghost in *Hamlet*, for example, is wonderfully complicated in part because he is a figure from Roman tragedy—the spirit of the dead returning to seek revenge—who at the same time inhabits a Christian hell (or purgatory); Hamlet's description of humankind reflects at one moment the Neoplatonic wonderment at mankind ("What a piece of work is a man!") and, at the next, the Christian disparagement of human sinners ("And yet, to me, what is this quintessence of dust?").

As intellectual horizons expanded, so also did geographical and cosmological horizons. New worlds—both North and South America—were explored, and in them were found human beings who lived and worshiped in ways radically different from those of Renaissance Europeans and Englishmen. The universe during these years also seemed to shift and expand. Copernicus had earlier theorized that the earth was not the center of the cosmos but revolved as a planet around the sun. Galileo's telescope, created in 1609, allowed scientists to see that Copernicus had been correct: the universe was not organized with the earth at the center, nor was it so nicely circumscribed as people had, until that time, thought. In terms of expanding horizons, the impact of these discoveries on people's beliefs—religious, scientific, and philosophical—cannot be overstated.

London, too, rapidly expanded and changed during the years (from the early 1590s to around 1610) that Shakespeare lived there. London—the center of England's government, its economy, its royal court, its overseas trade—was, during these years, becoming an exciting metropolis, drawing to it thousands of new citizens every year. Troubled by overcrowding, by poverty, by recurring epidemics of the plague, London was also a mecca for the wealthy and the aristocratic, and for those who sought advancement at court, or power in government or finance or trade. One hears in Shakespeare's plays the voices of London—the struggles for power, the fear of venereal disease, the language of buying and selling. One hears as well the voices of Stratford-upon-Avon—references to the nearby Forest of Arden, to sheep herding, to small-town gossip, to village fairs and markets. Part of the richness of Shakespeare's work is the influence felt there of the various worlds in which he lived: the world of metropolitan London, the world of small-town and rural England, the world of the theater, and the worlds of craftsmen and shepherds.

That Shakespeare inhabited such worlds we know from surviving London and Stratford documents, as well as from the evidence of the plays and poems themselves. From such records we can sketch the dramatist's life. We know from his works that he was a voracious reader. We know from legal and business documents that he was a multifaceted theater man who became a wealthy landowner. We know a bit about his family life and a fair amount about his legal and financial dealings. Most scholars today depend upon such evidence as they draw their picture of the world's greatest playwright. Such, however, has not always been the case. Until the late eighteenth century, the William Shakespeare who lived in most biographies was the creation of legend and tradition. This was the Shakespeare who was supposedly caught poaching deer at Charlecote, the estate of Sir Thomas Lucy close by Stratford; this was the Shakespeare who fled from Sir Thomas's vengeance and made his way in London by taking care of horses outside a playhouse; this was the Shakespeare who reportedly could barely read, but whose natural gifts were extraordinary, whose father was a butcher who allowed his gifted son sometimes to help in the butcher shop, where William supposedly killed calves "in a high style," making a speech for the occasion. It was this legendary William Shakespeare whose Falstaff (in *1* and *2 Henry IV*) so pleased Queen Elizabeth that she demanded a play about Falstaff in love, and demanded that it be written in fourteen days (hence the existence of *The Merry Wives of Windsor*). It was this legendary Shakespeare who reached the top of his acting career in the roles of the Ghost in *Hamlet* and old Adam in *As You Like It*—and who died of a fever contracted by drinking too hard at "a merry meeting" with the poets Michael Drayton and Ben Jonson. This legendary Shakespeare is a rambunctious, undisciplined man, as attractively "wild" as his plays were seen by earlier generations to be. Unfortunately, there is no trace of evidence to support these wonderful stories.

Perhaps in response to the disreputable Shakespeare of legend—or perhaps in response to the fragmentary and, for some, all-too-ordinary Shakespeare documented by surviving records—some people since the mid-nineteenth century have argued that William Shakespeare could not have written the plays that bear his name. These persons have put forward some dozen names as more likely authors, among them Queen Elizabeth, Sir Francis Bacon, Edward de Vere (earl of Oxford), and Christopher Marlowe. Such attempts to find what for these people is a more believable author of the plays is a tribute to the regard in which the plays are held. Unfortunately for their claims, the documents that exist that provide evidence for the facts of Shakespeare's life tie him inextricably to the body of plays and poems that bear his name. Unlikely as it seems to those who want the works to have been written by an aristocrat, a university graduate, or an "important" person, the plays and poems seem clearly to have been produced by a man from Stratford-upon-Avon with a very good "grammar-school" education and a life of experience in London and in the world of the London theater. How this particular man produced the works that dominate the cultures of much of the world almost four hundred years after his death is one of life's mysteries—and one that will continue to tease our imaginations as we continue to delight in his plays and poems.

Shakespeare's Theater

The actors of Shakespeare's time are known to have performed plays in a great variety of locations. They played at court (that is, in the great halls of such royal residences as Whitehall, Hampton Court, and Greenwich); they played in halls at the universities of Oxford and Cambridge, and at the Inns of Court (the residences in London of the legal societies); and they also played in the private houses of great lords and civic officials. Sometimes acting companies went on tour from London into the provinces, often (but not only) when outbreaks of bubonic plague in the capital forced the closing of theaters to reduce the possibility of contagion in crowded audiences. In the provinces the actors usually staged their plays in churches (until around 1600) or in guildhalls. While surviving records show only a handful of occasions when actors played at inns while on tour, London inns were important playing places up until the 1590s.

The building of theaters in London had begun only shortly before Shakespeare wrote his first plays in the 1590s. These theaters were of two kinds: outdoor or public playhouses that could accommodate large numbers of playgoers, and indoor or private theaters for much smaller audiences. What is usually regarded as the first London outdoor public playhouse was called simply the Theatre. James Burbage—the father of Richard Burbage, who was perhaps the most famous actor in Shakespeare's company—built it in 1576 in an area north of the city of London called Shoreditch. Among the more famous of the other public playhouses that capitalized on the new fashion were the Curtain and the Fortune (both also built north of the city), the Rose, the Swan, the Globe, and the Hope (all located on the Bankside, a region just across the Thames south of the city of London). All these playhouses had to be built outside the jurisdiction of the city of London because many civic officials were hostile to the performance of drama and repeatedly petitioned the royal council to abolish it.

The theaters erected on the Bankside (a region under the authority of the Church of England, whose head was the monarch) shared the neighborhood with houses of prostitution and with the Paris Garden, where the blood sports of bearbaiting and bullbaiting were carried on. There may have been no clear distinction between playhouses and buildings for such sports, for we know that the Hope was used for both plays and baiting and that Philip Henslowe, owner of the Rose and, later, partner in the ownership of the Fortune, was also a partner in a monopoly on baiting. All these forms of entertainment were easily accessible to Londoners by boat across the Thames or over London Bridge.

Evidently Shakespeare's company prospered on the Bankside. They moved there in 1599. Threatened by difficulties in renewing the lease on the land where their first theater (the Theatre) had been built, Shakespeare's company took advantage of the Christmas holiday in

1598 to dismantle the Theatre and transport its timbers across the Thames to the Bankside, where, in 1599, these timbers were used in the building of the Globe. The weather in late December 1598 is recorded as having been especially harsh. It was so cold that the Thames was "nigh [nearly] frozen," and there was heavy snow. Perhaps the weather aided Shakespeare's company in eluding their landlord, the snow hiding their activity and the freezing of the Thames allowing them to slide the timbers across to the Bankside without paying tolls for repeated trips over London Bridge. Attractive as this narrative is, it remains just as likely that the heavy snow hampered transport of the timbers in wagons through the London streets to the river. It also must be remembered that the Thames was, according to report, only "nigh frozen" and therefore as impassable as it ever was. Whatever the precise circumstances of this fascinating event in English theater history, Shakespeare's company was able to begin playing at their new Globe theater on the Bankside in 1599. After the first Globe burned down in 1613 during the staging of Shakespeare's *Henry VIII* (its thatch roof was set alight by cannon fire called for by the performance), Shakespeare's company immediately rebuilt on the same location. The second Globe seems to have been a grander structure than its predecessor. It remained in use until the beginning of the English Civil War in 1642, when Parliament officially closed the theaters. Soon thereafter it was pulled down.

The public theaters of Shakespeare's time were very different buildings from our theaters today. First of all, they were open-air playhouses. As recent excavations of the Rose and the Globe confirm, some were polygonal or roughly circular in shape; the Fortune, however, was square. The most recent estimates of their size put the diameter of these buildings at 72 feet (the Rose) to 100 feet (the Globe), but we know that they held vast audiences of two or three thousand, who must have been squeezed together quite tightly. Some of these spectators paid extra to sit or stand in the two or three levels of roofed galleries that extended, on the upper levels, all the way around the theater and surrounded an open space. In this space were the stage and, perhaps, the tiring house (what we would call dressing rooms), as well as the so-called yard. In the yard stood the spectators who chose to pay less, the ones whom Hamlet contemptuously called "groundlings." For a roof they had only the sky, and so they were exposed to all kinds of weather. They stood on a floor that was sometimes made of mortar and sometimes of ash mixed with the shells of hazelnuts. The latter provided a porous and therefore dry footing for the crowd, and the shells may have been more comfortable to stand on because they were not as hard as mortar. Availability of shells may not have been a problem if hazelnuts were a favorite food for Shakespeare's audiences to munch on as they watched his plays. Archaeologists who are today unearthing the remains of theaters from this period have discovered quantities of these nutshells on theater sites.

Unlike the yard, the stage itself was covered by a roof. Its ceiling, called "the heavens," is thought to have been elaborately painted to depict the sun, moon, stars, and planets. Just how big the stage was remains hard to determine. We have a single sketch of part of the interior of the Swan. A Dutchman named Johannes de Witt visited this theater around 1596 and sent a sketch of it back to his friend, Arend van Buchel. Because van Buchel found de Witt's letter and sketch of interest, he copied both into a book. It is van Buchel's copy, adapted, it seems, to the shape and size of the page in his book, that survives. In this sketch, the stage appears to be a large rectangular platform that thrusts far out into the yard, perhaps even as far as the center of the circle formed by the surrounding galleries. This drawing, combined with the specifications for the size of the stage in the building contract for the Fortune, has led scholars to conjecture that the stage on which Shakespeare's plays were performed must have measured approximately 43 feet in width and 27 feet in depth, a vast acting area. But the digging up of a large part of the Rose by archaeologists has provided evidence of a quite different stage design. The Rose stage was a platform tapered at the corners and much shallower than what seems to be depicted in the van Buchel sketch. Indeed, its measurements seem to be about 37.5 feet across at its widest point and only 15.5 feet deep. Because the surviving indications of stage size and design differ from each other so much, it is possible that the stages in other theaters, like the Theatre, the Curtain, and the Globe (the outdoor playhouses where we know that Shakespeare's plays were performed), were different from those at both the Swan and the Rose.

After about 1608 Shakespeare's plays were staged not only at the Globe but also at an indoor or private playhouse in Blackfriars. This theater had been constructed in 1596 by James Burbage in an upper hall of a former Dominican priory or monastic house. Although Henry VIII had dissolved all English monasteries in the 1530s (shortly after he had founded the Church of England), the area remained under church, rather than hostile civic, control. The hall that Burbage had purchased and renovated was a large one in which Parliament had once met. In the private theater that he constructed, the stage, lit by candles, was built across the narrow end of the hall, with boxes flanking it. The rest of the hall offered seating room only. Because there was no provision for standing room, the largest audience it could hold was less than a thousand, or about a quarter of what the Globe could accommodate. Admission to Blackfriars was correspondingly more expensive. Instead of a penny to stand in the yard at the Globe, it cost a minimum of sixpence to get into Blackfriars. The best seats at the Globe (in the Lords' Room in the gallery above and behind the stage) cost sixpence; but the boxes flanking the stage at Blackfriars were half a crown, or five times sixpence. Some spectators who were particularly interested in displaying themselves paid even more to sit on stools on the Blackfriars stage.

Whether in the outdoor or indoor playhouses, the stages of Shakespeare's time were different from ours. They were not separated from the audience by the dropping of a curtain between acts and scenes. Therefore the playwrights of the time had to find other ways of signaling to the audience that one scene (to be imagined as occurring in one location at a given time) had ended and the next (to be imagined at perhaps a diffcrent location at a later time) had begun. The customary way used by Shakespeare and many of his contemporaries was to have everyone on stage exit at the end of one scene and have one or more different characters enter to begin the next. In a few cases, where characters remain onstage from one scene to another, the dialogue or stage action makes the change of location clear, and the characters are generally to be imagined as having moved from one place to another. For example, in *Romeo and Juliet*, Romeo and his friends remain onstage in Act 1 from scene 4 to scene 5, but they are represented as having moved between scenes from the street that leads to Capulet's house into Capulet's house itself. The new location is signaled in part by the appearance onstage of Capulet's servingmen carrying napkins, something they would not take into the streets. Playwrights had to be quite resourceful in the use of hand properties, like the napkin, or in the use of dialogue to specify where the action was taking place in their plays because, in contrast to most of today's theaters, the playhouses of Shakespeare's time did not use movable scenery to dress the stage and make the setting precise. As another consequence of this difference, however, the playwrights of Shakespeare's time did not have to specify exactly where the action of their plays was set when they did not choose to do so, and much of the action of their plays is tied to no specific place.

Usually Shakespeare's stage is referred to as a "bare stage," to distinguish it from the stages of the last two or three centuries with their elaborate sets. But the stage in Shakespeare's time was not completely bare. Philip Henslowe, owner of the Rose, lists in his inventory of stage properties a rock, three tombs, and two mossy banks. Stage directions in plays of the time also call for such things as thrones (or "states"), banquets (presumably tables with plaster replicas of food on them), and beds and tombs to be pushed onto the stage. Thus the stage often held more than the actors.

The actors did not limit their performing to the stage alone. Occasionally they went beneath the stage, as the Ghost appears to do in the first act of *Hamlet*. From there they could emerge onto the stage through a trapdoor. They could retire behind the hangings across the back of the stage (or the front of the tiring house), as, for example, the actor playing Polonius does when he hides behind the arras. Sometimes the hangings could be drawn back during a performance to "discover" one or more actors behind them. When performance required that an actor appear "above," as when Juliet is imagined to stand at the window of her chamber in the famous and misnamed "balcony scene," then the actor probably climbed the stairs to the gallery over the back of the stage and temporarily shared it with some of the spectators. The stage was also provided with ropes and winches so that actors could descend from, and reascend to, the "heavens."

Perhaps the greatest difference between dramatic performances in Shakespeare's time and ours was that in Shakespeare's England the roles of women were played by boys. (Some of these boys grew up to take male roles in their maturity.) There were no women in the acting companies, only in the audience. It had not always been so in the history of the English stage. There are records of women on English stages in the thirteenth and fourteenth centuries, two hundred years before Shakespeare's plays were performed. After the accession of James I in 1603, the queen of England and her ladies took part in entertainments at court called masques, and with the reopening of the theaters in 1660 at the restoration of Charles II, women again took their place on the public stage.

The chief competitors for the companies of adult actors such as the one to which Shakespeare belonged and for which he wrote were companies of exclusively boy actors. The competition was most intense in the early 1600s. There were then two principal children's companies: the Children of Paul's (the choirboys from St. Paul's Cathedral, whose private playhouse was near the cathedral); and the Children of the Chapel Royal (the choirboys from the monarch's private chapel, who performed at the Blackfriars theater built by Burbage in 1596, which Shakespeare's company had been stopped from using by local residents who objected to crowds). In *Hamlet* Shakespeare writes of "an aerie [nest] of children, little eyases [hawks], that cry out on the top of question and are most tyrannically clapped for 't. These are now the fashion and . . . berattle the common stages [attack the public theaters]." In the long run, the adult actors prevailed. The Children of Paul's dissolved around 1606. By about 1608 the Children of the Chapel

Royal had been forced to stop playing at the Blackfriars theater, which was then taken over by the King's Men, Shakespeare's own troupe. Acting companies and theaters of Shakespeare's time were organized in different ways. For example, Philip Henslowe owned the Rose and leased it to companies of actors, who paid him from their takings. Henslowe would act as manager of these companies, initially paying playwrights for their plays and buying properties, recovering his outlay from the actors. Shakespeare's company, however, managed itself, with the principal actors, Shakespeare among them, having the status of "sharers" and the right to a share in the takings, as well as the responsibility for a part of the expenses. Five of the sharers themselves, Shakespeare among them, owned the Globe. As actor, as sharer in an acting company and in ownership of theaters, and as playwright, Shakespeare was about as involved in the theatrical industry as one could imagine. Although Shakespeare and his fellows prospered, their status under the law was conditional upon the protection of powerful patrons. "Common players"—those who did not have patrons or masters—were classed in the language of the law with "vagabonds and sturdy beggars." So the actors had to secure for themselves the official rank of servants of patrons. Among the patrons under whose protection Shakespeare's company worked were the lord chamberlain and, after the accession of King James in 1603, the king himself.

We are now perhaps on the verge of learning a great deal more about the theaters in which Shakespeare and his contemporaries performed—or at least of opening up new questions about them. Already about 70 percent of the Rose has been excavated, as has about 10 percent of the second Globe, the one built in 1614. It is to be hoped that soon more will be available for study. These are exciting times for students of Shakespeare's stage.

The Publication of Shakespeare's Plays

Eighteen of Shakespeare's plays found their way into print during the playwright's lifetime, but there is nothing to suggest that he took any interest in their publication. These eighteen appeared separately in editions called quartos. Their pages were not much larger than the one you are now reading, and these little books were sold unbound for a few pence. The earliest of the quartos that still survive were printed in 1594, the year that both *Titus Andronicus* and a version of the play now called *2 King Henry VI* became available. While almost every one of these early quartos displays on its title page the name of the acting company that performed the play, only about half provide the name of the playwright, Shakespeare. The first quarto edition to bear the name Shakespeare on its title page is *Love's Labor's Lost* of 1598. A few of these quartos were popular with the book-buying public of Shakespeare's lifetime; for example, quarto *Richard II* went through five editions between 1597 and 1615. But most of the quartos were far from best-sellers; *Love's Labor's Lost* (1598), for instance, was not reprinted in quarto until 1631. After Shakespeare's death, two more of his plays appeared in quarto format: *Othello* in 1622 and *The Two Noble Kinsmen*, coauthored with John Fletcher, in 1634.

In 1623, seven years after Shakespeare's death, *Mr. William Shakespeares Comedies, Histories, & Tragedies* was published. This printing offered readers in a single book thirty-six of the thirty-eight plays now thought to have been written by Shakespeare, including eighteen that had never been printed before. And it offered them in a style that was then reserved for serious literature and scholarship. The plays were arranged in double columns on pages nearly a foot high. This large page size is called "folio," as opposed to the smaller "quarto," and the 1623 volume is usually called the Shakespeare First Folio. It is reputed to have sold for the lordly price of a pound. (One copy at the Folger Library is marked fifteen shillings—that is, three-quarters of a pound.)

In a preface to the First Folio entitled "To the great Variety of Readers," two of Shakespeare's former fellow actors in the King's Men, John Heminge and Henry Condell, wrote that they themselves had collected their dead companion's plays. They suggested that they had seen his own papers: "we have scarce received from him a blot in his papers." The title page of the Folio declared that the plays within it had been printed "according to the True Original Copies." Comparing the Folio to the quartos, Heminge and Condell disparaged the quartos, advising their readers that "before you were abused with divers stolen and surreptitious copies, maimed, and deformed by the frauds and stealths of injurious impostors." Many Shakespeareans of the eighteenth and nineteenth centuries believed Heminge and Condell and regarded the Folio plays as superior to anything in the quartos.

Once we begin to examine the Folio plays in detail, it becomes less easy to take at face value the word of Heminge and Condell about the superiority of the Folio texts. For example, of the first nine plays in the Folio (one quarter of the entire collection), four were essentially reprinted from earlier quarto printings that Heminge and Condell had disparaged; and four have now been identified as printed from copies written in the hand of a professional scribe of the 1620s named Ralph Crane; the ninth, *The Comedy of Errors,* was apparently also printed from a manuscript, but one whose origin cannot be readily identified. Evidently then, eight of the first nine plays in the First Folio were not printed, in spite of what the Folio title page announces, "according to the True Original Copies," or Shakespeare's own papers, and the source of the ninth is unknown. Since today's editors have been forced to treat Heminge and Condell's pronouncements with skepticism, they must choose whether to base their own editions upon quartos or the Folio on grounds other than Heminge and Condell's story of where the quarto and Folio versions originated.

Editors have often fashioned their own narratives to explain what lies behind the quartos and Folio. They have said that Heminge and Condell meant to criticize only a few of the early quartos, the ones that offer much shorter and sometimes quite different, often garbled, versions of plays. Among the examples of these are the 1600 quarto of *Henry V* (the Folio offers a much fuller version) or the 1603 *Hamlet* quarto (in 1604 a different, much longer form of the play got into print as a quarto). Early in this century editors speculated that these questionable texts were produced when someone in the audience took notes from the plays' dialogue during performances and then employed "hack poets" to fill out the notes. The poor results were then sold to a publisher and presented in print as Shakespeare's plays. More recently this story has given way to another in which the shorter versions are said to be recreations from memory of Shakespeare's plays by actors who wanted to stage them in the provinces but lacked manuscript copies. Most of the quartos offer much better texts than these so-called bad quartos. Indeed, in most of the quartos we find texts that are at least equal to or better than what is printed in the Folio. Many of this century's Shakespeare enthusiasts have persuaded themselves that most of the quartos were set into type directly from Shakespeare's own papers, although there is nothing on which to base this conclusion except the desire for it to be true. Thus speculation continues about how the Shakespeare plays got to be printed. All that we have are the printed texts.

The book collector who was most successful in bringing together copies of the quartos and the First Folio was Henry Clay Folger, founder of the Folger Shakespeare Library in Washington, D.C. While it is estimated that there survive around the world only about 230 copies of the First Folio, Mr. Folger was able to acquire more than seventy-five copies, as well as a large number of fragments, for the library that bears his name. He also amassed a substantial number of quartos. For example, only fourteen copies of the First Quarto of *Love's Labor's Lost* are known to exist, and three are at the Folger Shakespeare Library. As a consequence of Mr. Folger's labors, twentieth-century scholars visiting the Folger Library have been able to learn a great deal about sixteenth- and seventeenth-century printing and, particularly, about the printing of Shakespeare's plays. And Mr. Folger did not stop at the First Folio, but collected many copies of later editions of Shakespeare, beginning with the Second Folio (1632), the Third (1663–64), and the Fourth (1685). Each of these later folios was based on its immediate predecessor and was edited anonymously. The first editor of Shakespeare whose name we know was Nicholas Rowe, whose first edition came out in 1709. Mr. Folger collected this edition and many, many more by Rowe's successors.

An Introduction to This Text

The play we call *Othello* was printed in two different versions in the first quarter of the seventeenth century. In 1622 appeared *The Tragœdy of Othello, The Moore of Venice, As it hath beene diuerse times acted at the Globe, and at the Black-Friers, by his Maiesties Seruants, Written by William Shakespeare*, a quarto or pocket-size book that provides a somewhat shorter version of the play than the one most readers know. The second version to be printed is found in the First Folio of Shakespeare's plays, published in 1623. Entitled simply *The Tragedie of Othello, the Moore of Venice*, the Folio play has about 160 lines that do not appear in the Quarto. Some of these cluster together in quite extensive passages. The Folio also lacks a scattering of about a dozen lines or part-lines that are to be found in the Quarto. These two versions also differ from each other in their readings of hundreds of words.

Usually twentieth-century editors of Shakespeare make the decision about which version of a play to prefer according to their theories about the origins of the early printed texts. In the case of *Othello*, however, there has emerged no consensus among editors about what kind of manuscripts can be imagined to lie behind the two early printed texts. Therefore almost all recent editors have relied, for the basis of their editions, upon what they regard as the more accurate text, namely, the Folio's. (Following a recent fashion in Shakespeare editing, some editors have speculated that there were once two distinct Shakespearean versions of the play. According to this view, the Quarto offers Shakespeare's unrevised version, the Folio his revised version. Since these editors are led by their hypothesis to prefer the

Folio, their speculations have made little difference to the kind of editions they have produced.)

For the present edition we have reexamined these early printed texts. This edition is based directly on the Folio printing of *Othello* rather than on any modern edition.* But our text offers an *edition* of the Folio because it prints such Quarto readings and such later editorial emendations as are, in our judgment, necessary to repair what may be errors and deficiencies in the Folio. The present edition also offers its readers the lines and part-lines and many of the words that are to be found only in the Quarto, marking them as such (see below).

Quarto words are *added* when their omission would seem to leave a gap in our text. For example, in the first scene of the play, a half-line found in the Quarto, "And in conclusion," seems to have been dropped from the Folio between the lines "Horribly stuffed with epithets of war" and "Nonsuits my mediators"; we have added that needed half-line. We also add Quarto words when they are oaths or declarations ("O God," "Zounds," etc.) that may be missing from the Folio through censorship. When the Folio lacks Quarto words that appear to add nothing of significance, we do not add these words to our text. For example, the Quarto's "O, then" in the line "If she be false, heaven mocks itself" (3.3.319) seems only to regularize the meter without adding anything of significance; we have therefore chosen not to alter the Folio line.

Occasionally Quarto readings are *substituted* for Folio words when a word in the Folio is unintelligible (i.e., is not a word) or is incorrect according to the standards of

---

*We have also consulted the computerized text of the First Folio provided by the Text Archive of the Oxford University Computing Centre, to which we are grateful.

that time for acceptable grammar, rhetoric, idiom, or usage, and the Quarto provides an intelligible and acceptable word. (Examples of such substitutions are the Quarto's "pains" for the Folio's "apines" [1.1.171], Q's "sometimes" for F's "sometime" [1.2.4], and Q's "these" for F's "this" in the line "There's no composition in ⟨these⟩ news" [1.3.1].) We recognize that our understanding of what was acceptable in Shakespeare's time is to some extent inevitably based on reading others' editions of *Othello*, but it is also based on reading other writing from the period and on historical dictionaries and studies of Shakespeare's grammar.

We also prefer the Quarto reading to the Folio's when a word in the Folio seems to be the result of censorship or "damping down" of an oath or solemn declaration, and the Quarto provides a stronger oath or declaration (for example, when the Quarto reads "God" in place of the Folio's "Heaven" or Q reads "By the Mass" in place of F's "in troth"). And, finally, we print a word from the Quarto rather than the Folio when a word in the Folio seems at odds with the story that the play tells and the Quarto supplies a word that coheres with the story. (For example, the Folio has Othello report that Desdemona gave him "a world of kisses" before he had declared his love and they had discussed marriage, while the Quarto has him refer to a "world of sighs" [1.3.183]. Like almost all modern editions, we here adopt the Quarto reading.)

In order to enable its readers to tell the difference between the Folio and Quarto versions, the present edition uses a variety of signals:

(1) All the words in this edition that are printed in the Quarto version but not in the Folio appear in pointed brackets (⟨ ⟩).

(2) All full lines that are found in the Folio and not in the Quarto are printed in square brackets ([ ]).

(3) Sometimes neither the Folio nor the Quarto seems to offer a satisfactory reading, and it is necessary to print a word different from what is offered by either. Such words (called "emendations" by editors) are printed within half square brackets (⌈ ⌉).

By observing these signals and by referring to the textual notes printed after the play, a reader can use this edition to read the play as it was printed in the Folio, or as it was printed in the Quarto, or as it has been presented in the editorial tradition, which has combined Folio and Quarto. (This tradition can be traced back, ultimately, to the anonymous editor of the Second Quarto of 1630.)

In this edition whenever we change the wording of the Folio or add anything to its stage directions, we mark the change. We want our readers to be immediately aware when we have intervened. (Only when we correct an obvious typographical error in the Quarto or Folio does the change not get marked in our text.) Whenever we change the wording of the Folio or Quarto, or change the punctuation so as to affect meaning, we list the change in the textual notes at the back of the book. Those who wish to find the Quarto's alternatives to the Folio's readings will be able to find these also in the textual notes.

For the convenience of the reader, we have modernized the punctuation and the spelling of both the Folio and the Quarto. Sometimes we go so far as to modernize certain old forms of words; for example, when *a* means "he," we change it to *he;* we change *mo* to *more* and *ye* to *you.* But it is not our practice in editing any of the plays to modernize some words that sound distinctly different from modern forms. For example, when the early printed texts read *sith* or *apricocks* or *porpentine,* we have not modernized to *since, apricots, porcupine.* When the forms *an, and,* or *and if* appear instead of the modern form *if,* we have reduced *and* to *an* but have not changed any of these forms to their modern equivalent, *if.* We also modernize and, where necessary, correct passages in foreign languages, unless an error in the early printed text can be reasonably explained as a joke. We correct or regularize a number of the proper names, as is the usual practice in editions of the play. For example, the Folio's spelling "Rodorigo" is changed to "Roderigo," and there are a number of other comparable adjustments in the names.

This edition differs from many earlier ones in its efforts to aid the reader in imagining the play as a performance rather than as a series of fictional events. Thus stage directions are written with reference to the stage. For example, the stage direction for Brabantio's first entrance is based on the Folio, *"Enter Brabantio above"* rather than on the Quarto, *"Enter Brabantio at a window."* While in the fiction of the play we are no doubt to imagine the old man appearing at a window in the upper storey of his house, there is little evidence that there were windows in the gallery of early-seventeenth-century theaters. We print the stage direction more likely to have reference to the stage rather than to the story. Whenever it is reasonably certain, in our view, that a speech is accompanied by a particular action, we provide a stage direction describing the action. (Occasional exceptions to this rule occur when the action is so obvious that to add a stage direction would insult the reader.) Stage directions for the entrance of characters in mid-scene are, with rare exceptions, placed so that they immediately precede the characters' participation in the scene, even though these entrances may appear somewhat earlier in the early printed texts. Whenever we move a stage direction, we record this change in the textual notes. Latin stage directions (e.g., *Exeunt*) are translated into English (e.g., *They exit*).

We expand the often severely abbreviated forms of names used as speech headings in early printed texts into the full names of the characters. We also regularize the speakers' names in speech headings, using only a single designation for each character, even though the early printed texts sometimes use a variety of designations. Variations in the speech headings of the early printed texts are recorded in the textual notes.

In the present edition, as well, we mark with a dash any change of address within a speech, unless a stage direction intervenes. When the *-ed* ending of a word is to be pronounced, we mark it with an accent. Like editors for the last two centuries, we print metrically linked lines in the following way:

IAGO
Are your doors locked?
BRABANTIO   Why, wherefore ask you this?

However, when there are a number of short verse-lines that can be linked in more than one way, we do not, with rare exceptions, indent any of them.

The Explanatory Notes

The notes that appear on the pages facing the text are designed to provide readers with the help they may need to enjoy the play. Whenever the meaning of a word in the text is not readily accessible in a good contemporary dictionary, we offer the meaning in a note. Sometimes we provide a note even when the relevant meaning is to be found in the dictionary but when the word has acquired since Shakespeare's time other potentially confusing meanings. In our notes, we try to offer modern synonyms for Shakespeare's words. We also try to indicate to the reader the connection between the word in the play and the modern synonym. For example, Shakespeare sometimes uses the word *head* to mean "source," but, for modern readers, there may be no connection evident between these two words. We provide the connection by explaining Shakespeare's usage as follows: "**head**: fountainhead, source." On some occasions, a whole phrase or clause needs explanation. Then we rephrase in our own words the difficult passage, and add at the end synonyms for individual words in the passage. When scholars have been unable to determine the meaning of a word or phrase, we acknowledge the uncertainty.

The Tragedy of

OTHELLO,
The Moor of Venice

Characters in the Play

OTHELLO, a Moorish general in the Venetian army
DESDEMONA, a Venetian lady
BRABANTIO, a Venetian senator, father to Desdemona

IAGO, Othello's standard-bearer, or "ancient"
EMILIA, Iago's wife and Desdemona's attendant

CASSIO, Othello's second-in-command, or lieutenant
RODERIGO, a Venetian gentleman

Duke of Venice
LODOVICO ⎫
GRATIANO ⎭ *Venetian gentlemen, kinsmen to Brabantio*
Venetian senators

MONTANO, an official in Cyprus
BIANCA, a woman in Cyprus in love with Cassio
Clown, a comic servant to Othello and Desdemona
Gentlemen of Cyprus
Sailors

Servants, Attendants, Officers, Messengers, Herald, Musicians, Torchbearers.

3

The Tragedy of

OTHELLO,
The Moor of Venice

ACT 1

1.1 In the streets of Venice, Iago tells Roderigo of his hatred for Othello, who has given Cassio the lieutenancy that Iago wanted and has made Iago a mere ensign. At Iago's suggestion, he and Roderigo, a former suitor to Desdemona, awake Desdemona's father to tell him that Desdemona has eloped with Othello. This news enrages Brabantio, who organizes an armed band to search out Othello.

---

1. **Tush:** an expression of impatience
2-3. **who . . . thine:** i.e., who have had complete access to my money   **purse:** bag or pouch   **strings:** i.e., the purse string that closes the pouch
4. **'Sblood:** Christ's blood (a strong oath); **hear:** listen to
9. **great ones of the city:** Venetian nobles
10. **suit:** petition; **lieutenant:** i.e., second in command
11. **Off-capped:** i.e., removed their hats
12. **price:** value; **place:** position, rank
13. **as loving:** i.e., loving
14. **bombast:** i.e., wordy, pompous (literally, cotton padding); **circumstance:** ceremonious talk
15. **stuffed:** filled
17. **Nonsuits my mediators:** i.e., fails to grant the suit (request) of my petitioners; **Certes:** certainly
19. **he:** i.e., the officer (Cassio) chosen by Othello
20. **Forsooth:** in truth; **arithmetician:** one skilled in working with numbers (with the implication that Cassio knows about battles only from books)
22. **almost . . . in:** cursed by being married to (the only reference in the play to Cassio's **wife**)

ACT 1

Scene 1
Enter Roderigo and Iago.

RODERIGO
⟨Tush,⟩ never tell me! I take it much unkindly
That thou, Iago, who hast had my purse
As if the strings were thine, shouldst know of this.
IAGO   ⟨'Sblood,⟩ but you'll not hear me!
If ever I did dream of such a matter,   5
Abhor me.
RODERIGO
Thou toldst me thou didst hold him in thy hate.
IAGO   Despise me
If I do not. Three great ones of the city,
In personal suit to make me his lieutenant,   10
Off-capped to him; and, by the faith of man,
I know my price, I am worth no worse a place.
But he, as loving his own pride and purposes,
Evades them with a bombast circumstance,
Horribly stuffed with epithets of war,   15
⟨And in conclusion,⟩
Nonsuits my mediators. For "Certes," says he,
"I have already chose my officer."
And what was he?
Forsooth, a great arithmetician,   20
One Michael Cassio, a Florentine,
A fellow almost damned in a fair wife,

7

23. **set a squadron:** i.e., stationed even so much as a small detachment of men; **field:** i.e., battlefield

25. **spinster:** one (usually a woman) who spins; **unless:** except for; **theoric:** theory

26. **togèd consuls:** civic officials whom Iago pictures as wearing Roman togas; **propose:** talk

28. **had th' election:** i.e., was the one chosen

30. **Rhodes, Cyprus:** embattled islands that were part of the Venetian empire

31–32. **beleed and calmed:** stopped in my progress (nautical terms in which Cassio and Iago are compared to sailing ships, Cassio coming between Iago and the wind [putting Iago in the lee] and thereby stopping him)

33. **By . . . creditor:** i.e., by a mere bookkeeper; **countercaster:** one who computes with tokens

34. **in good time:** i.e., "to be sure"

35. **God bless the mark:** an expression of impatient scorn; **his Moorship's:** i.e., Othello's (a sarcastic racial slur by analogy with the title "his Worship"); **ancient:** i.e., ensign, standard-bearer (the lowest-ranking commissioned officer in the infantry)

37. **service:** military service

38. **affection:** personal preference

39–40. **old gradation . . . first:** i.e., each second officer automatically succeeded each first officer

41. **affined:** i.e., bound, obliged (literally, related)

45. **serve . . . him:** i.e., use him for my own ends

47. **mark:** observe

48. **knee-crooking knave:** bowing menial

53. **Whip me:** i.e., I'd have them whip

54. **trimmed . . . duty:** i.e., appearing dutiful in manners and looks **trimmed:** dressed

That never set a squadron in the field,
Nor the division of a battle knows
More than a spinster—unless the bookish theoric,   25
Wherein the ⟨togèd⟩ consuls can propose
As masterly as he. Mere prattle without practice
Is all his soldiership. But he, sir, had th' election;
And I, of whom his eyes had seen the proof
At Rhodes, at Cyprus, and on ⟨other⟩ grounds   30
Christened and heathen, must be beeled and
   calmed
By debitor and creditor. This countercaster,
He, in good time, must his lieutenant be,
And I, ⟨God⟩ bless the mark, his Moorship's ancient.   35
RODERIGO
By heaven, I rather would have been his hangman.
IAGO
Why, there's no remedy. 'Tis the curse of service.
Preferment goes by letter and affection,
And not by old gradation, where each second
Stood heir to th' first. Now, sir, be judge yourself   40
Whether I in any just term am affined
To love the Moor.
RODERIGO
I would not follow him, then.
IAGO   O, sir, content you.
I follow him to serve my turn upon him.   45
We cannot all be masters, nor all masters
Cannot be truly followed. You shall mark
Many a duteous and knee-crooking knave
That, doting on his own obsequious bondage,
Wears out his time, much like his master's ass,   50
For naught but provender, and when he's old,
   cashiered.
Whip me such honest knaves! Others there are
Who, trimmed in forms and visages of duty,
Keep yet their hearts attending on themselves,   55

57–58. lined their coats: i.e., lined their pockets, gotten rich

59. Do themselves homage: show respect to themselves alone, rather than to their masters

64. I . . . myself: i.e., I serve my own interest

65–66. not I . . . seeming so: i.e., I do not follow him out of love and duty, though I seem to

66. peculiar end: personal goals

68. native act and figure: natural activity and form (i.e., what I really feel)

69. complement extern: external form

69–70. 'tis . . . But: i.e., soon afterward

71. daws: proverbially stupid birds; **I am not what I am:** i.e., I am not what I seem to be (Contrast God's words in Exodus 3.14: "I am that I am.")

72. owe: own, possess

73. carry 't thus: i.e., bring it off

74. Call up: i.e., arouse from bed

75. Make after him: i.e., go after Othello

76. Proclaim him: i.e., identify him publicly as a rebel or outlaw

77–78. though . . . flies: i.e., even though he is now fortunate (**in a fertile climate**), torment (**plague**) him with minor vexations

79. chances: possibilities

80. As it may lose some color: i.e., that his joy may pale or be diminished

82. like timorous accent: such dreadful sound

83. by night and negligence: i.e., resulting from someone's negligence at night

And, throwing but shows of service on their lords,
Do well thrive by them; and when they have lined
  their coats,
Do themselves homage. These fellows have some
  soul, 60
And such a one do I profess myself. For, sir,
It is as sure as you are Roderigo,
Were I the Moor I would not be Iago.
In following him, I follow but myself.
Heaven is my judge, not I for love and duty, 65
But seeming so for my peculiar end.
For when my outward action doth demonstrate
The native act and figure of my heart
In complement extern, 'tis not long after
But I will wear my heart upon my sleeve 70
For daws to peck at. I am not what I am.

RODERIGO
What a ⟨full⟩ fortune does the ⟨thick-lips⟩ owe
If he can carry 't thus!

IAGO   Call up her father.
Rouse him. Make after him, poison his delight, 75
Proclaim him in the streets; incense her kinsmen,
And, though he in a fertile climate dwell,
Plague him with flies. Though that his joy be joy,
Yet throw such chances of vexation on 't
As it may lose some color. 80

RODERIGO
Here is her father's house. I'll call aloud.

IAGO
Do, with like timorous accent and dire yell
As when, by night and negligence, the fire
Is spied in populous cities.

RODERIGO
What ho, Brabantio! Signior Brabantio, ho! 85

IAGO
Awake! What ho, Brabantio! Thieves, thieves!

87. **bags:** i.e., money bags

88 SD. **above:** i.e., in the gallery above the stage

89. **of:** for; **terrible:** terrifying

93. **wherefore ask you:** why do you ask

94. **Zounds:** i.e., Christ's wounds (a strong oath)

97. **very now:** i.e., at this very moment

98. **tupping:** copulating with (used, as here, in reference to sheep)

99. **snorting:** snoring

107. **charged:** ordered

110. **distemp'ring:** intoxicating

111. **Upon:** i.e., impelled by; **bravery:** impertinence, defiance

112. **start my quiet:** i.e., startle me from my peace

A gondolier. (1.1.140)
From Giovanni Ferro, *Teatro d'imprese* . . . (1623).

12

Look to your house, your daughter, and your bags!
Thieves, thieves!

⌜*Enter Brabantio,*⌝ *above.*

BRABANTIO
What is the reason of this terrible summons?
What is the matter there?   90
RODERIGO
Signior, is all your family within?
IAGO
Are your doors locked?
BRABANTIO   Why, wherefore ask you this?
IAGO
⟨Zounds,⟩ sir, you're robbed. For shame, put on your
    gown!   95
Your heart is burst. You have lost half your soul.
Even now, now, very now, an old black ram
Is tupping your white ewe. Arise, arise!
Awake the snorting citizens with the bell,
Or else the devil will make a grandsire of you.   100
Arise, I say!
BRABANTIO   What, have you lost your wits?
RODERIGO
Most reverend signior, do you know my voice?
BRABANTIO   Not I. What are you?
RODERIGO
My name is Roderigo.   105
BRABANTIO   The worser welcome.
I have charged thee not to haunt about my doors.
In honest plainness thou hast heard me say
My daughter is not for thee. And now in madness,
Being full of supper and distemp'ring draughts,   110
Upon malicious ⟨bravery⟩ dost thou come
To start my quiet.
RODERIGO   Sir, sir, sir—
BRABANTIO   But thou must needs be sure

115. **place:** i.e., social position
119. **grange:** a house in the country, isolated and therefore easily robbed
121. **simple:** sincere, honest
125. **have . . . horse:** i.e., allow your daughter to couple with an animal ("Covered," like "tupping," refers to the copulation of animals; "Barbary" is a region of Africa, and thus suggests Othello's homeland.)
126–27. **nephews, cousins, germans:** all terms for close relatives, here grandchildren; **coursers:** stallions; **jennets:** small Spanish horses
128. **profane:** foul-mouthed
134. **answer:** i.e., answer for
138. **odd-even . . . night:** around midnight—no longer night, strictly speaking, and not yet morning (hence **odd-even**) **dull:** i.e., sleeping **watch o' th' night:** nighttime
140. **But with:** i.e., than; **knave of common hire:** a servant offering himself for hire to anyone
142. **your allowance:** i.e., if you allowed this
143. **saucy:** insolent
146. **from:** i.e., contrary to

My ⟨spirit⟩ and my place have in ⟨them⟩ power   115
To make this bitter to thee.
RODERIGO
Patience, good sir.
BRABANTIO   What tell'st thou me of robbing?
This is Venice. My house is not a grange.
RODERIGO   Most grave Brabantio,   120
In simple and pure soul I come to you—
IAGO   ⟨Zounds,⟩ sir, you are one of those that will not
serve God if the devil bid you. Because we come to
do you service and you think we are ruffians, you'll
have your daughter covered with a Barbary horse,   125
you'll have your nephews neigh to you, you'll have
coursers for cousins and jennets for germans.
BRABANTIO   What profane wretch art thou?
IAGO   I am one, sir, that comes to tell you your daugh-
ter and the Moor are ⟨now⟩ making the beast with   130
two backs.
BRABANTIO   Thou art a villain.
IAGO   You are a senator.
BRABANTIO
This thou shalt answer. I know thee, Roderigo.
RODERIGO
Sir, I will answer anything. But I beseech you,   135
[If 't be your pleasure and most wise consent—
As partly I find it is—that your fair daughter,
At this odd-even and dull watch o' th' night,
Transported with no worse nor better guard
But with a knave of common hire, a gondolier,   140
To the gross clasps of a lascivious Moor:
If this be known to you, and your allowance,
We then have done you bold and saucy wrongs.
But if you know not this, my manners tell me
We have your wrong rebuke. Do not believe   145
That from the sense of all civility
I thus would play and trifle with your Reverence.

149. **gross:** great
150. **wit:** understanding, intellect
151. **In:** i.e., to; **extravagant and wheeling:** wandering, rootless (with perhaps an implication also of unrestrained, self-indulgent, changeable)
152. **Straight satisfy yourself:** i.e., inform yourself at once of the true state of affairs
156. **Strike . . . tinder:** i.e., light the **tinder** (a dry inflammable substance like partially charred linen)
157. **taper:** torch (lit from the **tinder**)
158. **accident:** unexpected event (i.e., Desdemona's elopement)
162. **not meet . . . place:** not proper nor "healthy" for someone in my position (as Othello's ensign)
163. **producted:** produced, brought forward
165. **gall:** irritate, annoy; **check:** (1) rebuke; (2) restraint
166. **cast:** dismiss
166–67. **embarked . . . to:** i.e., involved . . . in **loud:** clamorous, urgent
168. **stands in act:** is happening or about to happen; **for their souls:** i.e., even if they were to offer their souls in payment
169. **of his fathom:** i.e., with his capacity (as a military leader)
172. **life:** livelihood
174. **That:** i.e., in order that
176. **Sagittary:** the name of an inn, whose sign was Sagittarius, a centaur (See page 18.); **search:** search party
177 SD. **nightgown:** dressing gown
179. **what's . . . time:** the rest of my now-hated life

Your daughter, if you have not given her leave,
I say again, hath made a gross revolt,
Tying her duty, beauty, wit, and fortunes   150
In an extravagant and wheeling stranger
Of here and everywhere. Straight satisfy yourself.]
If she be in her chamber or your house,
Let loose on me the justice of the state
For thus deluding you.   155
BRABANTIO   Strike on the tinder, ho!
Give me a taper. Call up all my people.
This accident is not unlike my dream.
Belief of it oppresses me already.
Light, I say, light!   *He exits.* 160
IAGO, ⌈*to Roderigo*⌉   Farewell, for I must leave you.
It seems not meet nor wholesome to my place
To be producted, as if I stay I shall,
Against the Moor. For I do know the state,
However this may gall him with some check,   165
Cannot with safety cast him, for he's embarked
With such loud reason to the Cyprus wars,
Which even now stands in act, that, for their souls,
Another of his fathom they have none
To lead their business. In which regard,   170
Though I do hate him as I do hell ⟨pains,⟩
Yet, for necessity of present life,
I must show out a flag and sign of love—
Which is indeed but sign. That you shall surely find
    him,   175
Lead to the Sagittary the raisèd search,
And there will I be with him. So, farewell. *He exits.*

*Enter Brabantio ⟨in his nightgown,⟩ with Servants and
                    Torches.*

BRABANTIO
It is too true an evil. Gone she is,
And what's to come of my despisèd time

186. **thought:** comprehension
188. **Raise:** awake
191. **treason of the blood:** (1) betrayal of her father and family; (2) rebellion of the passions
192. **from hence:** from now on
193. **Is there not charms:** Singular verb with plural subject is not uncommon with Shakespeare and his contemporaries.
194. **property:** character, nature
195. **abused:** (1) deceived; (2) violated
201. **discover:** find
204. **I may . . . most:** i.e., I am so well respected at most houses that I can get help for the asking
205. **special officers of night:** i.e., officers who guard the city at night
206. **deserve:** i.e., requite, reward

Sagittarius. (1.1.176)
From Dirck Pietersz Pers, *Bellerophon, of Lust tot wysheyt* . . . (n.d.).

Is naught but bitterness.—Now, Roderigo,   180
Where didst thou see her?—O, unhappy girl!—
With the Moor, sayst thou?—Who would be a
   father?—
How didst thou know 'twas she?—O, she deceives
   me   185
Past thought!—What said she to you?—Get more
   tapers.
Raise all my kindred.—Are they married, think
   you?

RODERIGO   Truly, I think they are.   190

BRABANTIO
O heaven! How got she out? O treason of the blood!
Fathers, from hence trust not your daughters' minds
By what you see them act.—Is there not charms
By which the property of youth and maidhood
May be abused? Have you not read, Roderigo,   195
Of some such thing?

RODERIGO   Yes, sir, I have indeed.

BRABANTIO
Call up my brother.—O, would you had had her!—
Some one way, some another.—Do you know
Where we may apprehend her and the Moor?   200

RODERIGO
I think I can discover him, if you please
To get good guard and go along with me.

BRABANTIO
Pray you lead on. At every house I'll call.
I may command at most.—Get weapons, ho!
And raise some special officers of ⟨night⟩.—   205
On, good Roderigo. I will deserve your pains.

                                    They exit.

1.2 Iago warns Othello about Brabantio's anger, but Othello is confident in his own strength and in his love for Desdemona. Cassio arrives with orders for Othello: Othello is to meet with the duke and senators of Venice about a Turkish invasion of the Venetian colony of Cyprus. Brabantio and his armed band come to seize Othello, who persuades Brabantio to accompany him to the duke, where Othello has been summoned and where Brabantio can present his case against Othello for his "theft" of Desdemona.

---

2. **stuff . . . conscience:** material of which conscience is made
5. **yerked:** i.e., jabbed
9. **scurvy:** insulting
12. **full hard:** with great difficulty; **forbear him:** keep myself from injuring him
13. **fast:** securely
14. **the magnifico:** i.e., Brabantio, one of Venice's most prominent citizens
15–16. **hath in his effect . . . Duke's:** perhaps, has power and influence twice that of any other citizen and equal to the duke's
17. **grievance:** oppression
18. **might to enforce it on:** i.e., power to enforce it to its full extent
19. **cable:** i.e., scope (in modern slang, "rope")
21. **signiory:** Venice's governing body
22. **'Tis . . . to know:** i.e., it is not yet known
25. **siege:** a seat for a person of rank
25–27. **my demerits . . . reached:** my meritorious acts give me a social status comparable to Desdemona's family's

(continued)

Scene 2
Enter Othello, Iago, Attendants, with Torches.

IAGO
Though in the trade of war I have slain men,
Yet do I hold it very stuff o' th' conscience
To do no contrived murder. I lack iniquity
⟨Sometimes⟩ to do me service. Nine or ten times
I had thought t' have yerked him here under the 5
 ribs.
OTHELLO
'Tis better as it is.
IAGO   Nay, but he prated
And spoke such scurvy and provoking terms
Against your Honor,   10
That with the little godliness I have
I did full hard forbear him. But I pray you, sir,
Are you fast married? Be assured of this,
That the magnifico is much beloved,
And hath in his effect a voice potential 15
As double as the Duke's. He will divorce you
Or put upon you what restraint or grievance
The law (with all his might to enforce it on)
Will give him cable.
OTHELLO   Let him do his spite. 20
My services which I have done the signiory
Shall out-tongue his complaints. 'Tis yet to know
(Which, when I know that boasting is an honor,
I shall promulgate) I fetch my life and being
From men of royal siege, and my demerits 25
May speak unbonneted to as proud a fortune
As this that I have reached. For know, Iago,
But that I love the gentle Desdemona,
I would not my unhousèd free condition
Put into circumscription and confine 30
For the sea's worth. But look, what lights come
 yond?

28. **But:** except
29. **unhousèd:** unconfined
30. **circumscription and confine:** restraint and confinement
31. **sea's worth:** i.e., all the treasure in the sea
33. **raisèd:** perhaps, awakened from sleep, or, perhaps, aroused to action
36. **parts:** qualities; **perfect:** i.e., guiltless
38. **Janus:** Roman god with two faces
38 SD. **Torches:** men carrying torches
43. **haste-post-haste:** i.e., immediate
44. **on the instant:** instantly
47. **heat:** urgency
48. **sequent:** successive
50. **Consuls:** i.e., senators (see the next scene)
51. **hotly:** urgently
54. **several:** separate
59. **what makes he:** i.e., what is he doing
60. **boarded:** gone aboard and captured (with a sexual meaning); **carrack:** galleon, a great ship with a rich cargo
61. **prize:** booty

Janus. (1.2.38)
From Andrea Alciati, *Emblemata* . . . (1583).

22

IAGO
Those are the raisèd father and his friends.
You were best go in.
OTHELLO   Not I. I must be found.   35
My parts, my title, and my perfect soul
Shall manifest me rightly. Is it they?
IAGO   By Janus, I think no.

Enter Cassio, with ⟨Officers, and⟩ Torches.

OTHELLO
The servants of the ⟨Duke⟩ and my lieutenant!
The goodness of the night upon you, friends.   40
What is the news?
CASSIO   The Duke does greet you, general,
And he requires your haste-post-haste appearance,
Even on the instant.
OTHELLO   What is the matter, think you?   45
CASSIO
Something from Cyprus, as I may divine.
It is a business of some heat. The galleys
Have sent a dozen sequent messengers
This very night at one another's heels,
And many of the Consuls, raised and met,   50
Are at the Duke's already. You have been hotly
   called for.
When, being not at your lodging to be found,
The Senate hath sent about three several quests
To search you out.   55
OTHELLO   'Tis well I am found by you.
I will but spend a word here in the house
And go with you.   ⌜*He exits.*⌝
CASSIO   Ancient, what makes he here?
IAGO
Faith, he tonight hath boarded a land carrack.   60
If it prove lawful prize, he's made forever.
CASSIO   I do not understand.

65. **Marry:** i.e., indeed (originally an oath on the name of the Virgin Mary)
67. **Have with you:** i.e., I'll go with you
69. **advised:** wary
70. **to:** with
71. **stand:** halt
75. **I am for you:** Iago pretends to challenge Roderigo.
76. **Keep up:** i.e., sheathe; **bright:** shiny and unmarked, because unused
82. **enchanted:** cast a spell on
83. **refer me:** entrust my case; **things . . . sense:** evidence plain to the senses
85. **tender:** young
88. **a general mock:** everyone's mockery

IAGO　　　　　　　　　He's married.
CASSIO　　　　　　　　　　To who?
IAGO　Marry, to—　　　　　　　　　　65

⌐*Reenter Othello.*⌐

　　　　　Come, captain, will you go?
OTHELLO　Have with you.
CASSIO
　Here comes another troop to seek for you.

Enter Brabantio, Roderigo, with Officers, and Torches.

IAGO
　It is Brabantio. General, be advised,
　He comes to bad intent.　　　　　　70
OTHELLO　　　　　　　Holla, stand there!
RODERIGO　Signior, it is the Moor.
BRABANTIO　　　　　　　Down with him,
　thief!
　　　　　　　⌐*They draw their swords.*⌐
IAGO
　You, Roderigo! Come, sir, I am for you.　75
OTHELLO
　Keep up your bright swords, for the dew will rust
　them.
　Good signior, you shall more command with years
　Than with your weapons.
BRABANTIO
　O, thou foul thief, where hast thou stowed my　80
　daughter?
　Damned as thou art, thou hast enchanted her!
　For I'll refer me to all things of sense,
　[If she in chains of magic were not bound,]
　Whether a maid so tender, fair, and happy,　85
　So opposite to marriage that she shunned
　The wealthy curlèd ⟨darlings⟩ of our nation,
　Would ever have, t' incur a general mock,

89. **guardage:** perhaps, her protected situation (or, **her guardage:** i.e., my guardianship of her)

90. **fear:** frighten

91. **Judge me the world:** i.e., let the world be my judge; **gross in sense:** self-evident

92. **practiced on her:** tricked her

94. **motion:** impulse, inclination; **disputed on:** i.e., argued in court

96. **attach:** arrest

98. **arts . . . warrant:** i.e., black magic, forbidden by law

101. **Hold:** i.e., hold back

102. **you of my inclining:** i.e., my followers

104. **Whither will:** i.e., where do you wish

106–8. **fit . . . answer:** i.e., until the court is next in session **course of direct session:** either regular sessions of court or a specially convened (**direct**) session

119. **idle:** frivolous

"A practicer of arts inhibited." (1.2.97–98)
From Christopher Marlowe, *The tragicall historie of . . . Doctor Faustus . . .* (1631).

Run from her guardage to the sooty bosom
Of such a thing as thou—to fear, not to delight!   90
[Judge me the world, if 'tis not gross in sense
That thou hast practiced on her with foul charms,
Abused her delicate youth with drugs or minerals
That weakens motion. I'll have 't disputed on.
'Tis probable, and palpable to thinking.   95
I therefore apprehend and do attach thee]
For an abuser of the world, a practicer
Of arts inhibited and out of warrant.—
Lay hold upon him. If he do resist,
Subdue him at his peril.   100
OTHELLO   Hold your hands,
Both you of my inclining and the rest.
Were it my cue to fight, I should have known it
Without a prompter.—Whither will you that I go
To answer this your charge?   105
BRABANTIO   To prison, till fit time
Of law and course of direct session
Call thee to answer.
OTHELLO   What if ⟨I⟩ do obey?
How may the Duke be therewith satisfied,   110
Whose messengers are here about my side,
Upon some present business of the state,
To bring me to him?
OFFICER   'Tis true, most worthy signior.
The Duke's in council, and your noble self   115
I am sure is sent for.
BRABANTIO   How? The Duke in council?
In this time of the night? Bring him away;
Mine's not an idle cause. The Duke himself,
Or any of my brothers of the state,   120
Cannot but feel this wrong as 'twere their own.
For if such actions may have passage free,
Bondslaves and pagans shall our statesmen be.
                            They exit.

1.3 The duke and the senators discuss the movements of the Turkish fleet and conclude that its target is, indeed, Cyprus. When Brabantio and Othello arrive, the duke insists on evidence to support the old man's charge that Othello has bewitched Desdemona. At Othello's suggestion, the duke sends for Desdemona. Othello describes his courtship of Desdemona, who, when she enters, tells her father and the senators that she has married Othello because she loves him. She thereby vindicates Othello before the senate. The duke orders Othello immediately to Cyprus and grants Desdemona her wish to join him there. Othello gives Iago the duty of conveying Desdemona to Cyprus. Alone with Iago, Roderigo, now in despair of winning Desdemona's love, threatens suicide, but Iago persuades him instead to sell his lands for ready cash and to pursue Desdemona to Cyprus. Iago begins to plot to himself how he may use Othello's marriage to get back at Othello and to get Cassio's place as lieutenant.

---

1. **composition:** consistency; **these news:** these reports (**News** is sometimes treated as plural.)

2. **credit:** credibility

3. **disproportioned:** inconsistent

7. **jump not:** do not completely agree; **just account:** exact count

8. **aim:** estimate

12. **I do not . . . error:** i.e., the inconsistency does not reassure me

13–14. **But . . . sense:** I do believe—and fear— the main item of information   **approve:** confirm

(continued)

Scene 3
Enter Duke, Senators, and Officers.

DUKE, ⌜*reading a paper*⌝
There's no composition in ⟨these⟩ news
That gives them credit.
FIRST SENATOR, ⌜*reading a paper*⌝
Indeed, they are disproportioned.
My letters say a hundred and seven galleys.
DUKE
And mine, a hundred forty.   5
SECOND SENATOR, ⌜*reading a paper*⌝
                                      And mine, two hundred.
But though they jump not on a just account
(As in these cases, where the aim reports
'Tis oft with difference), yet do they all confirm
A Turkish fleet, and bearing up to Cyprus.   10
DUKE
Nay, it is possible enough to judgment.
I do not so secure me in the error,
But the main article I do approve
In fearful sense.
SAILOR, *within*   What ho, what ho, what ho!   15

Enter Sailor.

OFFICER   A messenger from the galleys.
DUKE   Now, what's the business?
SAILOR
The Turkish preparation makes for Rhodes.
So was I bid report here to the state
By Signior Angelo.   20
DUKE
How say you by this change?
FIRST SENATOR   This cannot be,
By no assay of reason. 'Tis a pageant
To keep us in false gaze. When we consider
Th' importancy of Cyprus to the Turk,   25

18. **preparation:** fleet prepared for war
21. **How . . . by:** i.e., what do you say about
23. **By no assay:** i.e., according to any test; **pageant:** a show designed to deceive us
24. **in false gaze:** i.e., looking the wrong way
26. **but:** only
27. **it:** i.e., Cyprus
28. **may he . . . bear it:** i.e., the Turk can more easily take Cyprus **question:** dispute, contest **bear it:** carry it, capture it
29. **For that:** because; **brace:** state of defense
31. **dressed in:** equipped with
34. **latest:** until last
39. **Ottomites:** Turks; **Reverend and Gracious:** addressed to the duke
41. **injointed them:** joined; **after:** i.e., second
43–44. **restem . . . course:** i.e., retrace their course
47. **servitor:** servant
48. **recommends:** informs
51. **Marcus . . . town?:** Is not Marcus Luccicos in town?
54. **Post-post-haste:** i.e., instantly; **Dispatch:** hurry

And let ourselves again but understand
That, as it more concerns the Turk than Rhodes,
So may he with more facile question bear it,
[For that it stands not in such warlike brace,
But altogether lacks th' abilities   30
That Rhodes is dressed in—if we make thought of
   this,
We must not think the Turk is so unskillful
To leave that latest which concerns him first,
Neglecting an attempt of ease and gain   35
To wake and wage a danger profitless.]
DUKE
Nay, in all confidence, he's not for Rhodes.
OFFICER   Here is more news.

Enter a Messenger.

MESSENGER
The Ottomites, Reverend and Gracious,
Steering with due course toward the isle of Rhodes,   40
Have there injointed them with an after fleet.
[FIRST SENATOR
Ay, so I thought. How many, as you guess?]
MESSENGER
Of thirty sail; and now they do restem
Their backward course, bearing with frank
   appearance   45
Their purposes toward Cyprus. Signior Montano,
Your trusty and most valiant servitor,
With his free duty recommends you thus,
And prays you to believe him.
DUKE   'Tis certain, then, for Cyprus.   50
Marcus Luccicos, is not he in town?
FIRST SENATOR
He's now in Florence.
DUKE   Write from us to him.
Post-post-haste. Dispatch.

56. **straight:** straightway, immediately
57. **general enemy Ottoman:** i.e., the Turks, the enemy of all Christians
58. **gentle:** noble (a title of respect)
62. **place:** official position; **aught:** i.e., anything
65. **particular:** personal
66. **floodgate:** torrentlike
67. **engluts:** i.e., swallows
74. **mountebanks:** wandering quacks
75–77. **nature . . . not:** i.e., nature could not err so preposterously without (**sans**) witchcraft **nature:** i.e., Desdemona's nature
80–82. **the bloody book . . . sense:** i.e., you shall be judge and pass sentence according to your own interpretation of the law, which provides for the death penalty (and therefore is called **the bloody book of law**)
82. **proper:** own
83. **Stood . . . action:** i.e., were the one charged

FIRST SENATOR
  Here comes Brabantio and the valiant Moor.   55

  Enter Brabantio, Othello, Cassio, Iago, Roderigo, and
          Officers.

DUKE
  Valiant Othello, we must straight employ you
  Against the general enemy Ottoman.
  ⌈*To Brabantio.*⌉ I did not see you. Welcome, gentle
    signior.
  We lacked your counsel and your help tonight.   60
BRABANTIO
  So did I yours. Good your Grace, pardon me.
  Neither my place nor aught I heard of business
  Hath raised me from my bed, nor doth the general
    care
  Take hold on me, for my particular grief   65
  Is of so floodgate and o'erbearing nature
  That it engluts and swallows other sorrows
  And it is still itself.
DUKE   Why, what's the matter?
BRABANTIO   My daughter! O, my daughter!   70
⌈FIRST SENATOR⌉   Dead?
BRABANTIO   Ay, to me.
  She is abused, stol'n from me, and corrupted
  By spells and medicines bought of mountebanks;
  For nature so prepost'rously to err—   75
  Being not deficient, blind, or lame of sense—
  Sans witchcraft could not.
DUKE
  Whoe'er he be that in this foul proceeding
  Hath thus beguiled your daughter of herself
  And you of her, the bloody book of law   80
  You shall yourself read in the bitter letter,
  After your own sense, yea, though our proper son
  Stood in your action.

89. **in your own part:** i.e., on behalf of yourself
90. **but:** except
92. **approved good:** i.e., demonstrably good in my experience
95. **The very head . . . offending:** i.e., the foremost, or chief, of my offenses   **front:** forehead
96. **Rude:** unrefined, unpolished
98. **pith:** strength
99. **some nine moons wasted:** i.e., nine months ago
100. **dearest:** most valuable; **tented field:** i.e., battlefield (on which armies also pitched their tents)
106. **round:** straightforward
110. **withal:** i.e., with
113–14. **her motion . . . herself:** i.e., her own natural impulses made her blush
115. **credit:** reputation

A "tented field." (1.3.100)
From Jacobus a. Bruck, *Emblemata . . .* (1615).

BRABANTIO   Humbly I thank your Grace.
Here is the man—this Moor, whom now it seems   85
Your special mandate for the state affairs
Hath hither brought.
ALL   We are very sorry for 't.
DUKE, ⌜to Othello⌝
What, in your own part, can you say to this?
BRABANTIO Nothing, but this is so.   90
OTHELLO
Most potent, grave, and reverend signiors,
My very noble and approved good masters:
That I have ta'en away this old man's daughter,
It is most true; true I have married her.
The very head and front of my offending   95
Hath this extent, no more. Rude am I in my speech,
And little blessed with the soft phrase of peace;
For since these arms of mine had seven years' pith,
Till now some nine moons wasted, they have used
Their dearest action in the tented field,   100
And little of this great world can I speak
More than pertains to feats of ⟨broil⟩ and battle.
And therefore little shall I grace my cause
In speaking for myself. Yet, by your gracious
     patience,   105
I will a round unvarnished tale deliver
Of my whole course of love—what drugs, what
     charms,
What conjuration, and what mighty magic
(For such proceeding I am charged withal)   110
I won his daughter.
BRABANTIO   A maiden never bold,
Of spirit so still and quiet that her motion
Blushed at herself. And she, in spite of nature,
Of years, of country, credit, everything,   115
To fall in love with what she feared to look on!
It is a judgment maimed and most imperfect

119. **must be driven:** i.e., judgment is forced
120. **practices . . . hell:** i.e., cunning hellish plots
121. **Why:** i.e., to explain why
122. **blood:** passions, sensual appetites
123. **dram . . . effect:** small quantity of liquid magically created for this purpose
126. **more wider . . . test:** fuller and clearer evidence
127. **thin habits:** i.e., insubstantial accusations (literally, light clothing); **likelihoods:** hypotheses
128. **modern:** ordinary, commonplace; **seeming:** perhaps, appearance; **prefer:** produce
130. **forcèd courses:** i.e., by means of force
132. **it:** i.e., Desdemona's affection; **question:** interchange, talk
133. **affordeth:** naturally yields
136. **before:** in the presence of
144. **vices of my blood:** my sins
145. **justly:** truly, exactly
150. **Still:** continually; **the story:** i.e., about the story

That will confess perfection so could err
Against all rules of nature, and must be driven
To find out practices of cunning hell   120
Why this should be. I therefore vouch again
That with some mixtures powerful o'er the blood,
Or with some dram conjured to this effect,
He wrought upon her.
⟨DUKE⟩   To vouch this is no proof   125
    Without more wider and more ⟨overt⟩ test
    Than these thin habits and poor likelihoods
    Of modern seeming do prefer against him.
⟨FIRST SENATOR⟩ But, Othello, speak:
    Did you by indirect and forcèd courses   130
    Subdue and poison this young maid's affections?
    Or came it by request, and such fair question
    As soul to soul affordeth?
OTHELLO   I do beseech you,
    Send for the lady to the Sagittary   135
    And let her speak of me before her father.
    If you do find me foul in her report,
    [The trust, the office I do hold of you,]
    Not only take away, but let your sentence
    Even fall upon my life.   140
DUKE Fetch Desdemona hither.
OTHELLO
    Ancient, conduct them. You best know the place.
                              ⌈*Iago and Attendants exit.*⌉
    And ⟨till⟩ she come, as truly as to heaven
    [I do confess the vices of my blood,]
    So justly to your grave ears I'll present   145
    How I did thrive in this fair lady's love,
    And she in mine.
DUKE Say it, Othello.
OTHELLO
    Her father loved me, oft invited me,
    Still questioned me the story of my life   150

152. **passed:** experienced, endured

156. **moving accidents:** stirring events or disasters

157–58. **imminent deadly breach:** a death-threatening gap in fortifications

160. **redemption:** being ransomed

161. **portance in:** conduct during

162. **antres:** caves; **idle:** empty

165. **hint:** occasion, opportunity; **process:** narrative

167. **Anthropophagi:** a race of cannibals mentioned in travelers' tales

177. **dilate:** relate in detail, expand upon

178. **by parcels:** in pieces

179. **intentively:** (1) attentively; (2) intently

184. **in faith:** a mild oath; **passing:** surpassingly

One of the "men whose heads do grow beneath their shoulders." (1.3.167–68)
From Conrad Lycosthenes, *Prodigiorum* . . . (1557).

From year to year—the ⟨battles,⟩ sieges, ⟨fortunes⟩
That I have passed.
I ran it through, even from my boyish days
To th' very moment that he bade me tell it,
Wherein I spoke of most disastrous chances: 155
Of moving accidents by flood and field,
Of hairbreadth 'scapes i' th' imminent deadly
    breach,
Of being taken by the insolent foe
And sold to slavery, of my redemption thence,   160
And portance in my traveler's history,
Wherein of antres vast and deserts idle,
Rough quarries, rocks, ⟨and⟩ hills whose ⟨heads⟩
    touch heaven,
It was my hint to speak—such was my process—   165
And of the cannibals that each ⟨other⟩ eat,
The Anthropophagi, and men whose heads
⟨Do grow⟩ beneath their shoulders. These things to
    hear
Would Desdemona seriously incline.   170
But still the house affairs would draw her ⟨thence,⟩
Which ever as she could with haste dispatch
She'd come again, and with a greedy ear
Devour up my discourse. Which I, observing,
Took once a pliant hour, and found good means   175
To draw from her a prayer of earnest heart
That I would all my pilgrimage dilate,
Whereof by parcels she had something heard,
But not ⟨intentively.⟩ I did consent,
And often did beguile her of her tears   180
When I did speak of some distressful stroke
That my youth suffered. My story being done,
She gave me for my pains a world of ⟨sighs.⟩
She swore, in faith, 'twas strange, 'twas passing
    strange,   185
'Twas pitiful, 'twas wondrous pitiful.

191. **but:** simply
194. **that:** because
196. **witness:** bear witness to
199. **Take . . . best:** make the best of this bad business (proverbial)
204. **Destruction . . . head:** i.e., let destruction fall on my head
210. **bound:** obliged; **education:** upbringing
211. **learn:** teach
212. **lord of duty:** i.e., the one to whom I owe obedience
217. **challenge:** claim
219. **have done:** i.e., am finished

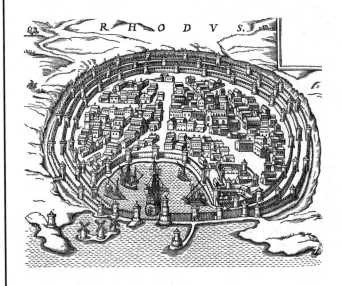

Rhodes. (1.3.18)
From Sebastian Münster, *La cosmographie vniuerselle* . . . (1575).

She wished she had not heard it, yet she wished
That heaven had made her such a man. She thanked
    me,
And bade me, if I had a friend that loved her,   190
I should but teach him how to tell my story,
And that would woo her. Upon this hint I spake.
She loved me for the dangers I had passed,
And I loved her that she did pity them.
This only is the witchcraft I have used.   195
Here comes the lady. Let her witness it.

        Enter Desdemona, Iago, Attendants.

DUKE
I think this tale would win my daughter, too.
Good Brabantio,
Take up this mangled matter at the best.
Men do their broken weapons rather use   200
Than their bare hands.
BRABANTIO   I pray you hear her speak.
If she confess that she was half the wooer,
Destruction on my head if my bad blame
Light on the man.—Come hither, gentle mistress.   205
Do you perceive in all this noble company
Where most you owe obedience?
DESDEMONA   My noble father,
I do perceive here a divided duty.
To you I am bound for life and education.   210
My life and education both do learn me
How to respect you. You are the lord of duty.
I am hitherto your daughter. But here's my
    husband.
And so much duty as my mother showed   215
To you, preferring you before her father,
So much I challenge that I may profess
Due to the Moor my lord.
BRABANTIO   God be with you! I have done.

220. **Please it:** i.e., if it please
221. **get:** beget, father
223. **here do give thee:** It is possible that at this point Brabantio may join their hands.
224. **but . . . already:** i.e., if you did not already have
225. **For your sake, jewel:** i.e., on account of you, Desdemona
227. **For:** because; **escape:** i.e., elopement
228. **clogs:** weights fastened to the legs of captives
229. **lay a sentence:** i.e., pronounce a maxim (Latin *sententia*)
230. **grise:** i.e., **step**
232–40. **When remedies . . . grief:** These sayings of the duke are involved and unclear, but each generally expands the proverb "What is past help should be past tears."
234. **mischief:** misfortune
235. **next:** nearest, quickest
237. **Patience . . . makes:** i.e., patience makes a mockery of fortune's damage
238. **The robbed:** i.e., the victim of robbery
240. **spends a bootless:** indulges in a profitless
243–46. **He . . . borrow:** Brabantio makes a distinction between someone, like the duke, who, free of sorrow, delivers platitudes, and someone, like himself, who, already grieving, must draw on his already exhausted patience to put up with these platitudes.
247. **gall:** bitterness
250. **piercèd:** lanced and thereby cured

Please it your Grace, on to the state affairs.   220
I had rather to adopt a child than get it.—
Come hither, Moor.
I here do give thee that with all my heart
[Which, but thou hast already, with all my heart]
I would keep from thee.—For your sake, jewel,   225
I am glad at soul I have no other child,
For thy escape would teach me tyranny,
To hang clogs on them.—I have done, my lord.
DUKE
Let me speak like yourself and lay a sentence,
Which as a grise or step may help these lovers   230
⟨Into your favor.⟩
When remedies are past, the griefs are ended
By seeing the worst, which late on hopes depended.
To mourn a mischief that is past and gone
Is the next way to draw new mischief on.   235
What cannot be preserved when fortune takes,
Patience her injury a mock'ry makes.
The robbed that smiles steals something from the
    thief;
He robs himself that spends a bootless grief.   240
BRABANTIO
So let the Turk of Cyprus us beguile,
We lose it not so long as we can smile.
He bears the sentence well that nothing bears
But the free comfort which from thence he hears;
But he bears both the sentence and the sorrow   245
That, to pay grief, must of poor patience borrow.
These sentences to sugar or to gall,
Being strong on both sides, are equivocal.
But words are words. I never yet did hear
That the bruised heart was piercèd through the   250
    ⟨ear.⟩
I humbly beseech you, proceed to th' affairs of
    state.

255. **fortitude:** strength

257. **substitute:** deputy; **allowed:** acknowledged

257–58. **a sovereign . . . effects:** i.e., which has a powerful influence over what we do

258–59. **throws . . . you:** i.e., says you are a safer person for the position

260. **slubber:** sully

261. **stubborn and boist'rous:** painfully rough

262–64. **custom . . . down:** i.e., habit has made the hard beds of war seem soft to me   **thrice-driven bed of down:** i.e., an exceedingly soft bed (The feathers, that is, have been winnowed [**driven**] three times so that only the smallest and softest remain.)

264. **agnize:** acknowledge

265–66. **alacrity . . . hardness:** i.e., eagerness to undergo hardships

267. **This . . . wars:** Such a combination of singular and plural was not unusual in Shakespeare's time.

268. **state:** rank and power

269. **fit disposition:** appropriate arrangements

270. **Due . . . exhibition:** i.e., assignment to her of a proper (**due**) residence and maintenance

271. **besort:** suitable company

272. **levels . . . breeding:** is consistent with her rank

279. **To . . . ear:** i.e., listen with favor as I unfold my plan

280–81. **And . . . simpleness:** i.e., grant me the privilege of your voice to compensate for my lack of skill (**simpleness**) as a speaker

282. **would you:** i.e., do you wish

284. **My . . . fortunes:** i.e., the openly violent way in which I took by storm the future (**fortunes**)

286. **quality:** i.e., that which makes him what he is

44

DUKE   The Turk with a most mighty preparation makes
       for Cyprus. Othello, the fortitude of the place is   255
       best known to you. And though we have there a
       substitute of most allowed sufficiency, yet opinion, a
       sovereign mistress of effects, throws a more safer
       voice on you. You must therefore be content to
       slubber the gloss of your new fortunes with this   260
       more stubborn and boist'rous expedition.
OTHELLO
    The tyrant custom, most grave senators,
    Hath made the flinty and steel ⌜couch⌝ of war
    My thrice-driven bed of down. I do agnize
    A natural and prompt alacrity   265
    I find in hardness, and do undertake
    This present wars against the Ottomites.
    Most humbly, therefore, bending to your state,
    I crave fit disposition for my wife,
    Due reference of place and exhibition,   270
    With such accommodation and besort
    As levels with her breeding.
DUKE
    Why, at her father's.
BRABANTIO   I will not have it so.
OTHELLO   Nor I.   275
DESDEMONA   Nor would I there reside
    To put my father in impatient thoughts
    By being in his eye. Most gracious duke,
    To my unfolding lend your prosperous ear
    And let me find a charter in your voice   280
    T' assist my simpleness.
DUKE   What would you, Desdemona?
DESDEMONA
    That I ⟨did⟩ love the Moor to live with him
    My downright violence and storm of fortunes
    May trumpet to the world. My heart's subdued   285
    Even to the very quality of my lord.

288. **parts:** qualities
291. **moth:** idle unimportant creature
293. **heavy:** sorrowful, tedious
293–94. **support / By:** i.e., undergo during
295. **voice:** approval
296. **Vouch:** declare
298. **heat:** sexual desire, which Othello may be associating with his past youth (**young affects**)
299. **In . . . satisfaction:** In the early printed texts, this line reads "In my defunct, and proper satisfaction."
300. **free and bounteous:** noble and liberal
301. **heaven . . . think:** i.e., heaven prevent you good souls from thinking that
302. **scant:** neglect
303. **For:** because
304. **feathered Cupid:** Roman god of love, usually depicted as a winged infant (hence **light-winged toys, toys** meaning erotic pleasures); **seel:** close (literally, sew up); **wanton:** lustful
305. **speculative . . . instruments:** i.e., eyes, and also eyes of the mind **officed:** given an office or function
306. **That:** i.e., so that; **disports:** amusements
307. **helm:** helmet
308. **indign:** disgraceful
309. **Make head . . . estimation:** collect as an army to attack my reputation
319–20. **quality . . . you:** i.e., of a kind to be of concern to you

I saw Othello's visage in his mind,
And to his honors and his valiant parts
Did I my soul and fortunes consecrate.
So that, dear lords, if I be left behind,   290
A moth of peace, and he go to the war,
The rites for why I love him are bereft me
And I a heavy interim shall support
By his dear absence. Let me go with him.
OTHELLO   Let her have your voice.   295
Vouch with me, heaven, I therefore beg it not
To please the palate of my appetite,
Nor to comply with heat (the young affects
In ⌈me⌉ defunct) and proper satisfaction,
But to be free and bounteous to her mind.   300
And heaven defend your good souls that you think
I will your serious and great business scant
⟨For⟩ she is with me. No, when light-winged toys
Of feathered Cupid seel with wanton dullness
My speculative and officed ⟨instruments,⟩   305
That my disports corrupt and taint my business,
Let housewives make a skillet of my helm,
And all indign and base adversities
Make head against my estimation.
DUKE
Be it as you shall privately determine,   310
Either for her stay or going. Th' affair cries haste,
And speed must answer it.
⌈FIRST⌉ SENATOR   You must away tonight.
OTHELLO   With all my
    heart.   315
DUKE
At nine i' th' morning here we'll meet again.
Othello, leave some officer behind
And he shall our commission bring to you,
⟨With⟩ such things else of quality and respect
As doth import you.   320

324. **conveyance:** escort
330. **delighted:** i.e., delightful
333. **Look to:** watch
335. **My . . . faith:** i.e., I would stake my life on her fidelity to me
336. **Honest:** Often, as here, a condescending term for a social inferior, **honest** is repeatedly attached to Iago's name. (Later, it plays against the word as applied to Desdemona, where, as it standardly does in referring to a woman, it always means "chaste.")
339. **advantage:** opportunity
341. **worldly . . . direction:** i.e., perhaps, domestic or financial instructions
347. **incontinently:** immediately

OTHELLO   So please your Grace, my
   ancient.
A man he is of honesty and trust.
To his conveyance I assign my wife,
With what else needful your good Grace shall think   325
To be sent after me.
DUKE   Let it be so.
Good night to everyone. ⌜*To Brabantio.*⌝ And, noble
   signior,
If virtue no delighted beauty lack,   330
Your son-in-law is far more fair than black.
⟨FIRST⟩ SENATOR
Adieu, brave Moor, use Desdemona well.
BRABANTIO
Look to her, Moor, if thou hast eyes to see.
She has deceived her father, and may thee. *He exits.*
OTHELLO
My life upon her faith!   335
   ⌜*The Duke, the Senators, Cassio, and Officers exit.*⌝
                    Honest Iago,
My Desdemona must I leave to thee.
I prithee let thy wife attend on her,
And bring them after in the best advantage.—
Come, Desdemona, I have but an hour   340
Of love, of ⟨worldly matters,⟩ and direction
To spend with thee. We must obey the time.
                    ⟨*Othello and Desdemona*⟩ *exit.*
RODERIGO Iago—
IAGO What sayst thou, noble heart?
RODERIGO What will I do, think'st thou?   345
IAGO Why, go to bed and sleep.
RODERIGO I will incontinently drown myself.
IAGO If thou dost, I shall never love thee after. Why,
   thou silly gentleman!
RODERIGO It is silliness to live, when to live is torment, 350
   and then have we a prescription to die when death is
   our physician.

357. **guinea hen:** i.e., female guinea fowl (Iago's contemptuous reference to Desdemona)
358. **change:** i.e., exchange
360. **fond:** doting; **virtue:** power
361. **fig:** term of contempt (To "give the fig" is to make an obscene gesture with the thumb.)
365. **gender:** kind
365–66. **distract it with:** i.e., divide it among
367–68. **corrigible:** corrective
368. **balance:** a weighing device with **scales**
369. **poise:** counterbalance
370. **blood:** passions
373. **motions:** emotions, impulses; **unbitted:** i.e., uncontrolled, like horses without bits in their mouths
374–75. **sect . . . scion:** cutting . . . shoot
382. **Put money . . . purse:** In these speeches, Iago urges Roderigo to turn his land and other material possessions into ready cash.
383–84. **defeat . . . beard:** i.e., disguise your face with a beard
388. **answerable sequestration:** comparable separation

A balance. (1.3.368)
From Silvestro Pietrasanta, *Symbola heroica* . . . (1682).

IAGO   O, villainous! I have looked upon the world for
   four times seven years, and since I could distinguish betwixt a benefit and an injury, I never found   355
   man that knew how to love himself. Ere I would say
   I would drown myself for the love of a guinea hen, I
   would change my humanity with a baboon.
RODERIGO   What should I do? I confess it is my shame
   to be so fond, but it is not in my virtue to amend it.   360
IAGO   Virtue? A fig! 'Tis in ourselves that we are thus or
   thus. Our bodies are our gardens, to the which our
   wills are gardeners. So that if we will plant nettles
   or sow lettuce, set hyssop and weed up thyme,
   supply it with one gender of herbs or distract it   365
   with many, either to have it sterile with idleness or
   manured with industry, why the power and corrigible authority of this lies in our wills. If the ⟨balance⟩
   of our lives had not one scale of reason to poise
   another of sensuality, the blood and baseness of our   370
   natures would conduct us to most prepost'rous
   conclusions. But we have reason to cool our raging
   motions, our carnal stings, ⟨our⟩ unbitted lusts—
   whereof I take this that you call love to be a sect, or
   scion.   375
RODERIGO   It cannot be.
IAGO   It is merely a lust of the blood and a permission
   of the will. Come, be a man! Drown thyself? Drown
   cats and blind puppies. I have professed me thy
   friend, and I confess me knit to thy deserving   380
   with cables of perdurable toughness. I could never
   better stead thee than now. Put money in thy purse.
   Follow thou the wars; defeat thy favor with an
   usurped beard. I say, put money in thy purse. It
   cannot be that Desdemona should ⟨long⟩ continue   385
   her love to the Moor—put money in thy purse—
   nor he his to her. It was a violent commencement in
   her, and thou shalt see an answerable sequestration

390. **wills:** desires

391. **locusts:** This seems to be an allusion to the "locusts and wild honey" that fed John the Baptist in the wilderness (Matthew 3.4). It is possible that, for both Matthew and Iago, **locusts** are the pods of the carob tree (called "locust beans" because of their resemblance to the insect). However, the Geneva Bible (1560), in its marginal note on Matthew 3.4, while glossing the phrase as "food that God does freely provide," glosses the word *locusts* as "grass-hoppers."

392. **coloquintida:** a bitter drug

393. **change for youth:** i.e., exchange (Othello) for a young man

395–96. **wilt needs:** must

397. **Make . . . money:** i.e., raise ready cash

397–98. **sanctimony:** religion (i.e., the marriage **vow**)

398. **erring:** wandering

401. **A pox of:** a plague on

402. **clean . . . way:** entirely beside the point

403. **compassing:** achieving

405. **fast:** steadfast

407. **Thou . . . me:** i.e., you can trust me

409. **hearted:** fixed in my heart

410. **be conjunctive:** i.e., unite

414. **Traverse:** i.e., march

418. **betimes:** early

419. **Go to:** an expression of impatience

—put but money in thy purse. These Moors are
changeable in their wills. Fill thy purse with money.   390
The food that to him now is as luscious as locusts
shall be to him shortly as bitter as coloquintida.
She must change for youth. When she is sated
with his body she will find the ⟨error⟩ of her choice.
Therefore, put money in thy purse. If thou wilt   395
needs damn thyself, do it a more delicate way than
drowning. Make all the money thou canst. If sanctimony and a frail vow betwixt an erring barbarian
and ⟨a⟩ supersubtle Venetian be not too hard for my
wits and all the tribe of hell, thou shalt enjoy her.   400
Therefore make money. A pox of drowning thyself!
It is clean out of the way. Seek thou rather to be
hanged in compassing thy joy than to be drowned
and go without her.
RODERIGO   Wilt thou be fast to my hopes if I depend on   405
the issue?
IAGO   Thou art sure of me. Go, make money. I have
told thee often, and I retell thee again and again, I
hate the Moor. My cause is hearted; thine hath no
less reason. Let us be conjunctive in our revenge   410
against him. If thou canst cuckold him, thou dost
thyself a pleasure, me a sport. There are many
events in the womb of time which will be delivered.
Traverse, go, provide thy money. We will have more
of this tomorrow. Adieu.   415
RODERIGO   Where shall we meet i' th' morning?
IAGO   At my lodging.
RODERIGO   I'll be with thee betimes.
IAGO   Go to, farewell. Do you hear, Roderigo?
⟨RODERIGO   What say you?   420
IAGO   No more of drowning, do you hear?
RODERIGO   I am changed.
IAGO   Go to, farewell. Put money enough in your
purse.⟩

427. **profane:** misuse
428. **snipe:** woodcock (figuratively, a fool)
431. **'Has:** i.e., he has; **my office:** i.e., my sexual duty as a husband
432. **in that kind:** in that regard
433. **as if . . . surety:** i.e., as if I were sure of it; **holds:** esteems
435. **proper:** attractive
439. **he:** i.e., Cassio; **his:** i.e., Othello's
440. **He:** i.e., Cassio; **dispose:** manner
442. **free:** sincere, straightforward
443. **that but:** who only
444. **tenderly:** easily, readily
446. **engendered:** conceived

[RODERIGO I'll sell all my land.]   *He exits.* 425
IAGO
  Thus do I ever make my fool my purse.
  For I mine own gained knowledge should profane
  If I would time expend with such ⟨a⟩ snipe
  But for my sport and profit. I hate the Moor,
  And it is thought abroad that 'twixt my sheets   430
  'Has done my office. I know not if 't be true,
  But I, for mere suspicion in that kind,
  Will do as if for surety. He holds me well.
  The better shall my purpose work on him.
  Cassio's a proper man. Let me see now: 435
  To get his place and to plume up my will
  In double knavery—How? how?—Let's see.
  After some time, to abuse Othello's ⟨ear⟩
  That he is too familiar with his wife.
  He hath a person and a smooth dispose   440
  To be suspected, framed to make women false.
  The Moor is of a free and open nature
  That thinks men honest that but seem to be so,
  And will as tenderly be led by th' nose
  As asses are.   445
  I have 't. It is engendered. Hell and night
  Must bring this monstrous birth to the world's light.
                                        ⟨*He exits.*⟩

The Tragedy of

OTHELLO,
The Moor of Venice

ACT 2

2.1   The Turkish fleet is destroyed in a storm, while Cassio and then Desdemona, Emilia, and Iago arrive safely at Cyprus. Desdemona anxiously waits for Othello. When his ship arrives, he and Desdemona joyfully greet each other. Iago, putting his plot into action, persuades Roderigo that Desdemona is in love with Cassio and that Roderigo should help get Cassio dismissed from the lieutenancy.

---

2. **high-wrought flood:** agitated sea

3. **main:** open sea

7. **ruffianed:** blustered, raged

8. **mountains:** i.e., mountainous waves

9. **hold the mortise:** i.e., hold together where they are joined

10. **segregation:** breaking up, scattering

12. **chidden billow:** i.e., the wave, which seems **chidden** (driven, rebuked) by the wind

15–16. **Seems . . . pole:** The constellation Ursa Minor (the Little **Bear**) contains two stars which are the **guards** of the polestar. (See page 60.)

17. **like molestation:** similar disturbance

18. **enchafèd flood:** raging sea

21. **bear it out:** i.e., endure the storm

ACT 2

Scene 1
Enter Montano and two Gentlemen.

MONTANO
What from the cape can you discern at sea?
FIRST GENTLEMAN
Nothing at all. It is a high-wrought flood.
I cannot 'twixt the heaven and the main
Descry a sail.
MONTANO
Methinks the wind hath spoke aloud at land.   5
A fuller blast ne'er shook our battlements.
If it hath ruffianed so upon the sea,
What ribs of oak, when mountains melt on them,
Can hold the mortise? What shall we hear of this?
SECOND GENTLEMAN
A segregation of the Turkish fleet.   10
For do but stand upon the foaming shore,
The chidden billow seems to pelt the clouds,
The wind-shaked surge, with high and monstrous
    mane,
Seems to cast water on the burning Bear   15
And quench the guards of th' ever-fixèd pole.
I never did like molestation view
On the enchafèd flood.
MONTANO   If that the Turkish fleet
Be not ensheltered and embayed, they are drowned.   20
It is impossible to bear it out.

59

24. **designment halts:** plan is crippled
25. **wrack and sufferance:** shipwreck and damage
27. **How:** i.e., what
28. **put in:** i.e., put into harbor
29. **A Veronesa:** i.e., a ship from Verona in the Venetian navy
35. **Touching:** regarding
40. **full:** complete
43–44. **we . . . regard:** i.e., we can no longer see the difference between sea and sky

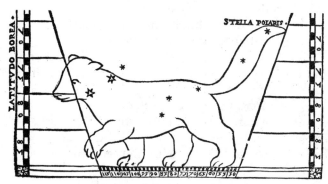

"The burning Bear." (2.1.15)
From Giovanni Paolo Gallucci, *Coelestium corporum . . . explicatio . . .* (1605).

Enter a ⟨third⟩ Gentleman.

THIRD GENTLEMAN   News, lads! Our wars are done.
The desperate tempest hath so banged the Turks
That their designment halts. A noble ship of Venice
Hath seen a grievous wrack and sufferance   25
On most part of their fleet.
MONTANO
How? Is this true?
THIRD GENTLEMAN   The ship is here put in,
A Veronesa. Michael Cassio,
Lieutenant to the warlike Moor Othello,   30
Is come on shore; the Moor himself at sea,
And is in full commission here for Cyprus.
MONTANO
I am glad on 't. 'Tis a worthy governor.
THIRD GENTLEMAN
But this same Cassio, though he speak of comfort
Touching the Turkish loss, yet he looks sadly   35
And ⟨prays⟩ the Moor be safe, for they were parted
With foul and violent tempest.
MONTANO   Pray ⟨heaven⟩ he be;
For I have served him, and the man commands
Like a full soldier. Let's to the seaside, ho!   40
As well to see the vessel that's come in
As to throw out our eyes for brave Othello,
[Even till we make the main and th' aerial blue
An indistinct regard.]
⟨THIRD⟩ GENTLEMAN   Come, let's do so;   45
For every minute is expectancy
Of more ⟨arrivance.⟩

Enter Cassio.

CASSIO
Thanks, you the valiant of ⟨this⟩ warlike isle,
That so approve the Moor! O, let the heavens

53. **bark:** ship
54. **Of . . . allowance:** i.e., reputed (or allowed) to be very expert and experienced
55–56. **my hopes . . . cure:** i.e., I am hopeful (about Othello's safety) **surfeited:** made sick through excess **Stand in bold cure:** i.e., are not beyond recovery
60. **My . . . for:** i.e., I hope that it is
61. **shot of courtesy:** courteous salute or volley
67. **achieved:** won
68. **paragons:** surpasses
69. **quirks:** figures of speech; **blazoning pens:** i.e., poets who itemize the beauties of a woman
70–71. **in . . . ingener:** i.e., in her natural beauty (she) would tire out any artist who would try to represent her **ingener:** contriver, artist (accent on first syllable)

Give him defense against the elements,   50
For I have lost him on a dangerous sea.
MONTANO   Is he well shipped?
CASSIO
His bark is stoutly timbered, and his pilot
Of very expert and approved allowance;
Therefore my hopes, not surfeited to death,   55
Stand in bold cure.
          ⌜*Voices cry*⌝ *within. "A sail, a sail, a sail!"*

          ⟨*Enter a Messenger.*⟩

CASSIO   What noise?
⟨MESSENGER⟩
The town is empty; on the brow o' th' sea
Stand ranks of people, and they cry "A sail!"
CASSIO
My hopes do shape him for the Governor.   60
                              ⟨*A shot.*⟩
⟨SECOND⟩ GENTLEMAN
They do discharge their shot of courtesy.
Our friends, at least.
CASSIO   I pray you, sir, go forth,
And give us truth who 'tis that is arrived.
⟨SECOND⟩ GENTLEMAN   I shall.   *He exits.*   65
MONTANO
But, good lieutenant, is your general wived?
CASSIO
Most fortunately. He hath achieved a maid
That paragons description and wild fame,
One that excels the quirks of blazoning pens,
And in th' essential vesture of creation   70
Does tire the ⌜ingener.⌝

          Enter ⟨*Second*⟩ *Gentleman.*

          How now? Who has put in?

74. **'Has:** i.e., he has; **happy:** fortunate
76. **guttered:** furrowed, jagged; **congregated:** massed
77. **ensteeped:** submerged
78. **As:** i.e., as if; **do omit:** i.e., do not act in accordance with
79. **mortal:** deadly
83. **conduct:** escort
84. **footing:** landing
85. **sennight's:** week's; **Jove:** king of the Roman gods
89. **extincted:** (1) extinguished; (2) dull (having lost their color or tincture)
93. **let . . . knees:** i.e., kneel to her
101. **How . . . company?:** i.e., how were you and Othello parted?

⟨SECOND⟩ GENTLEMAN
'Tis one Iago, ancient to the General.
CASSIO
'Has had most favorable and happy speed!
Tempests themselves, high seas, and howling winds,　75
The guttered rocks and congregated sands
(Traitors ensteeped to ⟨clog⟩ the guiltless keel),
As having sense of beauty, do omit
Their mortal natures, letting go safely by
The divine Desdemona.　80
MONTANO　　　　　　　　What is she?
CASSIO
She that I spake of, our great captain's captain,
Left in the conduct of the bold Iago,
Whose footing here anticipates our thoughts
A sennight's speed. Great Jove, Othello guard,　85
And swell his sail with thine own powerful breath,
That he may bless this bay with his tall ship,
Make love's quick pants in Desdemona's arms,
Give renewed fire to our extincted spirits,
⟨And bring all Cyprus comfort!⟩　90

Enter Desdemona, Iago, Roderigo, and Emilia.

　　　　　　　　　　　O, behold,
The riches of the ship is come on shore!
You men of Cyprus, let her have your knees.
　　　　　　　　　　　⌜*He kneels.*⌝
Hail to thee, lady, and the grace of heaven,
Before, behind thee, and on every hand　95
Enwheel thee round.　　　⌜*He rises.*⌝
DESDEMONA　　　　I thank you, valiant Cassio.
What tidings can you tell of my lord?
CASSIO
He is not yet arrived, nor know I aught
But that he's well and will be shortly here.　100
DESDEMONA
O, but I fear—How lost you company?

105. **their greeting:** i.e., the shot

110. **extend my manners:** i.e., extend my greeting to include a kiss

112. **would she:** i.e., if she would

115. **has no speech:** i.e., says nothing

117. **still:** always; **have list:** want to

118. **Marry:** a mild oath; **before:** i.e., in the presence of

120. **with thinking:** i.e., silently

122. **You:** i.e., women; **out of door:** in public

125. **huswifery:** skilled household management; **huswives:** (1) housewives; (2) hussies

CASSIO
The great contention of sea and skies
Parted our fellowship.
                  Within "A sail, a sail!" ⌜*A shot.*⌝
                  But hark, a sail!

⟨SECOND⟩ GENTLEMAN
They give ⟨their⟩ greeting to the citadel.   105
This likewise is a friend.

CASSIO   See for the news.
                  ⌜*Second Gentleman exits.*⌝
Good ancient, you are welcome. Welcome, mistress.
                     ⌜*He kisses Emilia.*⌝
Let it not gall your patience, good Iago,
That I extend my manners. 'Tis my breeding   110
That gives me this bold show of courtesy.

IAGO
Sir, would she give you so much of her lips
As of her tongue she oft bestows on me,
You would have enough.

DESDEMONA
Alas, she has no speech!   115

IAGO   In faith, too much.
I find it still when I have ⟨list⟩ to sleep.
Marry, before your Ladyship, I grant,
She puts her tongue a little in her heart
And chides with thinking.   120

EMILIA You have little cause to say so.

IAGO Come on, come on! You are pictures out of door,
bells in your parlors, wildcats in your kitchens,
saints in your injuries, devils being offended, players in your huswifery, and huswives in your beds. 125

DESDEMONA Oh, fie upon thee, slanderer.

IAGO
Nay, it is true, or else I am a Turk.
You rise to play, and go to bed to work.

EMILIA You shall not write my praise.

135. **assay:** try; **There's one gone:** i.e., has someone gone

137. **beguile:** divert (my) attention (and others') from

138. **The thing I am:** i.e., my anxiety

140. **about it:** i.e., trying to do it; **my invention:** i.e., what I am devising

141. **birdlime:** a sticky substance applied to bushes to catch birds; **frieze:** coarse woolen stuff (from which it would be hard to remove birdlime)

142. **muse:** The Muses were deities believed to inspire poets to write. **labors:** (1) works hard; (2) strains to give birth

143. **is delivered:** gives birth

144. **fair:** (1) light in complexion and therefore, by the standards of Shakespeare's day, (2) beautiful; **wit:** wisdom

145. **for use:** i.e., made to be used

146. **black:** dark in complexion and therefore, by the standards of Shakespeare's day, unattractive; **witty:** clever

147. **thereto have:** i.e., also has

148. **white:** (1) fair love; (2) wight (pronounced "white" and meaning "man"); (3) the bull's-eye in a target, which an archer tries to **hit**

152. **folly:** (1) foolishness; (2) wantonness

153. **fond:** foolish

155. **foul:** ugly

156. **thereunto:** besides

IAGO   No, let me not.   130
DESDEMONA
What wouldst write of me if thou shouldst praise
    me?
IAGO
O, gentle lady, do not put me to 't,
For I am nothing if not critical.
DESDEMONA
Come on, assay.—There's one gone to the harbor?   135
IAGO Ay, madam.
DESDEMONA, ⌈*aside*⌉
I am not merry, but I do beguile
The thing I am by seeming otherwise.—
Come, how wouldst thou praise me?
IAGO I am about it, but indeed my invention comes   140
    from my pate as birdlime does from frieze: it
    plucks out brains and all. But my muse labors, and
    thus she is delivered:
If she be fair and wise, fairness and wit,
The one's for use, the other useth it.   145
DESDEMONA
Well praised! How if she be black and witty?
IAGO
If she be black, and thereto have a wit,
She'll find a white that shall her blackness ⟨hit.⟩
DESDEMONA
Worse and worse.
EMILIA   How if fair and foolish?   150
IAGO
She never yet was foolish that was fair,
For even her folly helped her to an heir.
DESDEMONA These are old fond paradoxes to make
    fools laugh i' th' alehouse. What miserable praise
    hast thou for her that's foul and foolish?   155
IAGO
There's none so foul and foolish thereunto,
But does foul pranks which fair and wise ones do.

158. **heavy:** profound
160–61. **authority . . . merit:** her moral supremacy
161. **justly:** rightly, properly
161–62. **put on . . . itself:** i.e., demand the approval even of entirely malicious people
163. **ever:** always
164. **Had tongue at will:** perhaps, always knew what to say; or, perhaps, could speak when she wished
165. **gay:** i.e., gorgeously dressed
166. **Fled . . . may:** i.e., restrained her desires though she had power to satisfy them
168. **Bade . . . fly:** i.e., endured her injury (**wrong**) with patience **Bade:** ordered
170. **change . . . tail:** i.e., perhaps, exchange one worthless thing for another (Obscene meanings of **head** and **tail** may apply here, but the meaning of the line is obscure.)
173. **wight:** person
175. **suckle . . . beer:** i.e., nurse babies and keep household accounts **small beer:** light beer
177. **of:** i.e., from
178. **How say you:** i.e., what do you say
179. **profane:** irreverent, wicked; **liberal:** dissolute
180. **home:** i.e., bluntly
181. **in:** i.e., in the role of
185. **gyve . . . courtship:** i.e., shackle you with your own manners
188. **kissed . . . fingers:** a courtly gesture
189. **the sir:** the fine gentleman

DESDEMONA O heavy ignorance! Thou praisest the
worst best. But what praise couldst thou bestow on
a deserving woman indeed, one that in the authori- 160
ty of her merit did justly put on the vouch of very
malice itself?

IAGO
She that was ever fair and never proud,
Had tongue at will and yet was never loud,
Never lacked gold and yet went never gay, 165
Fled from her wish, and yet said "Now I may,"
She that being angered, her revenge being nigh,
Bade her wrong stay and her displeasure fly,
She that in wisdom never was so frail
To change the cod's head for the salmon's tail, 170
She that could think and ne'er disclose her mind,
[See suitors following and not look behind,]
She was a wight, if ever such ⟨wight⟩ were—

DESDEMONA To do what?

IAGO
To suckle fools and chronicle small beer. 175

DESDEMONA O, most lame and impotent conclusion!
—Do not learn of him, Emilia, though he be thy
husband.—How say you, Cassio? Is he not a most
profane and liberal counselor?

CASSIO He speaks home, madam. You may relish him 180
more in the soldier than in the scholar.

⌈*Cassio takes Desdemona's hand.*⌉

IAGO, ⌈*aside*⌉ He takes her by the palm. Ay, well said,
whisper. With as little a web as this will I ensnare as
great a fly as Cassio. Ay, smile upon her, do. I will
⌈gyve⌉ thee in thine own courtship. You say true, 'tis 185
so indeed. If such tricks as these strip you out of
your lieutenantry, it had been better you had not
kissed your three fingers so oft, which now again
you are most apt to play the sir in. Very good; well
kissed; ⟨an⟩ excellent courtesy! 'Tis so, indeed. Yet 190

192. **clyster pipes:** tubes used for enemas

204. **Olympus:** the mountain in Greece where, according to mythology, the gods lived

205. **If . . . die:** i.e., if I were to die this minute,

207. **hath . . . absolute:** i.e., is so perfectly content

208. **comfort:** delight

209. **Succeeds:** follows; **unknown fate:** i.e., what is destined to happen in the unknown future

218. **well tuned:** Iago picks up the musical image in Othello's reference to **discords.**

219. **set down . . . music:** i.e., destroy your harmony (Loosening the pegs of a stringed instrument slackens the strings and puts it out of tune.)

220. **As . . . I am:** i.e., in all my reputed "honesty"

again your fingers to your lips? Would they were
⟨clyster⟩ pipes for your sake!   ⟨*Trumpets within.*⟩
The Moor. I know his trumpet.
CASSIO   'Tis truly so.
DESDEMONA   Let's meet him and receive him.   195
CASSIO   Lo, where he comes!

                    Enter Othello and Attendants.

OTHELLO
O, my fair warrior!
DESDEMONA   My dear Othello!
OTHELLO
It gives me wonder great as my content
To see you here before me. O my soul's joy!   200
If after every tempest come such calms,
May the winds blow till they have wakened death,
And let the laboring bark climb hills of seas
Olympus high, and duck again as low
As hell's from heaven! If it were now to die,   205
'Twere now to be most happy, for I fear
My soul hath her content so absolute
That not another comfort like to this
Succeeds in unknown fate.
DESDEMONA   The heavens forbid   210
But that our loves and comforts should increase
Even as our days do grow!
OTHELLO   Amen to that, sweet powers!
I cannot speak enough of this content.
It stops me here; it is too much of joy.   ⟨*They kiss.*⟩ 215
And this, and this, the greatest discords be
That e'er our hearts shall make!
IAGO, ⌜*aside*⌝ O, you are well tuned now,
But I'll set down the pegs that make this music,
As honest as I am.   220
OTHELLO   Come. Let us to the castle.—
News, friends! Our wars are done. The Turks are
drowned.

225. **well desired:** much loved
227. **out of fashion:** inappropriately
229. **coffers:** chests, including strongboxes
230. **master:** i.e., ship's commander
232. **challenge:** claim, deserve
236. **base:** cowardly, worthless
238. **list:** listen to
239. **watches on the court of guard:** i.e., stands watch at the guardhouse (**the court of guard**)
240. **directly:** completely
242. **thus:** presumably, on your lips (i.e., keep silent)
243. **Mark me:** notice
244. **but:** only
245. **still:** always, forever; **prating:** mere talk
248. **blood:** sexual appetite; **act of sport:** i.e., lovemaking
250. **favor:** appearance; **sympathy:** agreement
254. **heave the gorge:** i.e., become ill, vomit; **disrelish:** have a distaste for
255. **Very nature:** i.e., nature itself
257. **pregnant:** obvious
258–59. **stands . . . fortune as:** i.e., is most likely to benefit than   **eminent in the degree:** i.e., high on the ladder

How does my old acquaintance of this isle?—
Honey, you shall be well desired in Cyprus.　　　225
I have found great love amongst them. O, my sweet,
I prattle out of fashion, and I dote
In mine own comforts.—I prithee, good Iago,
Go to the bay and disembark my coffers.
Bring thou the master to the citadel.　　　230
He is a good one, and his worthiness
Does challenge much respect.—Come, Desdemona.
Once more, well met at Cyprus.
　　　　　　　　　⌜*All but Iago and Roderigo*⌝ *exit.*
IAGO, ⌜*to a departing Attendant*⌝ Do thou meet me pres-
　ently at the harbor. ⌜*To Roderigo.*⌝ Come ⟨hither.⟩ If　235
　thou be'st valiant—as they say base men being in
　love have then a nobility in their natures more than
　is native to them—list me. The Lieutenant tonight
　watches on the court of guard. First, I must tell thee
　this: Desdemona is directly in love with him.　　　240
RODERIGO　With him? Why, 'tis not possible.
IAGO　Lay thy finger thus, and let thy soul be instructed.
　Mark me with what violence she first loved the
　Moor but for bragging and telling her fantastical
　lies. ⟨And will she⟩ love him still for prating? Let not　245
　thy discreet heart think it. Her eye must be fed. And
　what delight shall she have to look on the devil?
　When the blood is made dull with the act of sport,
　there should be, ⟨again⟩ to inflame it and to give
　satiety a fresh appetite, loveliness in favor, sympathy　250
　in years, manners, and beauties, all which the Moor
　is defective in. Now, for want of these required
　conveniences, her delicate tenderness will find it-
　self abused, begin to heave the gorge, disrelish and
　abhor the Moor. Very nature will instruct her in it　255
　and compel her to some second choice. Now, sir,
　this granted—as it is a most pregnant and unforced
　position—who stands so eminent in the degree of

261. **civil and humane:** polite and courteous

262. **compassing of:** attaining; **salt . . . loose:** lecherous

263. **slipper:** slippery

264. **knave:** villain

265. **stamp . . . advantages:** coin (or fraudulently manufacture) opportunities

268. **green:** unripe, inexperienced

269. **look after:** i.e., look for; **pestilent:** plaguey, confoundedly

272. **condition:** character, disposition

273–74. **wine . . . grapes:** i.e., she's just like the rest of us

275. **Blessed pudding:** Like **Blessed fig's end,** this oath shows contempt for the one who is being called "blessed." **pudding:** a kind of sausage

276. **paddle with:** i.e., play with her fingers on; **his:** i.e., Cassio's

279–80. **index . . . history:** i.e., the prefatory matter to the real story **index:** table of contents

283. **mutualities:** exchange of intimacies; **marshal the way:** clear and point out the way

283–84. **hard at hand:** immediately

284. **master and main exercise:** principal act

285. **incorporate:** i.e., corporal, bodily, carnal; **Pish:** term of disgust or contempt

286. **Watch you:** i.e., stand watch

287. **command:** i.e., your orders to stand watch

290. **tainting:** disparaging, mocking

292. **minister:** provide

294. **choler:** anger

this fortune as Cassio does? A knave very voluble, no
further conscionable than in putting on the mere   260
form of civil and humane seeming for the better
⟨compassing⟩ of his salt and most hidden loose
affection. Why, none, why, none! A slipper and
subtle knave, a ⟨finder-out of occasions,⟩ that ⟨has⟩ an
eye can stamp and counterfeit advantages, though   265
true advantage never present itself; a devilish knave!
Besides, the knave is handsome, young, and hath all
those requisites in him that folly and green minds
look after. A pestilent complete knave, and the
woman hath found him already.   270
RODERIGO   I cannot believe that in her. She's full of
most blessed condition.
IAGO   Blessed fig's end! The wine she drinks is made of
grapes. If she had been blessed, she would never
have loved the Moor. Blessed pudding! Didst thou   275
not see her paddle with the palm of his hand? Didst
not mark that?
RODERIGO   Yes, that I did. But that was but courtesy.
IAGO   Lechery, by this hand! An index and obscure
prologue to the history of lust and foul thoughts.   280
They met so near with their lips that their breaths
embraced together. Villainous thoughts, Roderigo!
When these ⟨mutualities⟩ so marshal the way, hard
at hand comes the master and main exercise, th'
incorporate conclusion. Pish! But, sir, be you ruled 285
by me. I have brought you from Venice. Watch you
tonight. For the command, I'll lay 't upon you.
Cassio knows you not. I'll not be far from you. Do
you find some occasion to anger Cassio, either by
speaking too loud, or tainting his discipline, or from 290
what other course you please, which the time shall
more favorably minister.
RODERIGO   Well.
IAGO   Sir, he's rash and very sudden in choler, and

295. **haply:** perhaps

297. **mutiny:** riot

297–98. **whose qualification . . . but by:** i.e., who will not be appeased except by **qualification:** appeasement

298. **displanting:** displacement, supplanting

300. **prefer:** promote

301. **impediment:** i.e., Cassio

303–4. **bring . . . opportunity:** i.e., arrange any opportunity for me

305. **warrant:** assure

306. **his:** i.e., Othello's

309. **apt:** likely; **of . . . credit:** i.e., quite believable

310. **howbeit that:** even though

314. **absolute:** mere

315. **accountant:** i.e., accountable

316. **diet:** feed

317. **For that:** because

319. **inwards:** "innards," inner parts

322. **yet that:** until

324. **judgment:** i.e., Othello's reason

325–26. **If . . . on:** i.e., if Roderigo can carry out what I need **whom I trace . . . hunting:** i.e., whose steps I pursue in order to make him hunt more quickly **the putting on:** that which I've put him up to

327. **have . . . on the hip:** i.e., have Cassio at a disadvantage—a wrestling term (See page 88.)

328. **Abuse:** slander, revile; **the rank garb:** i.e., language that makes him look coarse or lecherous

haply may strike at you. Provoke him that he may,   295
for even out of that will I cause these of Cyprus to
mutiny, whose qualification shall come into no
true taste again but by the displanting of Cassio. So
shall you have a shorter journey to your desires by
the means I shall then have to prefer them, and the   300
impediment most profitably removed, without the
which there were no expectation of our prosperity.
RODERIGO   I will do this, if you can bring it to any
opportunity.
IAGO   I warrant thee. Meet me by and by at the citadel. I   305
must fetch his necessaries ashore. Farewell.
RODERIGO   Adieu.   *He exits.*
IAGO
That Cassio loves her, I do well believe 't.
That she loves him, 'tis apt and of great credit.
The Moor, howbeit that I endure him not,   310
Is of a constant, loving, noble nature,
And I dare think he'll prove to Desdemona
A most dear husband. Now, I do love her too,
Not out of absolute lust (though peradventure
I stand accountant for as great a sin)   315
But partly led to diet my revenge
For that I do suspect the lusty Moor
Hath leaped into my seat—the thought whereof
Doth, like a poisonous mineral, gnaw my inwards,
And nothing can or shall content my soul   320
Till I am evened with him, wife for wife,
Or, failing so, yet that I put the Moor
At least into a jealousy so strong
That judgment cannot cure. Which thing to do,
If this poor trash of Venice, whom I trace   325
For his quick hunting, stand the putting on,
I'll have our Michael Cassio on the hip,
Abuse him to the Moor in the ⟨rank⟩ garb
(For I fear Cassio with my ⟨nightcap⟩ too),

332. **practicing upon:** plotting against, destroying
333. **'Tis . . . confused:** i.e., I have a plan, though the details are unclear

2.2

3. **importing:** making known; **mere perdition:** total destruction
4. **triumph:** festivity
6. **addition:** rank
9. **offices:** kitchens (from which food and drink could be obtained)
11. **have told:** i.e., has struck

2.3 Iago gets Cassio drunk, making it easy for Roderigo to provoke Cassio into a brawl, first with Roderigo, then with Montano, whom he wounds. Othello, called from his bed by the noise, stops the brawl and strips Cassio of his lieutenancy. Iago advises Cassio to seek Desdemona's help in getting reinstated. The next step in Iago's plan is to tell Othello that Desdemona supports Cassio because Cassio is her lover.

2. **stop:** check, self-restraint
3. **outsport:** i.e., celebrate past the point of

Make the Moor thank me, love me, and reward me   330
For making him egregiously an ass
And practicing upon his peace and quiet
Even to madness. 'Tis here, but yet confused.
Knavery's plain face is never seen till used.

He exits.

Scene 2
Enter Othello's Herald with a proclamation.

HERALD   It is Othello's pleasure, our noble and valiant
general, that upon certain tidings now arrived,
importing the mere perdition of the Turkish fleet,
every man put himself into triumph: some to
dance, some to make bonfires, each man to what   5
sport and revels his addition leads him. For besides
these beneficial news, it is the celebration of his
nuptial. So much was his pleasure should be pro-
claimed. All offices are open, and there is full
liberty of feasting from this present hour of five till   10
the bell have told eleven. (Heaven) bless the isle of
Cyprus and our noble general, Othello!

He exits.

Scene 3
Enter Othello, Desdemona, Cassio, and Attendants.

OTHELLO
Good Michael, look you to the guard tonight.
Let's teach ourselves that honorable stop
Not to outsport discretion.
CASSIO
Iago hath direction what to do,
But notwithstanding, with my personal eye   5
Will I look to 't.

8. **with your earliest:** i.e., at your earliest convenience

11. **purchase:** i.e., marriage; **fruits:** i.e., consummation

15. **Not this hour:** i.e., not for an hour

16. **cast:** dismissed

19. **sport:** a plaything; **Jove:** king of the Roman gods, famous for his sexual exploits with mortal women

21. **game:** amorous play

22. **fresh:** youthful

24. **parley:** a meeting between opposing forces before a battle (Battle was often used as a metaphor for love encounters in this period. The military language continues with **alarum** [line 28], meaning a summons to military action.)

26. **right:** very

31. **stoup:** a large drinking vessel; **without:** outside

32. **brace:** pair

32–33. **fain have a measure:** i.e., gladly drink a toast

35. **unhappy:** unfortunate

38. **But:** only

OTHELLO   Iago is most honest.
Michael, goodnight. Tomorrow with your earliest
Let me have speech with you. ⌜*To Desdemona.*⌝ Come,
   my dear love,   10
The purchase made, the fruits are to ensue;
That profit's yet to come 'tween me and you.—
Goodnight.
   ⟨*Othello and Desdemona*⟩ *exit,* ⌜*with Attendants.*⌝

                    Enter Iago.

CASSIO
Welcome, Iago. We must to the watch.
IAGO   Not this hour, lieutenant. 'Tis not yet ten o' th'   15
   clock. Our general cast us thus early for the love of
   his Desdemona—who let us not therefore blame;
   he hath not yet made wanton the night with her, and
   she is sport for Jove.
CASSIO   She's a most exquisite lady.   20
IAGO   And, I'll warrant her, full of game.
CASSIO   Indeed, she's a most fresh and delicate creature.
IAGO   What an eye she has! Methinks it sounds a parley
   to provocation.   25
CASSIO   An inviting eye, and yet methinks right mod-
   est.
IAGO   And when she speaks, is it not an alarum to love?
CASSIO   She is indeed perfection.
IAGO   Well, happiness to their sheets! Come, lieuten-   30
   ant, I have a stoup of wine; and here without are a
   brace of Cyprus gallants that would fain have a
   measure to the health of black Othello.
CASSIO   Not tonight, good Iago. I have very poor and
   unhappy brains for drinking. I could well wish   35
   courtesy would invent some other custom of entertainment.
IAGO   O, they are our friends! But one cup; I'll drink
   for you.

41. **qualified:** diluted; **innovation:** change
48. **dislikes:** displeases
51. **offense:** i.e., inclination to take offense
52. **my young mistress' dog:** i.e., a young girl's (spoiled) pet
55-56. **caroused . . . pottle-deep:** i.e., drunk up whole potfuls of drink   **pottle:** a small pot
57. **else:** i.e., others (Many editions substitute the quarto's "lads" for the Folio's "else.")
58. **That . . . distance:** i.e., who are anxious (and aggressive) about preserving their personal honor
60. **flustered:** i.e., made flush and excited
65. **If . . . dream:** i.e., if the future confirms my hopes
67. **rouse:** a deep drink

CASSIO   I have drunk but one cup tonight, and that was   40
craftily qualified too, and behold what innovation it
makes here. I am ⟨unfortunate⟩ in the infirmity and
dare not task my weakness with any more.
IAGO   What, man! 'Tis a night of revels. The gallants
desire it.   45
CASSIO   Where are they?
IAGO   Here at the door. I pray you, call them in.
CASSIO   I'll do 't, but it dislikes me.   *He exits.*
IAGO
If I can fasten but one cup upon him
With that which he hath drunk tonight already,   50
He'll be as full of quarrel and offense
As my young mistress' dog. Now my sick fool
    Roderigo,
Whom love hath turned almost the wrong side out,
To Desdemona hath tonight caroused   55
Potations pottle-deep; and he's to watch.
Three else of Cyprus, noble swelling spirits
That hold their honors in a wary distance,
The very elements of this warlike isle,
Have I tonight flustered with flowing cups;   60
And they watch too. Now, 'mongst this flock of
    drunkards
Am I ⟨to put⟩ our Cassio in some action
That may offend the isle. But here they come.
If consequence do but approve my dream,   65
My boat sails freely both with wind and stream.

Enter Cassio, Montano, and Gentlemen, ⌐followed by
Servants with wine.⌐

CASSIO   'Fore ⟨God,⟩ they have given me a rouse already.
MONTANO   Good faith, a little one; not past a pint, as I
am a soldier.   70
IAGO   Some wine, ho!

72. **cannikin:** little can
75. **span:** short time
80. **potting:** i.e., drinking; **Your Dane:** i.e., a typical Dane
81. **swag-bellied:** pot-bellied
83. **exquisite:** skilled
85. **drinks you:** i.e., drinks
86–87. **He sweats not . . . Almain:** i.e., it takes little effort for him to outdrink a typical German
90–91. **I'll do you justice:** i.e., I'll drink as much as you do
93–100. **King Stephen . . . thee:** part of a well-known ballad of the period entitled "Bell My Wife." **lown:** rogue **wight:** person **degree:** rank **auld:** old
105. **place:** social position, rank

"He gives your Hollander a vomit." (2.3.87)
From Jean Jacques Boissard, *Theatrum vitae humanae . . .* (1596).

⌐*Sings.*⌐ *And let me the cannikin clink, clink,*
   And let me the cannikin clink.
   A soldier's a man,
   O, man's life's but a span,   75
   Why, then, let a soldier drink.
Some wine, boys!
CASSIO 'Fore ⟨God,⟩ an excellent song.
IAGO I learned it in England, where indeed they are
most potent in potting. Your Dane, your German, 80
and your swag-bellied Hollander—drink, ho!—are
nothing to your English.
CASSIO Is your ⟨Englishman⟩ so exquisite in his drink-
ing?
IAGO Why, he drinks you, with facility, your Dane 85
dead drunk. He sweats not to overthrow your Al-
main. He gives your Hollander a vomit ere the next
pottle can be filled.
CASSIO To the health of our general!
MONTANO I am for it, lieutenant, and I'll do you 90
justice.
IAGO O sweet England!
  ⌐*Sings.*⌐ *King Stephen was and-a worthy peer,*
    His breeches cost him but a crown;
    He held them sixpence all too dear;   95
    With that he called the tailor lown.
    He was a wight of high renown,
    And thou art but of low degree;
    'Tis pride that pulls the country down,
    ⟨Then⟩ take thy auld cloak about thee. 100
Some wine, ho!
CASSIO ⟨'Fore God,⟩ this is a more exquisite song than
the other!
IAGO Will you hear 't again?
CASSIO No, for I hold him to be unworthy of his place 105
that does those things. Well, ⟨God's⟩ above all; and
there be souls must be saved, [and there be souls
must not be saved.]

111. **quality:** rank

124. **platform:** i.e., where they will set the guard (**watch**)

128. **just equinox:** i.e., exact equivalent

129. **pity of:** i.e., a pity about

131. **On . . . infirmity:** i.e., at some time or another when he is the victim of his weakness

135–36. **watch . . . cradle:** i.e., be awake all night as well as all day if he doesn't drink himself to sleep **horologe:** clock, hourglass

"I'll have our Michael Cassio on the hip." (2.1.327)
From Romein de Hoogue, *L'academie de l'admirable art de la lutte* . . . (1712).

IAGO   It's true, good lieutenant.
CASSIO   For mine own part—no offense to the General,   110
  nor any man of quality—I hope to be saved.
IAGO   And so do I too, lieutenant.
CASSIO   Ay, but, by your leave, not before me. The
  Lieutenant is to be saved before the Ancient. Let's
  have no more of this. Let's to our affairs. ⟨God⟩   115
  forgive us our sins! Gentlemen, let's look to our
  business. Do not think, gentlemen, I am drunk. This
  is my ancient, this is my right hand, and this is my
  left. I am not drunk now. I can stand well enough,
  and I speak well enough.   120
GENTLEMEN   Excellent well.
CASSIO   Why, very well then. You must not think then
  that I am drunk.   *He exits.*
MONTANO
  To th' platform, masters. Come, let's set the watch.
                                      ⌜*Gentlemen exit.*⌝
IAGO, ⌜*to Montano*⌝
  You see this fellow that is gone before?   125
  He's a soldier fit to stand by Caesar
  And give direction; and do but see his vice.
  'Tis to his virtue a just equinox,
  The one as long as th' other. 'Tis pity of him.
  I fear the trust Othello puts him in,   130
  On some odd time of his infirmity,
  Will shake this island.
MONTANO   But is he often thus?
IAGO
  'Tis evermore ⟨the⟩ prologue to his sleep.
  He'll watch the horologe a double set   135
  If drink rock not his cradle.
MONTANO   It were well
  The General were put in mind of it.
  Perhaps he sees it not, or his good nature
  Prizes the virtue that appears in Cassio   140
  And looks not on his evils. Is not this true?

145. **second:** second in command, lieutenant
146. **engraffed infirmity:** a weakness that has grown to be part of him in the same way a shoot becomes part of the plant to which it is grafted
151 SD. **within:** i.e., offstage
153. **Zounds:** i.e., Christ's wounds (a strong oath)
156. **twiggen bottle:** a bottle encased in woven twigs or wicker work
159–60. **hold your hand:** i.e., do not strike
162. **mazard:** slang for "head"
165. **mutiny:** riot

Enter Roderigo.

IAGO, ⌜*aside to Roderigo*⌝ How now, Roderigo?
I pray you, after the Lieutenant, go.
                                    ⟨*Roderigo exits.*⟩
MONTANO
And 'tis great pity that the noble Moor
Should hazard such a place as his own second   145
With one of an engraffed infirmity.
It were an honest action to say so
To the Moor.
IAGO   Not I, for this fair island.
I do love Cassio well and would do much   150
To cure him of this evil—   ⟨*"Help, help!" within.*⟩
                    But hark! What noise?

Enter Cassio, pursuing Roderigo.

CASSIO ⟨Zounds,⟩ you rogue, you rascal!
MONTANO What's the matter, lieutenant?
CASSIO A knave teach me my duty? I'll beat the knave 155
    into a twiggen bottle.
RODERIGO Beat me?
CASSIO Dost thou prate, rogue?   ⌜*He hits Roderigo.*⌝
MONTANO Nay, good lieutenant. I pray you, sir, hold
    your hand.   160
CASSIO Let me go, sir, or I'll knock you o'er the
    mazard.
MONTANO Come, come, you're drunk.
CASSIO Drunk?
                                    ⟨*They fight.*⟩
IAGO, ⌜*aside to Roderigo*⌝
Away, I say! Go out and cry a mutiny.   165
                              ⌜*Roderigo exits.*⌝
Nay, good lieutenant.—⟨God's will,⟩ gentlemen!—
Help, ho! Lieutenant—sir—Montano—⟨sir⟩—
Help, masters!—Here's a goodly watch indeed!
                              ⟨*A bell is rung.*⟩

169. **bell:** i.e., alarm bell; **Diablo:** i.e., the devil
170. **rise:** rebel, riot; **hold:** i.e., stop
182–83. **to ourselves . . . Ottomites:** i.e., bring ourselves to the destruction that divine providence (**heaven**), by wrecking the Turkish fleet, has prevented the Turks from bringing down on us
184. **put by:** i.e., give up
185. **to carve . . . rage:** i.e., to indulge his rage
186. **Holds . . . light:** regards . . . as of little value
188. **propriety:** i.e., proper condition
190. **On . . . thee:** i.e., by your love for me, I order you (to speak)
192. **In quarter and in terms:** i.e., in relation to each other
194. **As if . . . men:** i.e., as if the influence of some planet had driven them mad
195. **tilting one at other's:** i.e., charging or thrusting at one another's
196. **speak:** i.e., speak of
197. **odds:** strife
198. **would:** i.e., I wish

Who's that which rings the bell? Diablo, ho!
The town will rise. ⟨God's will,⟩ lieutenant, ⟨hold!⟩   170
You ⟨will be shamed⟩ forever.

Enter Othello and Attendants.

OTHELLO   What is the matter here?
MONTANO   ⟨Zounds,⟩ I bleed
    still.
I am hurt to th' death. He dies! ⌜*He attacks Cassio.*⌝   175
OTHELLO   Hold, for your lives!
IAGO
    Hold, ho! Lieutenant—sir—Montano—
        gentlemen—
    Have you forgot all ⌜sense of place⌝ and duty?
    Hold! The General speaks to you. Hold, for shame!   180
OTHELLO
    Why, how now, ho! From whence ariseth this?
    Are we turned Turks, and to ourselves do that
    Which heaven hath forbid the Ottomites?
    For Christian shame, put by this barbarous brawl!
    He that stirs next to carve for his own rage   185
    Holds his soul light; he dies upon his motion.
    Silence that dreadful bell. It frights the isle
    From her propriety. What is the matter, masters?
    Honest Iago, that looks dead with grieving,
    Speak. Who began this? On thy love, I charge thee.   190
IAGO
    I do not know. Friends all but now, even now,
    In quarter and in terms like bride and groom
    Divesting them for bed; and then but now,
    As if some planet had unwitted men,
    Swords out, and tilting one at other's ⟨breast,⟩   195
    In opposition bloody. I cannot speak
    Any beginning to this peevish odds,
    And would in action glorious I had lost
    Those legs that brought me to a part of it!

200. **you . . . forgot:** i.e., that you have so forgotten yourself

202. **were wont be:** used to be

203. **gravity and stillness:** i.e., dignified manner

204. **name:** reputation

205. **censure:** judgment

206. **unlace:** undo

207. **spend your rich opinion:** i.e., squander your valuable reputation

209. **hurt to danger:** i.e., dangerously injured

211. **something . . . offends:** i.e., somewhat . . . hurts (i.e., because of my wounds, speaking is painful)

214. **By me . . . amiss:** i.e., that I said or did wrong

215. **self-charity:** i.e., care of oneself

219. **My blood . . . to rule:** i.e., my passion (anger) is overcoming my reason and judgment

220. **collied:** darkened (literally, blackened with coal)

221. **Assays:** tries

224. **rout:** uproar, disturbance

225. **approved in:** i.e., proved to be guilty of

227. **lose me:** i.e., lose my favor; **town of war:** fortified place

228. **Yet:** still

229. **manage:** engage in

230. **on . . . safety:** i.e., in the chief guardhouse and while on duty

OTHELLO
How comes it, Michael, you are thus forgot?   200
CASSIO
I pray you pardon me; I cannot speak.
OTHELLO
Worthy Montano, you were wont be civil.
The gravity and stillness of your youth
The world hath noted. And your name is great
In mouths of wisest censure. What's the matter   205
That you unlace your reputation thus,
And spend your rich opinion for the name
Of a night-brawler? Give me answer to it.
MONTANO
Worthy Othello, I am hurt to danger.
Your officer Iago can inform you,   210
While I spare speech, which something now offends
     me,
Of all that I do know; nor know I aught
By me that's said or done amiss this night,
Unless self-charity be sometimes a vice,   215
And to defend ourselves it be a sin
When violence assails us.
OTHELLO   Now, by heaven,
My blood begins my safer guides to rule,
And passion, having my best judgment collied,   220
Assays to lead the way. ⟨Zounds, if I⟩ stir,
Or do but lift this arm, the best of you
Shall sink in my rebuke. Give me to know
How this foul rout began, who set it on;
And he that is approved in this offense,   225
Though he had twinned with me, both at a birth,
Shall lose me. What, in a town of war
Yet wild, the people's hearts brimful of fear,
To manage private and domestic quarrel,
In night, and on the court and guard of safety?   230
'Tis monstrous. Iago, who began 't?

232. **partially affined:** i.e., partial, biased
235. **Touch . . . near:** i.e., there's no need to allude to what concerns me so closely (my soldiership)
237. **offense:** harm
243. **execute upon:** i.e., use against
246. **fell out:** happened
248. **the rather:** the more quickly
249. **For that:** because; **fall:** downward stroke
253. **even:** just
257. **him:** i.e., Montano
260. **strange indignity:** i.e., unusual insult
261. **pass:** i.e., allow to pass
263. **mince:** extenuate or make light of

MONTANO
  If partially affined, or ⌜leagued⌝ in office,
  Thou dost deliver more or less than truth,
  Thou art no soldier.
IAGO   Touch me not so near.   235
  I had rather have this tongue cut from my mouth
  Than it should do offense to Michael Cassio.
  Yet I persuade myself, to speak the truth
  Shall nothing wrong him. ⟨Thus⟩ it is, general:
  Montano and myself being in speech,   240
  There comes a fellow crying out for help,
  And Cassio following him with determined sword
  To execute upon him. Sir, this gentleman
  ⌜*Pointing to Montano.*⌝
  Steps in to Cassio and entreats his pause.
  Myself the crying fellow did pursue,   245
  Lest by his clamor—as it so fell out—
  The town might fall in fright. He, swift of foot,
  Outran my purpose, and I returned ⟨the⟩ rather
  For that I heard the clink and fall of swords
  And Cassio high in oath, which till tonight   250
  I ne'er might say before. When I came back—
  For this was brief—I found them close together
  At blow and thrust, even as again they were
  When you yourself did part them.
  More of this matter cannot I report.   255
  But men are men; the best sometimes forget.
  Though Cassio did some little wrong to him,
  As men in rage strike those that wish them best,
  Yet surely Cassio, I believe, received
  From him that fled some strange indignity   260
  Which patience could not pass.
OTHELLO   I know, Iago,
  Thy honesty and love doth mince this matter,
  Making it light to Cassio.—Cassio, I love thee,
  But nevermore be officer of mine.   265

280. **Marry:** i.e., indeed

286. **sense:** (1) feeling; (2) reason (for being concerned)

288. **imposition:** ascription, something put on someone by others

291. **recover:** win back

292. **cast in his mood:** i.e., dismissed because he is angry

292–93. **punishment . . . malice:** i.e., a punishment imposed for political motives (i.e., perhaps, to placate the Cypriots), rather than out of personal ill-feeling toward Cassio

293. **even so as:** just as

293–95. **one would beat . . . lion:** i.e., punish the weak in order to scare the strong (Iago refers to the proverb "Beat the dog in the presence of the lion.")

295. **Sue to:** petition

Enter Desdemona attended.

Look if my gentle love be not raised up!
I'll make thee an example.

DESDEMONA   What is the matter, dear?

OTHELLO   All's well ⟨now,⟩
  sweeting.   270
Come away to bed. ⌜*To Montano.*⌝ Sir, for your hurts,
Myself will be your surgeon.—Lead him off.
                      ⌜*Montano is led off.*⌝
Iago, look with care about the town
And silence those whom this vile brawl
  distracted.—   275
Come, Desdemona. 'Tis the soldier's life
To have their balmy slumbers waked with strife.
                  ⌜*All but Iago and Cassio*⌝ *exit.*

IAGO   What, are you hurt, lieutenant?

CASSIO   Ay, past all surgery.

IAGO   Marry, ⟨God⟩ forbid!   280

CASSIO   Reputation, reputation, reputation! O, I have
  lost my reputation! I have lost the immortal part of
  myself, and what remains is bestial. My reputation,
  Iago, my reputation!

IAGO   As I am an honest man, I thought you had   285
  received some bodily wound. There is more sense
  in that than in reputation. Reputation is an idle and
  most false imposition, oft got without merit and lost
  without deserving. You have lost no reputation at
  all, unless you repute yourself such a loser. What,   290
  man, there are ways to recover the General again!
  You are but now cast in his mood—a punishment
  more in policy than in malice, even so as one would
  beat his offenseless dog to affright an imperious
  lion. Sue to him again and he's yours.   295

CASSIO   I will rather sue to be despised than to deceive
  so good a commander with so slight, so drunken,

298–99. **speak parrot:** i.e., speak without knowing what one is saying

299–300. **discourse fustian:** i.e., speak bombastic rant

308. **nothing wherefore:** i.e., not the cause of it **wherefore:** why

311. **pleasance:** pleasure

316. **unperfectness:** imperfection

318. **moraler:** moralizer

322. **my place:** i.e., as Othello's lieutenant

324. **Hydra:** the many-headed monster slain by Hercules; **stop:** i.e., silence

325. **by and by:** i.e., the next moment; **presently:** immediately

328–29. **familiar creature:** i.e., not a devil (as Cassio calls it) but a spirit (a **familiar**) that is serviceable to its master

331. **approved it:** tested it and found it true

Hydra. (2.3.324)
From Jacob Typot, *Symbola diuina* . . . (1652).

x

100

and so indiscreet an officer. [Drunk? And speak
parrot? And squabble? Swagger? Swear? And discourse fustian with one's own shadow?] O thou 300
invisible spirit of wine, if thou hast no name to be
known by, let us call thee devil!

IAGO What was he that you followed with your sword?
What had he done to you?

CASSIO I know not. 305

IAGO Is 't possible?

CASSIO I remember a mass of things, but nothing
distinctly; a quarrel, but nothing wherefore. O
⟨God,⟩ that men should put an enemy in their
mouths to steal away their brains! That we should 310
with joy, pleasance, revel, and applause transform
ourselves into beasts!

IAGO Why, but you are now well enough. How came
you thus recovered?

CASSIO It hath pleased the devil drunkenness to give 315
place to the devil wrath. One unperfectness shows
me another, to make me frankly despise myself.

IAGO Come, you are too severe a moraler. As the time,
the place, and the condition of this country stands,
I could heartily wish this had not ⟨so⟩ befallen. But 320
since it is as it is, mend it for your own good.

CASSIO I will ask him for my place again; he shall tell
me I am a drunkard! Had I as many mouths as
Hydra, such an answer would stop them all. To be
now a sensible man, by and by a fool, and presently 325
a beast! O, strange! Every inordinate cup is un-
blessed, and the ingredient is a devil.

IAGO Come, come, good wine is a good familiar creature, if it be well used. Exclaim no more against it.
And, good lieutenant, I think you think I love you. 330

CASSIO I have well approved it, sir.—I drunk!

IAGO You or any man living may be drunk at a time,
man. ⟨I'll⟩ tell you what you shall do. Our general's

335. **for that:** because
336. **mark:** notice, attention
336-37. **denotement:** description
337. **parts:** accomplishments; **graces:** attractive qualities
339. **free:** noble; **apt:** ready (to help)
343. **splinter:** set with splints; **my fortunes . . . lay:** i.e., I will bet all my possessions against any stake (**lay**)
344-45. **this crack . . . stronger:** It was proverbial that a broken bone, when healed, was stronger than before, if it was well set.
349. **I think it freely:** i.e., I entirely believe it; **betimes:** early
351. **desperate:** in despair
351-52. **check me here:** hold me back now
357. **free:** honorable
358. **Probal to thinking:** i.e., probable
360. **inclining:** i.e., always inclined to help; **subdue:** prevail upon
361. **suit:** petition; **framed:** created; **fruitful:** productive (of good works)
363. **win:** persuade; **were 't:** i.e., even if she were to ask him
364. **seals . . . sin:** In Christianity, baptism and the other sacraments are both the guarantees (**seals**) and the outward manifestations (**symbols**) that humankind may be redeemed, or ransomed, from sin.
365. **enfettered:** enslaved
366. **list:** likes
367. **her appetite:** her fancy; or, his desire for her
368. **weak function:** i.e., his capacity to act, diminished by his attachment to Desdemona

wife is now the general: I may say so in this
respect, for that he hath devoted and given up   335
himself to the contemplation, mark, and ⌐denote-
ment⌐ of her parts and graces. Confess yourself
freely to her. Importune her help to put you in your
place again. She is of so free, so kind, so apt, so
blessed a disposition she holds it a vice in her   340
goodness not to do more than she is requested. This
broken joint between you and her husband entreat
her to splinter, and, my fortunes against any lay
worth naming, this crack of your love shall grow
stronger than it was before.   345
CASSIO You advise me well.
IAGO I protest, in the sincerity of love and honest
kindness.
CASSIO I think it freely; and betimes in the morning I
will beseech the virtuous Desdemona to undertake   350
for me. I am desperate of my fortunes if they check
me ⟨here⟩.
IAGO You are in the right. Good night, lieutenant. I
must to the watch.
CASSIO Good night, honest Iago.   *Cassio exits.* 355
IAGO
And what's he, then, that says I play the villain,
When this advice is free I give and honest,
Probal to thinking, and indeed the course
To win the Moor again? For 'tis most easy
Th' inclining Desdemona to subdue   360
In any honest suit. She's framed as fruitful
As the free elements. And then for her
To win the Moor—⟨were 't⟩ to renounce his baptism,
All seals and symbols of redeemèd sin—
His soul is so enfettered to her love   365
That she may make, unmake, do what she list,
Even as her appetite shall play the god
With his weak function. How am I then a villain

369–70. **this parallel . . . good:** i.e., this course that parallels exactly the one that would lead to his good

370. **Divinity of hell:** i.e., the kind of argument you would expect from Satan   **Divinity:** theology

371. **put on:** i.e., urge

372. **suggest:** i.e., tempt; **shows:** appearances

374. **Plies:** begs (repeatedly and forcefully)

376. **pestilence:** i.e., poison

377. **repeals:** i.e., wishes to have him recalled (as if from banishment)

379. **undo . . . Moor:** i.e., destroy Othello's confidence in her

380. **pitch:** Pitch is black, malodorous, and extremely sticky; it is thus the perfect substance for Iago to imagine as helping him "enmesh" his victims.

384. **chase:** hunt

384–85. **not . . . cry:** i.e., not one of the hounds following the scent but merely one at the back of the pack adding his voice to the cry

387. **issue:** result

388. **so much:** i.e., a certain amount of

389. **wit:** good sense

393. **wit:** intelligence

396. **cashiered:** i.e., gotten (him) dismissed

397–98. **Though . . . ripe:** These lines sound like proverbs that ought to persuade Roderigo of Iago's wisdom, but the lines themselves are obscure.

To counsel Cassio to this parallel course
Directly to his good? Divinity of hell!   370
When devils will the blackest sins put on,
They do suggest at first with heavenly shows,
As I do now. For whiles this honest fool
Plies Desdemona to repair his fortune,
And she for him pleads strongly to the Moor,   375
I'll pour this pestilence into his ear:
That she repeals him for her body's lust;
And by how much she strives to do him good,
She shall undo her credit with the Moor.
So will I turn her virtue into pitch,   380
And out of her own goodness make the net
That shall enmesh them all.

Enter Roderigo.

                                        How now, Roderigo?
RODERIGO I do follow here in the chase, not like a
hound that hunts, but one that fills up the cry. My   385
money is almost spent, I have been tonight exceed-
ingly well cudgeled, and I think the issue will be I
shall have so much experience for my pains, and so,
with no money at all and a little more wit, return
again to Venice.   390
IAGO
How poor are they that have not patience!
What wound did ever heal but by degrees?
Thou know'st we work by wit and not by witchcraft,
And wit depends on dilatory time.
Dost not go well? Cassio hath beaten thee,   395
And thou, by that small hurt, ⟨hast⟩ cashiered Cassio.
Though other things grow fair against the sun,
Yet fruits that blossom first will first be ripe.
Content thyself awhile. ⟨By th' Mass,⟩ 'tis morning!
Pleasure and action make the hours seem short.   400
Retire thee; go where thou art billeted.

405. **move . . . mistress:** i.e., intercede with Desdemona on Cassio's behalf

408. **jump when:** i.e., at exactly the moment

410. **device:** ingenious plot; **coldness:** i.e., slowness to act.

"Works," or fortified walls. (3.2.3)
From Johann Amos Comenius, *Orbis sensualium
pictus* . . . (1685).

Away, I say! Thou shalt know more hereafter.
Nay, get thee gone.   *Roderigo exits.*
                    Two things are to be done.
My wife must move for Cassio to her mistress.   405
I'll set her on.
Myself ⌜the⌝ while to draw the Moor apart
And bring him jump when he may Cassio find
Soliciting his wife. Ay, that's the way.
Dull not device by coldness and delay.   410
                              He exits.

The Tragedy of

OTHELLO,
The Moor of Venice

ACT 3

3.1 Cassio arrives with musicians to honor Othello and Desdemona. As Iago has recommended, Cassio asks Emilia to arrange a meeting with Desdemona, even though Emilia assures him that Desdemona is already urging Othello to reinstate him.

---

1. **content your pains:** i.e., reward your efforts
2. **morrow:** morning (By employing musicians to awaken Othello and Desdemona after their wedding night, Cassio is following Renaissance custom.)
3 SD. **Clown:** comic servant
4–5. **have . . . nose thus:** The Clown alludes to Naples's reputation for being a likely place to contract syphilis, which would eat away the bridge of the nose.

ACT 3

Scene 1
Enter Cassio ⟨with⟩ Musicians.

CASSIO
Masters, play here (I will content your pains)
Something that's brief; and bid "Good morrow,
general." ⌐*They play.*⌐

⌐*Enter the Clown.*⌐

CLOWN Why masters, have your instruments been in
Naples, that they speak i' th' nose thus?   5
MUSICIAN How, sir, how?
CLOWN Are these, I pray you, wind instruments?
MUSICIAN Ay, marry, are they, sir.
CLOWN O, thereby hangs a tail.
MUSICIAN Whereby hangs a tale, sir?   10
CLOWN Marry, sir, by many a wind instrument that I
know. But, masters, here's money for you; and the
General so likes your music that he desires you, for
love's sake, to make no more noise with it.
MUSICIAN Well, sir, we will not.   15
CLOWN If you have any music that may not be heard, to
't again. But, as they say, to hear music the General
does not greatly care.
MUSICIAN We have none such, sir.
CLOWN Then put up your pipes in your bag, for I'll   20
away. Go, vanish into air, away!

111

22. **mine:** i.e., my

24. **Prithee . . . quillets:** i.e., I pray you to put away your quibbles

27–28. **a . . . speech:** i.e., the favor of a little conversation

30. **seem to notify:** i.e., tell (The Clown mockingly affects extravagantly courtly language.)

32. **In happy time:** i.e., at just the right time

36. **send in:** i.e., send a message; **suit:** petition

38. **access:** accent on the second syllable

39. **presently:** immediately

40. **a mean:** i.e., some means

45. **A Florentine:** Cassio, a citizen of Florence (a **Florentine**), comments that Iago is as kind and honest as one of Cassio's own townsmen.

47. **displeasure:** unhappiness, trouble

Musicians exit.

CASSIO Dost thou hear, mine honest friend?
CLOWN No, I hear not your honest friend. I hear you.
CASSIO Prithee, keep up thy quillets. ⌜*Giving money.*⌝
  There's a poor piece of gold for thee. If the gentle-   25
  woman that attends the ⟨General's wife⟩ be stirring,
  tell her there's one Cassio entreats her a little favor
  of speech. Wilt thou do this?
CLOWN She is stirring, sir. If she will stir hither, I shall
  seem to notify unto her.   30
⟨CASSIO
  Do, good my friend.⟩   *Clown exits.*

Enter Iago.

  In happy time, Iago.
IAGO You have not been abed, then?
CASSIO Why, no. The day had broke
  Before we parted. I have made bold, Iago,   35
  To send in to your wife. My suit to her
  Is that she will to virtuous Desdemona
  Procure me some access.
IAGO I'll send her to you presently,
  And I'll devise a mean to draw the Moor   40
  Out of the way, that your converse and business
  May be more free.
CASSIO
  I humbly thank you for 't. ⌜*Iago*⌝ *exits.* I never
  knew
  A Florentine more kind and honest.   45

Enter Emilia.

EMILIA
  Good morrow, good lieutenant. I am sorry
  For your displeasure, but all will sure be well.
  The General and his wife are talking of it,
  And she speaks for you stoutly. The Moor replies

51. **affinity:** kindred, connections
52. **might not but:** i.e., could only
54. **suitor:** petitioner
55. **occasion:** opportunity; **front:** forelock (Proverbial: "Seize occasion by the forelock.")
56. **bring . . . again:** i.e., restore you to your position
58. **or that:** i.e., and if
62. **bestow:** place; **time:** i.e., the chance
63. **bosom:** i.e., your innermost thoughts

3.2

1. **pilot:** i.e., of the ship that bore Othello to Cyprus
2. **by him:** i.e., through his agency; **do my duties:** i.e., pay my respects
3. **works:** fortifications (See page 106.)
4. **Repair:** return
7. **wait upon:** attend upon

That he you hurt is of great fame in Cyprus   50
And great affinity, and that in wholesome wisdom
He might not but refuse you. But he protests he
  loves you
And needs no other suitor but his likings
⟨To take the safest occasion by the front⟩   55
To bring you in again.
CASSIO   Yet I beseech you,
  If you think fit, or that it may be done,
  Give me advantage of some brief discourse
  With Desdemon alone.   60
EMILIA   Pray you come in.
  I will bestow you where you shall have time
  To speak your bosom freely.
[CASSIO   I am much bound to you.]
                                        ⟨*They exit.*⟩

Scene 2
Enter Othello, Iago, and Gentlemen.

OTHELLO
  These letters give, Iago, to the pilot
  And by him do my duties to the Senate.
                    ⌈*He gives Iago some papers.*⌉
  That done, I will be walking on the works.
  Repair there to me.
IAGO   Well, my good lord, I'll do 't.   5
OTHELLO
  This fortification, gentlemen, shall we see 't?
GENTLEMEN
  ⟨We⟩ wait upon your Lordship.
                                        They exit.

3.3 Desdemona's interview with Cassio is cut short by the arrival of Othello. Cassio leaves hastily in order to avoid speaking with Othello. Desdemona pleads to Othello on Cassio's behalf. When she exits, Iago says that Cassio's avoidance of Othello is suspicious and that Cassio may not be honorable, all the while insinuating that he, Iago, knows more than he is willing to say. He warns Othello against becoming jealous of Desdemona.

When Desdemona enters and Othello complains of an aching head, Desdemona offers to bind his head with her handkerchief. As they exit, the handkerchief drops unnoticed by either of them. Emilia picks it up and gives it to Iago, who has often asked for it. Othello reenters and, now tormented by jealousy, threatens Iago with death unless he provides proof of Desdemona's infidelity. Iago alleges that Cassio one night talked in his sleep about making love to Desdemona and that Cassio once wiped his beard with the lost handkerchief. Othello is convinced by this "proof" and vows to kill Desdemona; Iago agrees to kill Cassio. Othello then appoints Iago to the lieutenancy.

---

2. **All my abilities:** i.e., all I can
13–14. **in strangeness . . . distance:** i.e., stand aloof from you only so far as is politically expedient
17–18. **Or feed . . . circumstance:** These lines seem to give reasons why Cassio fears to wait for Othello to take him back into his good graces, but neither line is clear. **nice:** fastidious **waterish:** thin, diluted **circumstance:** details

(continued)

Scene 3
Enter Desdemona, Cassio, and Emilia.

DESDEMONA
  Be thou assured, good Cassio, I will do
  All my abilities in thy behalf.
EMILIA
  Good madam, do. I warrant it grieves my husband
  As if the cause were his.
DESDEMONA
  O, that's an honest fellow! Do not doubt, Cassio,   5
  But I will have my lord and you again
  As friendly as you were.
CASSIO   Bounteous madam,
  Whatever shall become of Michael Cassio,
  He's never anything but your true servant.   10
DESDEMONA
  I know 't. I thank you. You do love my lord;
  You have known him long; and be you well assured
  He shall in strangeness stand no farther off
  Than in a politic distance.
CASSIO   Ay, but, lady,   15
  That policy may either last so long,
  Or feed upon such nice and waterish diet,
  Or breed itself so out of ⟨circumstance,⟩
  That, I being absent and my place supplied,
  My general will forget my love and service.   20
DESDEMONA
  Do not doubt that. Before Emilia here,
  I give thee warrant of thy place. Assure thee,
  If I do vow a friendship, I'll perform it
  To the last article. My lord shall never rest:
  I'll watch him tame and talk him out of patience;   25
  His bed shall seem a school, his board a shrift;
  I'll intermingle everything he does
  With Cassio's suit. Therefore be merry, Cassio,

19. **supplied:** filled
21. **doubt:** fear; **Before:** in the presence of
22. **give thee warrant of:** i.e., guarantee you; **thy place:** i.e., your position (as lieutenant); **Assure thee:** rest assured
23. **a friendship:** i.e., an act of friendship
25. **watch him tame:** i.e., keep him awake at night until he is agreeable (a method of taming falcons)
26. **his board a shrift:** i.e., his table (shall seem) a confessional
30. **give thy cause away:** abandon your case; or, lose your case
36. **do:** i.e., act according to
46. **suitor:** petitioner
50. **grace:** favor in your eyes; **move:** persuade
51. **His present reconciliation take:** i.e., effect his immediate restoration to office
53. **in cunning:** deliberately
54. **in:** i.e., of

For thy solicitor shall rather die
Than give thy cause away.   30

Enter Othello and Iago.

EMILIA Madam, here comes my lord.
CASSIO Madam, I'll take my leave.
DESDEMONA Why, stay, and hear me speak.
CASSIO
Madam, not now. I am very ill at ease,
Unfit for mine own purposes.   35
DESDEMONA Well, do your discretion.   *Cassio exits.*
IAGO
Ha, I like not that.
OTHELLO   What dost thou say?
IAGO
Nothing, my lord; or if—I know not what.
OTHELLO
Was not that Cassio parted from my wife?   40
IAGO
Cassio, my lord? No, sure, I cannot think it
That he would steal away so guiltylike,
Seeing your coming.
OTHELLO I do believe 'twas he.
DESDEMONA How now, my lord?   45
I have been talking with a suitor here,
A man that languishes in your displeasure.
OTHELLO Who is 't you mean?
DESDEMONA
Why, your lieutenant, Cassio. Good my lord,
If I have any grace or power to move you,   50
His present reconciliation take;
For if he be not one that truly loves you,
That errs in ignorance and not in cunning,
I have no judgment in an honest face.
I prithee call him back.   55
OTHELLO   Went he hence now?

57. **faith:** i.e., in faith (a very mild oath)

65. **dinner:** the midday meal

72. **in our common reason:** i.e., according to ordinary judgment

73. **Save:** i.e., except

73-74. **the wars . . . best:** i.e., the military profession must punish (and thus make examples of) even its best members (**Her** refers to the **wars,** which is considered a singular noun.)

74. **not almost:** i.e., scarcely

75. **a private check:** i.e., even an unofficial censure

78. **mamm'ring on:** i.e., dithering about

82. **bring him in:** i.e., restore him to office; **By'r Lady:** an oath on the name of the Virgin Mary

85. **boon:** favor

86. **as:** i.e., as if

DESDEMONA ⟨Yes, faith,⟩ so humbled
  That he hath left part of his grief with me
  To suffer with him. Good love, call him back.
OTHELLO
  Not now, sweet Desdemon. Some other time.   60
DESDEMONA
  But shall 't be shortly?
OTHELLO   The sooner, sweet, for you.
DESDEMONA
  Shall 't be tonight at supper?
OTHELLO   No, not tonight.
DESDEMONA Tomorrow dinner, then?   65
OTHELLO I shall not dine at home;
  I meet the captains at the citadel.
DESDEMONA
  Why then tomorrow night, ⟨or⟩ Tuesday morn,
  On Tuesday noon or night; on Wednesday morn.
  I prithee name the time, but let it not   70
  Exceed three days. In faith, he's penitent;
  And yet his trespass, in our common reason—
  Save that, they say, the wars must make example
  Out of her best—is not almost a fault
  T' incur a private check. When shall he come?   75
  Tell me, Othello. I wonder in my soul
  What you would ask me that I should deny,
  Or stand so mamm'ring on? What? Michael Cassio,
  That came a-wooing with you, and so many a time,
  When I have spoke of you dispraisingly,   80
  Hath ta'en your part—to have so much to do
  To bring him in! ⟨By'r Lady,⟩ I could do much—
OTHELLO
  Prithee, no more. Let him come when he will;
  I will deny thee nothing.
DESDEMONA Why, this is not a boon!   85
  'Tis as I should entreat you wear your gloves,
  Or feed on nourishing dishes, or keep you warm,

88. **a peculiar profit:** something advantageous to yourself (**To your own person** repeats, and thus insists on, this notion.)

89. **suit:** petition

90. **touch:** put to the test

91. **poise:** weight, significance

94. **Whereon:** i.e., in return for what I have just said

97. **straight:** straightway, at once

98. **fancies:** inclinations, wishes

100. **wretch:** apparently a term of affection

101. **But:** unless

101–2. **when . . . again:** i.e., perhaps, I will love you until the universe is again swallowed up in Chaos, out of which it is said to have been created

Or sue to you to do a peculiar profit
To your own person. Nay, when I have a suit
Wherein I mean to touch your love indeed,   90
It shall be full of poise and difficult weight,
And fearful to be granted.
OTHELLO   I will deny thee nothing!
Whereon, I do beseech thee, grant me this,
To leave me but a little to myself.   95
DESDEMONA
Shall I deny you? No. Farewell, my lord.
OTHELLO
Farewell, my Desdemona. I'll come to thee straight.
DESDEMONA
Emilia, come.—Be as your fancies teach you.
Whate'er you be, I am obedient.
                         ⟨*Desdemona and Emilia*⟩ *exit.*
OTHELLO
Excellent wretch! Perdition catch my soul   100
But I do love thee! And when I love thee not,
Chaos is come again.
IAGO   My noble lord—
OTHELLO
What dost thou say, Iago?
IAGO   Did Michael Cassio,   105
When ⟨you⟩ wooed my lady, know of your love?
OTHELLO
He did, from first to last. Why dost thou ask?
IAGO
But for a satisfaction of my thought,
No further harm.
OTHELLO   Why of thy thought, Iago?   110
IAGO
I did not think he had been acquainted with her.
OTHELLO
O yes, and went between us very oft.
IAGO   Indeed?

126. **didst:** i.e., didst thou
127. **of my counsel:** i.e., in my confidence
132. **conceit:** conception, idea
136. **for:** i.e., because
139. **stops:** pauses, hesitations in your speaking
141. **tricks of custom:** i.e., usual or habitual tricks
142. **close dilations:** perhaps, expressions the speaker tries to hide
143. **That passion cannot rule:** i.e., that is not controlled by the emotions
144. **For:** i.e., as for

OTHELLO
Indeed? Ay, indeed! Discern'st thou aught in that?
Is he not honest?   115
IAGO   Honest, my lord?
OTHELLO   Honest—ay, honest.
IAGO
My lord, for aught I know.
OTHELLO   What dost thou think?
IAGO   Think, my lord?   120
OTHELLO
"Think, my lord?" ⟨By heaven,⟩ thou echo'st me
As if there were some monster in thy thought
Too hideous to be shown. Thou dost mean
    something.
I heard thee say even now, thou lik'st not that,   125
When Cassio left my wife. What didst not like?
And when I told thee he was of my counsel
⟨In⟩ my whole course of wooing, thou cried'st
    "Indeed?"
And didst contract and purse thy brow together   130
As if thou then hadst shut up in thy brain
Some horrible conceit. If thou dost love me,
Show me thy thought.
IAGO   My lord, you know I love you.
OTHELLO   I think thou dost;   135
And for I know thou 'rt full of love and honesty
And weigh'st thy words before thou giv'st them
    breath,
Therefore these stops of thine fright me the more.
For such things in a false, disloyal knave   140
Are tricks of custom; but in a man that's just,
They're close dilations working from the heart
That passion cannot rule.
IAGO   For Michael Cassio,
I dare be sworn I think that he is honest.   145
OTHELLO
I think so too.

149. **Certain:** i.e., certainly
158. **that all slaves are free to:** i.e., that which even slaves are free with respect to
161. **whereinto:** into which
164. **uncleanly apprehensions:** impure thoughts
165. **Keep . . . days:** i.e., hold court   **leets:** courts held by lords of the manor   **law days:** days on which courts were in session
165–66. **in sessions . . . With:** i.e., sit together with
171. **vicious:** imperfect, defective, mistaken
173. **jealousy:** suspiciousness
174. **Shapes:** imagines
174–76. **that your wisdom . . . notice:** i.e., that you therefore, in your wisdom, would take no notice of one who so mistakenly imagines things
177. **observance:** observation
178. **It were not for:** i.e., it is not in the interest of

IAGO　　　　　Men should be what they seem;
　　Or those that be not, would they might seem none!
OTHELLO　Certain, men should be what they seem.
IAGO
　　Why then, I think Cassio's an honest man.　　　　150
OTHELLO　Nay, yet there's more in this.
　　I prithee speak to me as to thy thinkings,
　　As thou dost ruminate, and give thy worst of
　　　　thoughts
　　The worst of words.　　　　　　　　　　　　155
IAGO　　　　　　　　Good my lord, pardon me.
　　Though I am bound to every act of duty,
　　I am not bound to ⟨that all slaves are free to.⟩
　　Utter my thoughts? Why, say they are vile and
　　　　false—　　　　　　　　　　　　　　160
　　As where's that palace whereinto foul things
　　Sometimes intrude not? Who has that breast so
　　　　pure
　　⟨But some⟩ uncleanly apprehensions
　　Keep leets and law days and in sessions sit　　165
　　With meditations lawful?
OTHELLO
　　Thou dost conspire against thy friend, Iago,
　　If thou but think'st him wronged and mak'st his ear
　　A stranger to thy thoughts.
IAGO　　　　　　　　　I do beseech you,　　170
　　Though I perchance am vicious in my guess—
　　As, I confess, it is my nature's plague
　　To spy into abuses, and ⟨oft⟩ my jealousy
　　Shapes faults that are not—that your wisdom
　　From one that so imperfectly conceits　　　　175
　　Would take no notice, nor build yourself a trouble
　　Out of his scattering and unsure observance.
　　It were not for your quiet nor your good,
　　Nor for my manhood, honesty, and wisdom,
　　To let you know my thoughts.　　　　　　180

182–83. Good . . . souls: proverbial **immediate:** nearest, i.e., most precious

192. if: i.e., even if

196–97. doth mock . . . feeds on: i.e., toys with its victim (as a cat plays with a mouse)

198. certain . . . fate: i.e., knowing that his wife is unfaithful; **his wronger:** i.e., his unfaithful wife

199. tells he o'er: i.e., does he count

202. Poor: i.e., the person who is poor

203. fineless: unlimited

204. ever: always

209. still: continually

211. once . . . resolved: i.e., at once to find out the truth

A falconer with his tamed falcon. (3.3.301–4)
From George Turbeville, *The booke of faulconrie or hauking* . . . (1575).

OTHELLO   What dost thou mean?

IAGO

Good name in man and woman, dear my lord,
Is the immediate jewel of their souls.
Who steals my purse steals trash. 'Tis something,
    nothing;   185
'Twas mine, 'tis his, and has been slave to
    thousands.
But he that filches from me my good name
Robs me of that which not enriches him
And makes me poor indeed.   190

OTHELLO   ⟨By heaven,⟩ I'll know thy thoughts.

IAGO

You cannot, if my heart were in your hand,
Nor shall not, whilst 'tis in my custody.

OTHELLO

Ha?

IAGO   O, beware, my lord, of jealousy!   195
It is the green-eyed monster which doth mock
The meat it feeds on. That cuckold lives in bliss
Who, certain of his fate, loves not his wronger;
But O, what damnèd minutes tells he o'er
Who dotes, yet doubts; suspects, yet ⟨strongly⟩ loves!   200

OTHELLO   O misery!

IAGO

Poor and content is rich, and rich enough;
But riches fineless is as poor as winter
To him that ever fears he shall be poor.
Good ⟨God,⟩ the souls of all my tribe defend   205
From jealousy!

OTHELLO   Why, why is this?
Think'st thou I'd make a life of jealousy,
To follow still the changes of the moon
With fresh suspicions? No. To be once in doubt   210
Is ⟨once⟩ to be resolved. Exchange me for a goat
When I shall turn the business of my soul

213. **exsufflicate:** Since this is the only recorded use of the word, its meaning is uncertain. (In Latin *exsufflare* means "to blow away.") **exsufflicate and blown:** perhaps, inflated; or, perhaps, spat out and flyblown

214. **Matching thy inference:** i.e., corresponding to your description of a jealous man

215. **fair:** beautiful; **feeds:** eats

217. **Where . . . virtuous:** i.e., when a woman is virtuous, these are virtuous accomplishments

219. **doubt of her revolt:** i.e., suspicion of her inconstancy

221. **prove:** i.e., put my doubt to the test

222. **on the proof:** i.e., directly I have the results of the test

229. **not jealous nor secure:** i.e., neither suspicious nor wholly trustful

231. **self-bounty:** inherent goodness; **abused:** deceived; **Look to 't:** i.e., be on your guard

232. **country:** native (i.e., Venetian)

242. **go to:** an expression of impatience or annoyance

243. **give out such a seeming:** i.e., present such a false appearance

244. **seel:** i.e., close up (literally, sew shut, as with the eyes of a falcon being tamed); **oak:** i.e., the grain in oak

To such exsufflicate and ⟨blown⟩ surmises,
Matching thy inference. 'Tis not to make me jealous
To say my wife is fair, feeds well, loves company,   215
Is free of speech, sings, plays, and dances ⟨well.⟩
Where virtue is, these are more virtuous.
Nor from mine own weak merits will I draw
The smallest fear or doubt of her revolt,
For she had eyes, and chose me. No, Iago,   220
I'll see before I doubt; when I doubt, prove;
And on the proof, there is no more but this:
Away at once with love or jealousy.

IAGO
I am glad of this, for now I shall have reason
To show the love and duty that I bear you   225
With franker spirit. Therefore, as I am bound,
Receive it from me. I speak not yet of proof.
Look to your wife; observe her well with Cassio;
Wear your eyes thus, not jealous nor secure.
I would not have your free and noble nature,   230
Out of self-bounty, be abused. Look to 't.
I know our country disposition well.
In Venice they do let ⟨God⟩ see the pranks
They dare not show their husbands. Their best
   conscience   235
Is not to leave 't undone, but ⌈keep 't⌉ unknown.

OTHELLO   Dost thou say so?

IAGO
She did deceive her father, marrying you,
And when she seemed to shake and fear your looks,
She loved them most.   240

OTHELLO   And so she did.

IAGO   Why, go to, then!
She that, so young, could give out such a seeming,
To seel her father's eyes up close as oak,
He thought 'twas witchcraft! But I am much to   245
   blame.

247. **of:** for
254. **moved:** disturbed, troubled
255. **am to:** i.e., must
255–57. **strain . . . suspicion:** i.e., force what I say to have greater consequences or broader scope than to raise suspicion
260. **fall into . . . success:** i.e., have such a hateful outcome or result
265. **I do not think but:** i.e., I think that; **honest:** chaste (This was the standard meaning of "honest" when applied to a woman.)
267. **erring from itself:** (1) wandering from itself; (2) sinning by departing from one's supposedly God-given nature
269. **affect:** like, be attracted to
270. **clime:** region; **complexion:** (1) temperament; (2) skin color; **degree:** social rank
271. **Whereto:** i.e., to which
272. **such:** i.e., such a one; **will:** desire; **rank:** offensively strong; loathsome; violent
274. **in position:** i.e., in establishing this general proposition
276. **recoiling:** returning
277. **match:** compare; **country forms:** i.e., the appearance of her countrymen
278. **happily:** haply, perhaps

I humbly do beseech you of your pardon
For too much loving you.
OTHELLO   I am bound to thee forever.
IAGO
I see this hath a little dashed your spirits.   250
OTHELLO
Not a jot, not a jot.
IAGO   ⟨I' faith,⟩ I fear it has.
I hope you will consider what is spoke
Comes from ⟨my⟩ love. But I do see you're moved.
I am to pray you not to strain my speech   255
To grosser issues nor to larger reach
Than to suspicion.
OTHELLO   I will not.
IAGO   Should you do so, my lord,
My speech should fall into such vile success   260
⟨As my thoughts aim not at.⟩ Cassio's my worthy
   friend.
My lord, I see you're moved.
OTHELLO   No, not much moved.
I do not think but Desdemona's honest.   265
IAGO
Long live she so! And long live you to think so!
OTHELLO
And yet, how nature erring from itself—
IAGO
Ay, there's the point. As, to be bold with you,
Not to affect many proposèd matches
Of her own clime, complexion, and degree,   270
Whereto we see in all things nature tends—
Foh! One may smell in such a will most rank,
Foul ⟨disproportion,⟩ thoughts unnatural—
But pardon me—I do not in position
Distinctly speak of her, though I may fear   275
Her will, recoiling to her better judgment,
May fall to match you with her country forms
And happily repent.

281. **Set on:** i.e., instruct, urge
284. **unfolds:** discloses, reveals
285. **would I might:** i.e., I would like to
287. **place:** position (as lieutenant)
290. **his means:** i.e., perhaps, the means he uses to recover his lieutenancy
291. **strain:** insist upon; **entertainment:** i.e., (return to) service, i.e., reinstatement
294. **busy:** prying, inquisitive
295. **As . . . am:** i.e., as I have great cause to fear that I am
296. **hold her free:** i.e., regard her as guiltless
297. **Fear . . . government:** i.e., do not have doubts about my discreet behavior
300. **qualities:** sorts, kinds
300-1. **with a learnèd . . . dealings:** i.e., with a mind experienced in all kinds of human behavior
301. **haggard:** i.e., uncontrolled, unchaste (A **haggard** is a wild female falcon.)
302. **Though that:** i.e., even though; **jesses:** the straps that link a trained falcon's legs to its leash
303. **whistle her off . . . wind:** i.e., turn her loose, abandon her (A falcon being let loose was "whistled down the wind," i.e., cast off to go with the wind.)
304. **prey at fortune:** i.e., fend for herself; **Haply, for:** perhaps because
305. **soft parts:** i.e., ingratiating qualities; **conversation:** i.e., way of dealing with others
306. **chamberers:** gallants
307. **vale:** valley
308. **abused:** deceived

OTHELLO   Farewell, farewell!
If more thou dost perceive, let me know more.   280
Set on thy wife to observe. Leave me, Iago.
IAGO, ⌐*beginning to exit*⌐ My lord, I take my leave.
OTHELLO
Why did I marry? This honest creature doubtless
Sees and knows more, much more, than he unfolds.
IAGO, ⌐*returning*⌐
My lord, I would I might entreat your Honor   285
To scan this thing no farther. Leave it to time.
Although 'tis fit that Cassio have his place—
For sure he fills it up with great ability—
Yet, if you please to ⟨hold⟩ him off awhile,
You shall by that perceive him and his means.   290
Note if your lady strain his entertainment
With any strong or vehement importunity.
Much will be seen in that. In the meantime,
Let me be thought too busy in my fears—
As worthy cause I have to fear I am—   295
And hold her free, I do beseech your Honor.
OTHELLO Fear not my government.
IAGO I once more take my leave.   *He exits.*
OTHELLO
This fellow's of exceeding honesty,
And knows all ⟨qualities⟩ with a learnèd spirit   300
Of human dealings. If I do prove her haggard,
Though that her jesses were my dear heartstrings,
I'd whistle her off and let her down the wind
To prey at fortune. Haply, for I am black
And have not those soft parts of conversation   305
That chamberers have, or for I am declined
Into the vale of years—yet that's not much—
She's gone, I am abused, and my relief
Must be to loathe her. O curse of marriage,
That we can call these delicate creatures ours   310
And not their appetites! I had rather be a toad

314. **great ones:** i.e., those of high social rank
315. **Prerogatived . . . base:** i.e., men of the higher ranks do not enjoy the privilege of exemption from wifely infidelity as much as those of lower rank
317. **this forkèd plague:** i.e., the plague of wearing cuckolds' horns (See page 174.)
318. **do quicken:** are conceived
319. **false, heaven:** Many editions include words from the quarto to make this phrase read "false, O then heaven." This addition regularizes the meter, but the line as it stands in the Folio is a strong poetic line.
322. **generous:** high-born, noble
324. **to blame:** i.e., blameworthy, at fault
326. **upon my forehead:** i.e., where cuckolds' horns supposedly grow
327. **with watching:** i.e., from lack of sleep
330. **napkin:** handkerchief
335. **remembrance:** i.e., token of remembrance, keepsake
338. **conjured:** implored (accent on second syllable); **ever:** always
339. **reserves it evermore:** i.e., always keeps it

And live upon the vapor of a dungeon
Than keep a corner in the thing I love
For others' uses. Yet 'tis the plague ⟨of⟩ great ones;
Prerogatived are they less than the base.   315
'Tis destiny unshunnable, like death.
Even then this forkèd plague is fated to us
When we do quicken. Look where she comes.

Enter Desdemona and Emilia.

If she be false, heaven ⟨mocks⟩ itself!
I'll not believe 't.   320
DESDEMONA   How now, my dear Othello?
Your dinner, and the generous islanders
By you invited, do attend your presence.
OTHELLO   I am to blame.
DESDEMONA
Why do you speak so faintly? Are you not well?   325
OTHELLO
I have a pain upon my forehead, here.
DESDEMONA
⟨Faith,⟩ that's with watching. 'Twill away again.
Let me but bind it hard; within this hour
It will be well.
OTHELLO   Your napkin is too little.   330
   Let it alone.   ⌐*The handkerchief falls, unnoticed.*¬
     Come, I'll go in with you.
DESDEMONA
I am very sorry that you are not well.
               ⟨*Othello and Desdemona*⟩ *exit.*
EMILIA, ⌐*picking up the handkerchief*¬
I am glad I have found this napkin.
This was her first remembrance from the Moor.   335
My wayward husband hath a hundred times
Wooed me to steal it. But she so loves the token
(For he conjured her she should ever keep it)
That she reserves it evermore about her

340. **work:** i.e., needlework, embroidery pattern; **ta'en out:** taken out (i.e., copied)

343. **nothing but to:** i.e., only; **fantasy:** fancy, whim

357. **to th' advantage:** i.e., fortunately

364. **purpose of import:** important purpose

To kiss and talk to. I'll have the work ta'en out   340
And give 't Iago. What he will do with it
Heaven knows, not I.
I nothing but to please his fantasy.

                Enter Iago.

IAGO How now? What do you here alone?
EMILIA
Do not you chide. I have a thing for you.   345
IAGO
You have a thing for me? It is a common thing—
EMILIA Ha?
IAGO To have a foolish wife.
EMILIA
O, is that all? What will you give me now
For that same handkerchief?   350
IAGO   What handkerchief?
EMILIA What handkerchief?
Why, that the Moor first gave to Desdemona,
That which so often you did bid me steal.
IAGO Hast stol'n it from her?   355
EMILIA
No, ⟨faith,⟩ she let it drop by negligence,
And to th' advantage I, being here, took 't up.
Look, here 'tis.
IAGO   A good wench! Give it me.
EMILIA
What will you do with 't, that you have been so   360
   earnest
To have me filch it?
IAGO, ⌜*snatching it*⌝ Why, what is that to you?
EMILIA
If it be not for some purpose of import,
Give 't me again. Poor lady, she'll run mad   365
When she shall lack it.

367. **Be not acknown on 't:** i.e., do not admit to knowing about it

374. **conceits:** conceptions, ideas

375. **are . . . distaste:** i.e., scarcely offend the taste

376. **act:** action

377. **the mines of sulfur:** Sulfur mines were famous for the fact that, once on fire, they seemed unquenchable.

379. **poppy:** i.e., opium; **mandragora:** the mandrake plant, which yields a narcotic syrup

380. **drowsy:** i.e., sleep-inducing, soporific

382. **owedst:** i.e., did own, did experience

385. **Avaunt:** i.e., away (used to send away witches and devils); **the rack:** an instrument of torture that tore the body apart

386. **abused:** deceived

394. **wanting:** missing

"Thou hast set me on the rack." (3.3.385)
From Girolamo Maggi, *De tintinnabulis liber . . .* (1689).

IAGO   Be not acknown on 't.
I have use for it. Go, leave me.   *Emilia exits.*
I will in Cassio's lodging lose this napkin
And let him find it. Trifles light as air   370
Are to the jealous confirmations strong
As proofs of holy writ. This may do something.
[The Moor already changes with my poison;]
Dangerous conceits are in their natures poisons,
Which at the first are scarce found to distaste,   375
But with a little act upon the blood
Burn like the mines of sulfur.

                    Enter Othello.

                            I did say so.
Look where he comes. Not poppy nor mandragora
Nor all the drowsy syrups of the world   380
Shall ever medicine thee to that sweet sleep
Which thou owedst yesterday.
OTHELLO   Ha, ha, false to me?
IAGO
Why, how now, general? No more of that!
OTHELLO
Avaunt! Begone! Thou hast set me on the rack.   385
I swear 'tis better to be much abused
Than but to know 't a little.
IAGO   How now, my lord?
OTHELLO
What sense had I ⟨of⟩ her stol'n hours of lust?
I saw 't not, thought it not; it harmed not me.   390
I slept the next night well, fed well, was free and
    merry.
I found not Cassio's kisses on her lips.
He that is robbed, not wanting what is stol'n,
Let him not know 't, and he's not robbed at all.   395
IAGO   I am sorry to hear this.

397. **the general camp:** the whole army

398. **Pioners:** pioneers; i.e., trench-diggers, the soldiers of lowest status in the army

399. **So:** i.e., so long as

403. **trump:** i.e., trumpet

405. **royal:** i.e., splendid

406. **Pride:** i.e., proud display; **circumstance:** pageantry

407. **mortal engines:** i.e., deadly cannons **engines:** literally, machines

408. **Jove's . . . counterfeit:** imitate (i.e., sound like) the thunderbolts thrown by Jove, the king of the Roman gods

415. **answer:** i.e., be made to defend yourself against

418. **probation:** proof

422. **remorse:** pity

423. **On horror's . . . accumulate:** i.e., pile up horrors on the horror you have already committed

424. **amazed:** astounded (with horror)

426. **that:** i.e., the slander of Desdemona and torture of Othello

OTHELLO
I had been happy if the general camp,
Pioners and all, had tasted her sweet body,
So I had nothing known. O, now, forever
Farewell the tranquil mind! Farewell content!   400
Farewell the plumèd troops and the big wars
That makes ambition virtue! O, farewell!
Farewell the neighing steed and the shrill trump,
The spirit-stirring drum, th' ear-piercing fife,
The royal banner, and all quality,   405
Pride, pomp, and circumstance of glorious war!
And O you mortal engines, whose rude throats
Th' immortal Jove's dread clamors counterfeit,
Farewell! Othello's occupation's gone!
IAGO   Is 't possible, my lord?   410
OTHELLO
Villain, be sure thou prove my love a whore!
Be sure of it. Give me the ocular proof,
Or, by the worth of mine eternal soul,
Thou hadst been better have been born a dog
Than answer my waked wrath.   415
IAGO   Is 't come to this?
OTHELLO
Make me to see 't, or at the least so prove it
That the probation bear no hinge nor loop
To hang a doubt on, or woe upon thy life!
IAGO   My noble lord—   420
OTHELLO
If thou dost slander her and torture me,
Never pray more. Abandon all remorse;
On horror's head horrors accumulate;
Do deeds to make heaven weep, all earth amazed;
For nothing canst thou to damnation add   425
Greater than that.
IAGO   O grace! O heaven forgive me!
Are you a man? Have you a soul or sense?

429. **God b' wi' you:** God be with you, i.e., good-bye

430. **vice:** fault, failing

433. **profit:** i.e., profitable lesson

434. **sith:** since

435. **Nay, stay:** Iago probably has begun to exit, and Othello calls him back. **shouldst be honest:** (1) ought to tell the truth; (2) should be, if appearance and experience can be believed, an honest man

437. **that:** i.e., that which

439. **honest:** chaste

442. **Dian:** Diana, goddess of chastity (See page 198.)

445. **Would:** i.e., if only

447. **put it to you:** i.e., raised with you the question of Desdemona's fidelity

451. **supervisor:** spectator

452. **topped:** "covered" in coition, i.e., "tupped" (a term describing the mating of ram and ewe)

456. **bolster:** This seems to mean "copulate." (A bolster is a long pillow. It is possible that "to bolster" means "to share a bolster.")

457. **More:** i.e., other

460–61. **prime, hot, salt:** lustful, lecherous

God b' wi' you. Take mine office.—O wretched fool,
That ⟨liv'st⟩ to make thine honesty a vice!— 430
O monstrous world! Take note, take note, O world:
To be direct and honest is not safe.—
I thank you for this profit, and from hence
I'll love no friend, sith love breeds such offense.
OTHELLO Nay, stay. Thou shouldst be honest. 435
IAGO
I should be wise; for honesty's a fool
And loses that it works for.
[OTHELLO   By the world,
I think my wife be honest and think she is not.
I think that thou art just and think thou art not. 440
I'll have some proof! ⌐Her⌐ name, that was as fresh
As Dian's visage, is now begrimed and black
As mine own face. If there be cords, or knives,
Poison, or fire, or suffocating streams,
I'll not endure it. Would I were satisfied!] 445
IAGO
I see you are eaten up with passion.
I do repent me that I put it to you.
You would be satisfied?
OTHELLO Would? Nay, and I will.
IAGO
And may; but how? How satisfied, my lord? 450
Would you, the ⟨supervisor,⟩ grossly gape on,
Behold her topped?
OTHELLO   Death and damnation! O!
IAGO
It were a tedious difficulty, I think,
To bring them to that prospect. Damn them then 455
If ever mortal eyes do see them bolster
More than their own! What then? How then?
What shall I say? Where's satisfaction?
It is impossible you should see this,
Were they as prime as goats, as hot as monkeys, 460

461. **pride:** heat
463. **imputation and strong circumstances:** i.e., a charge based on circumstantial evidence
467. **office:** duty
469. **Pricked:** spurred
477. **gripe:** i.e., grip, clutch
484. **but:** only
486. **denoted . . . conclusion:** i.e., indicated something that had actually happened
487. **shrewd doubt:** i.e., cause for keen suspicion
491. **Yet:** up to this point

An asp. (3.3.510)
From Edward Topsell, *The historie of serpents* . . . (1608).

As salt as wolves in pride, and fools as gross
As ignorance made drunk. But yet I say,
If imputation and strong circumstances
Which lead directly to the door of truth
Will give you satisfaction, you might have 't.   465
OTHELLO
Give me a living reason she's disloyal.
IAGO   I do not like the office,
But sith I am entered in this cause so far,
Pricked to 't by foolish honesty and love,
I will go on. I lay with Cassio lately,   470
And being troubled with a raging tooth
I could not sleep. There are a kind of men
So loose of soul that in their sleeps will mutter
Their affairs. One of this kind is Cassio.
In sleep I heard him say "Sweet Desdemona,   475
Let us be wary, let us hide our loves."
And then, sir, would he gripe and wring my hand,
Cry "O sweet creature!" then kiss me hard,
As if he plucked up kisses by the roots
That grew upon my lips; ⟨then⟩ laid his leg   480
O'er my thigh, and ⟨sighed,⟩ and ⟨kissed,⟩ and then
⟨Cried⟩ "Cursèd fate that gave thee to the Moor!"
OTHELLO
O monstrous! Monstrous!
IAGO   Nay, this was but his
     dream.   485
OTHELLO
But this denoted a foregone conclusion.
'Tis a shrewd doubt, though it be but a dream.
IAGO
And this may help to thicken other proofs
That do demonstrate thinly.
OTHELLO   I'll tear her all to pieces.   490
IAGO
Nay, ⟨but⟩ be wise. Yet we see nothing done.

492. **yet:** despite everything
494. **Spotted with strawberries:** i.e., embroidered with a strawberry pattern
502. **the slave:** probably Cassio, since this term of contempt was usually applied to males
505. **fond:** foolish
508. **hearted throne:** i.e., throne seated in the heart
509. **fraught:** load, burden
510. **aspics' tongues:** i.e., the tongues of poisonous snakes **aspics:** asps (See page 146.)
514–17. **the Pontic Sea . . . Hellespont:** The Black Sea (**the Pontic Sea**) empties into the Sea of Marmora (**the Propontic**) and through the Dardanelles (the **Hellespont**) into the Mediterranean. This outward current seems never to be reversed, never to feel "retiring ebb," because the water that flows back into the Black Sea does so in a very deep undercurrent far below the surface. **compulsive:** onward-driving **due:** straight
520. **capable:** capacious, full
521–22. **marble heaven:** perhaps the sky, shining or streaked (with clouds) like marble; or, perhaps heaven, providing unrelenting justice, as hard as marble

She may be honest yet. Tell me but this:
Have you not sometimes seen a handkerchief
Spotted with strawberries in your wife's hand?
OTHELLO
I gave her such a one. 'Twas my first gift.   495
IAGO
I know not that; but such a handkerchief—
I am sure it was your wife's—did I today
See Cassio wipe his beard with.
OTHELLO   If it be that—
IAGO
If it be that, or any ⌜that⌝ was hers,   500
It speaks against her with the other proofs.
OTHELLO
O, that the slave had forty thousand lives!
One is too poor, too weak for my revenge.
Now do I see 'tis true. Look here, Iago,
All my fond love thus do I blow to heaven.   505
'Tis gone.
Arise, black vengeance, from the hollow hell!
Yield up, O love, thy crown and hearted throne
To tyrannous hate! Swell, bosom, with thy fraught,
For 'tis of aspics' tongues!   510
IAGO   Yet be content.
OTHELLO   O, blood, blood, blood!
IAGO
Patience, I say. Your mind ⟨perhaps⟩ may change.
OTHELLO
Never, [Iago. Like to the Pontic Sea,
Whose icy current and compulsive course   515
Ne'er ⌜feels⌝ retiring ebb, but keeps due on
To the Propontic and the Hellespont,
Even so my bloody thoughts, with violent pace
Shall ne'er look back, ne'er ebb to humble love,
Till that a capable and wide revenge   520
Swallow them up. ⟨*He kneels.*⟩ Now by yond marble
     heaven,]

524. **engage:** pledge
527. **clip:** embrace
528–29. **give up . . . wit:** turn over the activities of his mind
531. **remorse:** a solemn obligation
532. **What bloody business ever:** i.e., however bloody the business
535. **bounteous:** i.e., unrestrained
536. **put thee to 't:** i.e., put you to the test
541. **minx:** promiscuous woman, whore

3.4 Desdemona, still actively seeking to have Cassio reinstated, is worried about the loss of her handkerchief. Her anxiety about it increases when Othello asks her for it and then sternly rebukes her when she cannot produce it. Cassio approaches her, but she must now, because of Othello's anger, postpone her efforts on his behalf. As he waits, Bianca, his lover, appears. Cassio has found Desdemona's handkerchief in his room (placed there by Iago) and he asks Bianca to copy the embroidery work for him.

1. **sirrah:** term of address to a male social inferior
2. **lies:** dwells, lodges
5. **lies:** i.e., does not tell the truth
6. **'tis stabbing:** i.e., he will surely stab me

In the due reverence of a sacred vow,
I here engage my words.
IAGO   Do not rise yet. ⟨*Iago kneels.*⟩ 525
Witness, you ever-burning lights above,
You elements that clip us round about,
Witness that here Iago doth give up
The execution of his wit, hands, heart
To wronged Othello's service! Let him command, 530
And to obey shall be in me remorse,
What bloody business ever.   ⌜*They rise.*⌝
OTHELLO   I greet thy love
Not with vain thanks but with acceptance
    bounteous,   535
And will upon the instant put thee to 't.
Within these three days let me hear thee say
That Cassio's not alive.
IAGO   My friend is dead.
'Tis done at your request. But let her live. 540
OTHELLO Damn her, lewd minx! O, damn her, damn
    her!
Come, go with me apart. I will withdraw
To furnish me with some swift means of death
For the fair devil. Now art thou my lieutenant. 545
IAGO I am your own forever.
                                        They exit.

Scene 4
Enter Desdemona, Emilia, and Clown.

DESDEMONA Do you know, sirrah, where Lieutenant
    Cassio lies?
CLOWN I dare not say he lies anywhere.
DESDEMONA Why, man?
CLOWN He's a soldier, and for me to say a soldier lies, 5
    'tis stabbing.

7. **Go to:** an expression of impatience
12. **devise:** i.e., make up
13. **lie in mine own throat:** i.e., tell a big lie
14. **edified:** instructed
19. **moved:** appealed to
21. **compass:** scope
23. **should I lose:** i.e., can I have lost
26. **crusadoes:** Portuguese gold coins, each stamped with a cross (**crux**); **but:** i.e., except that
32. **humors:** i.e., the bodily fluids then believed to cause such characteristics as jealousy (The word *humor* could refer either to the fluid or to the characteristic, but the idea of the sun drawing the humor from the person suggests that here the black bile that causes jealousy is the humor referred to.)

DESDEMONA   Go to! Where lodges he?
[CLOWN   To tell you where he lodges is to tell you
where I lie.
DESDEMONA   Can anything be made of this?]   10
CLOWN   I know not where he lodges; and for me to
devise a lodging and say he lies here, or he lies
there, were to lie in mine own throat.
DESDEMONA   Can you inquire him out, and be edified
by report?   15
CLOWN   I will catechize the world for him—that is,
make questions, and by them answer.
DESDEMONA   Seek him, bid him come hither. Tell him I
have moved my lord on his behalf and hope all will
be well.   20
CLOWN   To do this is within the compass of man's wit,
and therefore I will attempt the doing it.
Clown exits.
DESDEMONA
Where should I lose ⟨that⟩ handkerchief, Emilia?
EMILIA   I know not, madam.
DESDEMONA
Believe me, I had rather have lost my purse   25
Full of crusadoes. And but my noble Moor
Is true of mind and made of no such baseness
As jealous creatures are, it were enough
To put him to ill thinking.
EMILIA   Is he not jealous?   30
DESDEMONA
Who, he? I think the sun where he was born
Drew all such humors from him.
EMILIA   Look where he
comes.

Enter Othello.

DESDEMONA
I will not leave him now till Cassio   35
Be called to him.—How is 't with you, my lord?

37. **hardness:** i.e., how difficult

44. **liberal:** generous (with a play on "dissolute," "licentious")

46. **sequester:** seclusion

47. **castigation:** corrective discipline or punishment; **exercise devout:** acts of devotion

50. **frank:** open, generous (with a suggestion again of dissoluteness)

53–54. **The hearts . . . hearts:** Othello responds to Desdemona's "'twas that hand that gave away my heart." In the past, he says, people's hearts controlled the giving of hands (in marriage); now it is hands that (all too liberally) give away hearts.

56. **chuck:** a term of affection

57. **sent:** i.e., sent a messenger

58. **a salt and sorry rheum:** perhaps, a bad cold—though in Shakespeare "salt rheum" often refers to salt water (tears, or the sea); **offends:** troubles

OTHELLO
Well, my good lady. ⌜*Aside.*⌝ O, hardness to
  dissemble!—
How do you, Desdemona?
DESDEMONA   Well, my good lord.   40
OTHELLO
Give me your hand. ⌜*He takes her hand.*⌝ This hand
  is moist, my lady.
DESDEMONA
It ⟨yet has⟩ felt no age nor known no sorrow.
OTHELLO
This argues fruitfulness and liberal heart.
Hot, hot, and moist. This hand of yours requires   45
A sequester from liberty, fasting and prayer,
Much castigation, exercise devout;
For here's a young and sweating devil here
That commonly rebels. 'Tis a good hand,
A frank one.   50
DESDEMONA   You may indeed say so,
For 'twas that hand that gave away my heart.
OTHELLO
A liberal hand! The hearts of old gave hands,
But our new heraldry is hands, not hearts.
DESDEMONA
I cannot speak of this. Come now, your promise.   55
OTHELLO   What promise, chuck?
DESDEMONA
I have sent to bid Cassio come speak with you.
OTHELLO
I have a salt and sorry rheum offends me.
Lend me thy handkerchief.
DESDEMONA   Here, my lord.   60
OTHELLO
That which I gave you.
DESDEMONA   I have it not about me.
OTHELLO   Not?

67. **charmer:** sorceress, enchantress
68. **She:** the enchantress; **her, she:** my mother
70. **amiable:** desirable
73. **hold her:** regard her as
74. **fancies:** loves
76. **her:** i.e., to my wife; **heed on 't:** i.e., care of it
77. **Make it a darling:** i.e., cherish it
78. **perdition:** loss, ruin
81. **web:** weave, fabric
82–83. **A sybil . . . compasses:** i.e., a 200-year-old prophetess (See page 158.) **course:** travel **compasses:** i.e., yearly circuits
84. **fury:** inspired state
86. **mummy:** a preparation made from mummified bodies, thought to have medicinal or magic power
87. **Conserved of:** prepared from
90. **would:** i.e., I wish
91. **Wherefore:** why
92. **startingly:** i.e., in fits and starts; **rash:** i.e., urgently
93. **out o' th' way:** missing

DESDEMONA   No, ⟨faith,⟩ my lord.
OTHELLO   That's a fault. That handkerchief   65
Did an Egyptian to my mother give.
She was a charmer, and could almost read
The thoughts of people. She told her, while she kept
   it,
'Twould make her amiable and subdue my father   70
Entirely to her love. But if she lost it,
Or made a gift of it, my father's eye
Should hold her loathèd, and his spirits should hunt
After new fancies. She, dying, gave it me,
And bid me, when my fate would have me wived,   75
To give it her. I did so; and take heed on 't,
Make it a darling like your precious eye.
To lose 't or give 't away were such perdition
As nothing else could match.
DESDEMONA   Is 't possible?   80
OTHELLO
'Tis true. There's magic in the web of it.
A sybil that had numbered in the world
The sun to course two hundred compasses,
In her prophetic fury sewed the work.
The worms were hallowed that did breed the silk,   85
And it was dyed in mummy, which the skillful
Conserved of maidens' hearts.
DESDEMONA   ⟨I' faith,⟩ is 't true?
OTHELLO
Most veritable. Therefore, look to 't well.
DESDEMONA
Then would to ⟨God⟩ that I had never seen 't!   90
OTHELLO   Ha? Wherefore?
DESDEMONA
Why do you speak so startingly and rash?
OTHELLO
Is 't lost? Is 't gone? Speak, is 't out o' th' way?
DESDEMONA   ⟨Heaven⟩ bless us!
OTHELLO   Say you?   95

96. **an if:** i.e., if
101. **suit:** petition
106. **sufficient:** capable
114. **to blame:** blameworthy (for speaking to me like this)
115. **Zounds:** i.e., by Christ's wounds (a very strong oath)
119. **unhappy:** (1) sad; (2) unlucky
121. **all but:** i.e., nothing but
122. **hungerly:** i.e., hungrily

A sibyl. (3.4.82)
From Philippus de Barberiis, *Quattuor hic compressa . . .* (1495).

DESDEMONA
  It is not lost, but what an if it were?
OTHELLO How?
DESDEMONA I say it is not lost.
OTHELLO Fetch 't. Let me see 't!
DESDEMONA
  Why, so I can. But I will not now.   100
  This is a trick to put me from my suit.
  Pray you, let Cassio be received again.
OTHELLO
  Fetch me the handkerchief! ⌜*Aside.*⌝ My mind
    misgives.
DESDEMONA Come, come.   105
  You'll never meet a more sufficient man.
OTHELLO
  The handkerchief!
⟨DESDEMONA   I pray, talk me of Cassio.
OTHELLO The handkerchief!⟩
DESDEMONA   A man that all his time   110
  Hath founded his good fortunes on your love;
  Shared dangers with you—
OTHELLO
  The handkerchief!
DESDEMONA   ⟨I' faith,⟩ you are to blame.
OTHELLO ⟨Zounds!⟩   *Othello exits.* 115
EMILIA Is not this man jealous?
DESDEMONA I ne'er saw this before.
  Sure, there's some wonder in this handkerchief!
  I am most unhappy in the loss of it.
EMILIA
  'Tis not a year or two shows us a man.   120
  They are all but stomachs, and we all but food;
  They eat us hungerly, and when they are full
  They belch us.

          Enter Iago and Cassio.

  Look you—Cassio and my husband.

126. **importune:** accent on the second syllable
131. **office:** service, duty
132. **would not:** i.e., do not wish to
133. **mortal:** deadly
134. **nor . . . nor:** i.e., neither . . . nor
137. **But:** i.e., only
139–40. **shut myself . . . fortune's alms:** i.e., confine myself to some other career, taking what fortune gives me
142. **advocation:** i.e., advocacy
144. **favor:** appearance
147. **stood within the blank:** i.e., become the target **blank:** the white center of an archery target
148. **free:** frank, open
153. **unquietness:** perturbed state

Aiming at "the blank." (3.4.147)
From Gilles Corrozet, *Hecatongraphie* . . . (1543).

IAGO, ⌐*to Cassio*⌐
    There is no other way; 'tis she must do 't,   125
    And, lo, the happiness! Go and importune her.
DESDEMONA
    How now, good Cassio, what's the news with you?
CASSIO
    Madam, my former suit. I do beseech you
    That by your virtuous means I may again
    Exist, and be a member of his love   130
    Whom I with all the office of my heart
    Entirely honor. I would not be delayed.
    If my offense be of such mortal kind
    That nor my service past nor present sorrows
    Nor purposed merit in futurity   135
    Can ransom me into his love again,
    But to know so must be my benefit.
    So shall I clothe me in a forced content,
    And shut myself up in some other course
    To fortune's alms.   140
DESDEMONA   Alas, thrice-gentle Cassio,
    My advocation is not now in tune.
    My lord is not my lord; nor should I know him
    Were he in favor as in humor altered.
    So help me every spirit sanctified   145
    As I have spoken for you all my best,
    And stood within the blank of his displeasure
    For my free speech! You must awhile be patient.
    What I can do I will; and more I will
    Than for myself I dare. Let that suffice you.   150
IAGO
    Is my lord angry?
EMILIA   He went hence but now,
    And certainly in strange unquietness.
IAGO
    Can he be angry? I have seen the cannon

161. **Something . . . of state:** i.e., affairs . . . of state

162. **unhatched practice:** hitherto undisclosed intrigue

163. **Made demonstrable:** i.e., shown, revealed

164. **puddled:** muddied

166. **object:** i.e., the object of their concern

167. **let . . . and:** i.e., when our finger hurts

167–69. **it endues . . . Of pain:** i.e., it makes the rest of the body hurt too   **endues:** endows, supplies **healthful members:** healthy parts of the body

170. **observancy:** i.e., observant attention

171. **bridal:** wedding, or wedding feast; **Beshrew me:** curse me (a mild oath)

172. **unhandsome:** inexpert; i.e., clumsy

173. **Arraigning . . . soul:** i.e., bringing him into my soul's court of justice on the charge of being unkind (The legal metaphor continues in the next two lines with **suborned the witness** and **indicted.**)

175. **he's:** i.e., Othello is

178 **toy:** whim

182. **for:** because

183. **Begot:** i.e., conceived

When it hath blown his ranks into the air   155
And, like the devil, from his very arm
Puffed his own brother—and is he angry?
Something of moment then. I will go meet him.
There's matter in 't indeed if he be angry.

DESDEMONA
I prithee do so.   *He exits.*   160
              Something, sure, of state,
Either from Venice, or some unhatched practice
Made demonstrable here in Cyprus to him,
Hath puddled his clear spirit; and in such cases
Men's natures wrangle with inferior things,   165
Though great ones are their object. 'Tis even so.
For let our finger ache, and it endues
Our other healthful members even to a sense
Of pain. Nay, we must think men are not gods,
Nor of them look for such observancy   170
As fits the bridal. Beshrew me much, Emilia,
I was—unhandsome warrior as I am!—
Arraigning his unkindness with my soul.
But now I find I had suborned the witness,
And he's indicted falsely.   175

EMILIA   Pray heaven it be
State matters, as you think, and no conception
Nor no jealous toy concerning you.

DESDEMONA
Alas the day, I never gave him cause!

EMILIA
But jealous souls will not be answered so.   180
They are not ever jealous for the cause,
But jealous for they're jealous. It is a monster
Begot upon itself, born on itself.

DESDEMONA
Heaven keep ⟨that⟩ monster from Othello's mind!

EMILIA Lady, amen.   185

187. **fit:** i.e., receptive
190. **'Save:** i.e., God save (a commonplace greeting)
191–92. **What . . . home?:** i.e., what are you doing away from home
197. **Eightscore eight hours:** 160 plus eight hours (i.e., seven days and nights)
197–98. **lovers' absent . . . times:** i.e., an hour of a lover's absence is 160 times more tedious than all the hours on a clock's face (**dial**)
201. **pressed:** oppressed, weighed down
202. **more continuate:** less interrupted
203. **Strike off . . . absence:** i.e., pay off my debt of absence **score:** a debt which was originally marked on a post by cutting or scoring it with notches (with a pun on Bianca's use of **score** to mean "twenty")
204. **Take . . . out:** i.e., copy this embroidered pattern for me
206. **friend:** i.e., mistress
213. **remembrance:** keepsake

DESDEMONA
I will go seek him.—Cassio, walk hereabout.
If I do find him fit, I'll move your suit
And seek to effect it to my uttermost.
CASSIO   I humbly thank your Ladyship.
                    ⟨Desdemona and Emilia⟩ exit.

                    Enter Bianca.

BIANCA
'Save you, friend Cassio!   190
CASSIO   What make you from
   home?
How is 't with you, my most fair Bianca?
⟨I' faith,⟩ sweet love, I was coming to your house.
BIANCA
And I was going to your lodging, Cassio.   195
What, keep a week away? Seven days and nights,
Eightscore eight hours, and lovers' absent hours
More tedious than the dial eightscore times?
O weary reck'ning!
CASSIO   Pardon me, Bianca.   200
I have this while with leaden thoughts been pressed,
But I shall in a more continuate time
Strike off this score of absence. Sweet Bianca,
          ⌜Giving her Desdemona's handkerchief.⌝
Take me this work out.
BIANCA   O, Cassio, whence came this?   205
This is some token from a newer friend.
To the felt absence now I feel a cause.
Is 't come to this? Well, well.
CASSIO   Go to, woman!
Throw your vile guesses in the devil's teeth,   210
From whence you have them. You are jealous now
That this is from some mistress, some
   remembrance.
No, ⟨by my faith,⟩ Bianca.

217. Ere . . . demanded: i.e., before it is asked for by its owner

 218. like: i.e., likely
 221. attend . . . on: wait for
 222. addition: mark of honor
 223. womaned: i.e., with a woman
 227. bring me: i.e., go with me
 228. at night: i.e., tonight
 231. be circumstanced: i.e., accept your terms and conditions

BIANCA   Why, whose is it?   215
CASSIO
   I know not neither. I found it in my chamber.
   I like the work well. Ere it be demanded,
   As like enough it will, I would have it copied.
   Take it, and do 't, and leave me for this time.
BIANCA   Leave you? Wherefore?   220
CASSIO
   I do attend here on the General,
   And think it no addition, nor my wish,
   To have him see me womaned.
[BIANCA   Why, I pray you?
CASSIO   Not that I love you not.]   225
BIANCA   But that you do not love me!
   I pray you bring me on the way a little,
   And say if I shall see you soon at night.
CASSIO
   'Tis but a little way that I can bring you,
   For I attend here. But I'll see you soon.   230
BIANCA
   'Tis very good. I must be circumstanced.
                              ⟨*They exit.*⟩

The Tragedy of

OTHELLO,
The Moor of Venice

ACT 4

4.1 Iago continues to torment Othello with vivid descriptions of Desdemona's alleged sexual activity until Othello blacks out. Iago then places Othello where he can see (but not hear) a conversation with Cassio about Bianca, telling Othello that the bawdy conversation is about Cassio and Desdemona. Othello's fury grows.

Lodovico arrives from Venice with orders from the duke and senators that Othello return to Venice and that Cassio be appointed in his place. Othello strikes Desdemona in Lodovico's presence, then rudely dismisses her, and leaves in a jealous rage. Lodovico expresses his astonishment at the change in Othello.

---

8. **hypocrisy . . . devil:** i.e., if to seem good while doing evil is hypocrisy against God, then to seem evil while "meaning no harm" is hypocrisy against the devil

10-11. **tempt heaven:** i.e., put to the test God's grace to keep them from sin

12. **venial slip:** pardonable fault

ACT 4

Scene 1
Enter Othello and Iago.

IAGO Will you think so?

OTHELLO Think so, Iago?

IAGO What, to kiss in private?

OTHELLO An unauthorized kiss!

IAGO
Or to be naked with her friend in bed   5
An hour or more, not meaning any harm?

OTHELLO
Naked in bed, Iago, and not mean harm?
It is hypocrisy against the devil!
They that mean virtuously, and yet do so,
The devil their virtue tempts, and they tempt   10
   heaven.

IAGO
If they do nothing, 'tis a venial slip.
But if I give my wife a handkerchief—

OTHELLO What then?

IAGO
Why then, 'tis hers, my lord, and being hers,   15
She may, I think, bestow 't on any man.

OTHELLO
She is protectress of her honor, too.
May she give that?

20. **it . . . it:** i.e., the reputation for honor . . . honor itself

24. **raven:** a bird which was itself a bad omen and which was believed to spread infection; **infectious:** infected

25. **Boding:** ominous

31. **voluntary dotage:** i.e., willing but foolish affection

32. **Convincèd or supplied them:** conquered them (through **importunate suit**) or sexually satisfied them (those in **voluntary dotage**)

44. **belie:** tell lies about

45. **fulsome:** obscene

46. **To . . . hanged:** Proverbial: "Confess and be hanged."

48. **invest:** clothe

48–49. **shadowing:** (1) darkening, overshadowing; (2) image-making

IAGO
Her honor is an essence that's not seen;
They have it very oft that have it not.　　　　20
But for the handkerchief—
OTHELLO
By heaven, I would most gladly have forgot it.
Thou saidst—O, it comes o'er my memory
As doth the raven o'er the infectious house,
Boding to all—he had my handkerchief.　　　　25
IAGO　Ay, what of that?
OTHELLO　That's not so good now.
IAGO
What if I had said I had seen him do you wrong?
Or heard him say (as knaves be such abroad,
Who having, by their own importunate suit　　　　30
Or voluntary dotage of some mistress,
Convincèd or supplied them, cannot choose
But they must blab)—
OTHELLO　Hath he said anything?
IAGO
He hath, my lord, but be you well assured,　　　　35
No more than he'll unswear.
OTHELLO　　　　　　　　What hath he said?
IAGO
⟨Faith,⟩ that he did—I know not what he did.
OTHELLO　What? What?
IAGO
Lie—　　　　40
OTHELLO　With her?
IAGO　　　　　　　With her—on her—what you will.
OTHELLO　Lie with her? Lie on her? We say "lie on her"
when they belie her. Lie with her—⟨Zounds,⟩ that's
fulsome!　Handkerchief—confessions—handker-　　　　45
chief. [To confess and be hanged for his labor.
First to be hanged and then to confess—I tremble
at it. Nature would not invest herself in such shad-
owing passion without some instruction. It is not

65. **lethargy:** fit of unconsciousness; **his:** i.e., its
66. **by and by:** at once
69. **straight:** straightway, immediately
70. **great occasion:** i.e., an important subject
72. **mock me:** i.e., in referring to my head, suggesting that I wear the horns of a cuckold
74. **Would:** i.e., I wish
75. **hornèd man:** i.e., a cuckold
77. **civil:** civilized

"A hornèd man," or cuckold. (4.1.75)
From *The Bagford Ballads* (printed in 1878).

words that shakes me thus. Pish! Noses, ears, and   50
lips—is't possible? Confess—handkerchief—O,
devil!]   ⟨He⟩ *falls in a trance.*
IAGO Work on,
My medicine, ⟨work!⟩ Thus credulous fools are
    caught,   55
And many worthy and chaste dames even thus,
All guiltless, meet reproach.—What ho! My lord!
My lord, I say. Othello!

                    Enter Cassio.

                    How now, Cassio?
CASSIO What's the matter?   60
IAGO
My lord is fall'n into an epilepsy.
This is his second fit. He had one yesterday.
CASSIO
Rub him about the temples.
IAGO   ⟨No, forbear.⟩
The lethargy must have his quiet course.   65
If not, he foams at mouth, and by and by
Breaks out to savage madness. Look, he stirs.
Do you withdraw yourself a little while.
He will recover straight. When he is gone,
I would on great occasion speak with you.   70
                              ⌜*Cassio exits.*⌝
How is it, general? Have you not hurt your head?
OTHELLO
Dost thou mock me?
IAGO   I mock you not, by heaven!
Would you would bear your fortune like a man!
OTHELLO
A hornèd man's a monster and a beast.   75
IAGO
There's many a beast, then, in a populous city,
And many a civil monster.

80–81. **every bearded . . . you:** i.e., like you, every married man is a cuckold (Iago compares married men to yoked oxen pulling a load.)   **bearded:** i.e., old enough to have a beard   **yoked:** (1) married; (2) literally, under a yoke for horned oxen   **draw:** pull

82. **unproper:** not exclusively their own (because of their wives' lovers)

83. **peculiar:** exclusively theirs

85. **lip a wanton:** kiss an unchaste woman; **secure couch:** bed free of suspicion

90. **in a patient list:** within the bounds of calmness **list:** boundary, limit

93. **shifted him away:** got him out of the way

94. **laid . . . ecstasy:** i.e., provided good explanations for your trance

95. **anon:** soon

96. **encave:** hide

97. **fleers, gibes:** i.e., sneers

101. **cope:** (1) meet; (2) copulate with

102. **but . . . patience:** i.e., just observe his manner, indeed, be calm

103. **all in all in spleen:** i.e., consumed in anger

109. **keep time:** i.e., stay in control (a figure of speech from music)

110. **of:** i.e., about

111. **huswife:** hussy (pronounced "hussif")

OTHELLO
  Did he confess it?
IAGO   Good sir, be a man!
  Think every bearded fellow that's but yoked   80
  May draw with you. There's millions now alive
  That nightly lie in those unproper beds
  Which they dare swear peculiar. Your case is better.
  O, 'tis the spite of hell, the fiend's arch-mock,
  To lip a wanton in a secure couch   85
  And to suppose her chaste! No, let me know,
  And knowing what I am, I know what she shall be.
OTHELLO   O, thou art wise, 'tis certain.
IAGO   Stand you awhile apart.
  Confine yourself but in a patient list.   90
  Whilst you were here, o'erwhelmèd with your grief—
  A passion most ⟨unsuiting⟩ such a man—
  Cassio came hither. I shifted him away
  And laid good 'scuses upon your ecstasy,
  Bade him anon return and here speak with me,   95
  The which he promised. Do but encave yourself,
  And mark the fleers, the gibes, and notable scorns
  That dwell in every region of his face.
  For I will make him tell the tale anew—
  Where, how, how oft, how long ago, and when   100
  He hath and is again to cope your wife.
  I say but mark his gesture. Marry, patience,
  Or I shall say you're all in all in spleen,
  And nothing of a man.
OTHELLO   Dost thou hear, Iago,   105
  I will be found most cunning in my patience,
  But (dost thou hear?) most bloody.
IAGO   That's not amiss.
  But yet keep time in all. Will you withdraw?
                           ⌜*Othello withdraws.*⌝
  Now will I question Cassio of Bianca,   110
  A huswife that by selling her desires
  Buys herself bread and ⟨clothes.⟩ It is a creature

118. **unbookish:** ignorant
119. **light:** frivolous
121. **worser:** i.e., worse; **addition:** title (i.e., lieutenant)
122. **want:** lack
125. **speed:** succeed
126. **caitiff:** wretch
132. **importunes:** accent on second syllable
133. **o'er:** i.e., over again
137. **Roman:** i.e., perhaps, conqueror (through association with the word **triumph,** the name of the public celebrations of victory held by the ancient Romans)
138. **customer:** prostitute
138–39. **Prithee . . . wit:** i.e., please think charitably of my intelligence
139–40. **unwholesome:** tainted, corrupted

That dotes on Cassio—as 'tis the strumpet's plague
To beguile many and be beguiled by one.
He, when he hears of her, cannot restrain   115
From the excess of laughter. Here he comes.

Enter Cassio.

As he shall smile, Othello shall go mad,
And his unbookish jealousy must ⟨construe⟩
Poor Cassio's smiles, gestures, and light behaviors
Quite in the wrong.—How do you, lieutenant?   120

CASSIO
The worser that you give me the addition
Whose want even kills me.

IAGO
Ply Desdemona well, and you are sure on 't.
Now, if this suit lay in Bianca's ⟨power,⟩
How quickly should you speed!   125

CASSIO, ⌈*laughing*⌉   Alas, poor caitiff!

OTHELLO   Look how he laughs already!

IAGO   I never knew woman love man so.

CASSIO
Alas, poor rogue, I think ⟨i' faith⟩ she loves me.

OTHELLO
Now he denies it faintly and laughs it out.   130

IAGO
Do you hear, Cassio?

OTHELLO   Now he importunes him
To tell it o'er. Go to, well said, well said.

IAGO
She gives it out that you shall marry her.
Do you intend it?   135

CASSIO   Ha, ha, ha!

OTHELLO
Do you triumph, Roman? Do you triumph?

CASSIO   I marry ⟨her?⟩ What, a customer? Prithee bear
some charity to my wit! Do not think it so unwholesome. Ha, ha, ha!   140

141. **They . . . wins:** Proverbial: "He laughs that wins."

142. **cry:** common talk

144. **very:** true; **else:** otherwise

145. **scored:** struck, wounded

146. **the monkey's . . . giving out:** i.e., what Bianca says

147-48. **love and flattery:** i.e., love of me and flattery of herself

150. **even:** i.e., just

153. **bauble:** i.e., silly woman; **falls thus:** Cassio may here demonstrate how Bianca embraced him.

156. **imports:** signifies

163. **Before me:** a mild oath in imitation of "Before God"

164. **such another fitchew:** i.e., such a prostitute (Literally, **fitchew** means polecat.)

167. **Let:** i.e., may; **dam:** mother (Proverbially, the "devil's dam" was more evil than the devil.)

169-70. **take out:** copy

170. **piece of work:** i.e., story

OTHELLO So, so, so, so. They laugh that wins.

IAGO
⟨Faith,⟩ the cry goes that you marry her.

CASSIO Prithee say true!

IAGO I am a very villain else.

OTHELLO Have you scored me? Well. 145

CASSIO This is the monkey's own giving out. She is
persuaded I will marry her out of her own love and
flattery, not out of my promise.

OTHELLO
Iago ⟨beckons⟩ me. Now he begins the story.

CASSIO She was here even now. She haunts me in 150
every place. I was the other day talking on the
sea-bank with certain Venetians, and thither comes
the bauble. ⟨By this hand, she falls⟩ thus about my
neck!

OTHELLO Crying, "O dear Cassio," as it were; his 155
gesture imports it.

CASSIO So hangs and lolls and weeps upon me, so
shakes and pulls me. Ha, ha, ha!

OTHELLO Now he tells how she plucked him to my
chamber.—O, I see that nose of yours, but not that 160
dog I shall throw it to.

CASSIO Well, I must leave her company.

IAGO Before me, look where she comes.

Enter Bianca.

CASSIO 'Tis such another fitchew—marry, a per-
fumed one!—What do you mean by this haunting 165
of me?

BIANCA Let the devil and his dam haunt you! What did
you mean by that same handkerchief you gave me
even now? I was a fine fool to take it! I must take
out the work? A likely piece of work, that you 170
should find it in your chamber and know not who

173. **hobbyhorse:** i.e., mistress
174. **on 't:** i.e., from it
176. **should:** i.e., must
178-79. **when . . . next prepared for:** perhaps, when I next invite you, which will be never
185. **fain:** gladly
187. **Go to:** an expression of impatience
194. **prizes:** regards
202. **I strike it:** presumably accompanied by the appropriate gesture

left it there! This is some minx's token, and I must
take out the work! There, give it your hobbyhorse.
Wheresoever you had it, I'll take out no work on 't.
CASSIO
How now, my sweet Bianca? How now? How now?   175
OTHELLO
By heaven, that should be my handkerchief!
BIANCA If you'll come to supper tonight you may. If
you will not, come when you are next prepared
for.   *She exits.*
IAGO After her, after her!   180
CASSIO ⟨Faith,⟩ I must. She'll rail in the streets else.
IAGO Will you sup there?
CASSIO ⟨Faith,⟩ I intend so.
IAGO Well, I may chance to see you, for I would very
fain speak with you.   185
CASSIO Prithee come. Will you?
IAGO Go to; say no more.   ⟨*Cassio exits.*⟩
OTHELLO, ⌜*coming forward*⌝ How shall I murder him,
Iago?
IAGO Did you perceive how he laughed at his vice?   190
OTHELLO O Iago!
IAGO And did you see the handkerchief?
OTHELLO Was that mine?
[IAGO Yours, by this hand! And to see how he prizes
the foolish woman your wife! She gave it him, and   195
he hath giv'n it his whore.]
OTHELLO I would have him nine years a-killing! A fine
woman, a fair woman, a sweet woman!
IAGO Nay, you must forget that.
OTHELLO Ay, let her rot and perish and be damned   200
tonight, for she shall not live. No, my heart is turned
to stone. I strike it, and it hurts my hand. O, the
world hath not a sweeter creature! She might lie by
an emperor's side and command him tasks.

205. **your way:** i.e., the way you should think

209. **wit and invention:** intelligence and inventiveness

212. **gentle:** (1) noble; (2) kind; **condition:** nature, character

216. **fond over:** foolish about, doting on

217. **patent:** permission, license

217–18. **touch, comes near:** affects

219. **messes:** pieces (literally, individual servings of food)

225. **unprovide my mind:** i.e., make me unwilling

227. **even the:** i.e., the very

230. **his undertaker:** i.e., the one who undertakes to kill him

235. **This:** i.e., this delegation

IAGO   Nay, that's not your way.   205
OTHELLO   Hang her, I do but say what she is! So
    delicate with her needle, an admirable musi-
    cian—O, she will sing the savageness out of a bear!
    Of so high and plenteous wit and invention!
IAGO   She's the worse for all this.   210
OTHELLO   O, a thousand, a thousand times!—And then
    of so gentle a condition!
IAGO   Ay, too gentle.
OTHELLO   Nay, that's certain. But yet the pity of it,
    Iago! O, Iago, the pity of it, Iago!   215
IAGO   If you are so fond over her iniquity, give her
    patent to offend, for if it touch not you, it comes
    near nobody.
OTHELLO   I will chop her into messes! Cuckold me?
IAGO   O, 'tis foul in her.   220
OTHELLO   With mine officer!
IAGO   That's fouler.
OTHELLO   Get me some poison, Iago, this night. I'll not
    expostulate with her lest her body and beauty
    unprovide my mind again. This night, Iago.   225
IAGO   Do it not with poison. Strangle her in her bed,
    even the bed she hath contaminated.
OTHELLO   Good, good. The justice of it pleases. Very
    good.
IAGO   And for Cassio, let me be his undertaker. You   230
    shall hear more by midnight.
OTHELLO
    Excellent good.   ⟨*A trumpet sounds.*⟩
            What trumpet is that same?
IAGO   I warrant something from Venice.

    Enter Lodovico, Desdemona, and Attendants.

'Tis Lodovico. This comes from the Duke.   235
See, your wife's with him.
LODOVICO   ⟨God⟩ save you, worthy general.

238. **With . . . heart:** perhaps an emphatic "amen" to Lodovico's prayer; perhaps only an ordinary courtly greeting

240. **instrument of their pleasures:** i.e., the letter that contains their wishes or orders

242. **signior:** i.e., sir

246. **fall'n:** i.e., befallen, happened

247. **unkind:** unfortunate; unnatural, awkward

252. **in:** i.e., with

253. **'twixt:** i.e., between

255. **atone:** reconcile

262. **Deputing . . . government:** i.e., appointing Cassio as governor in Othello's place

263. **troth:** faith; **on 't:** i.e., of it

OTHELLO   With all my heart, sir.
LODOVICO
The Duke and the Senators of Venice greet you.
                              ⌜*He hands Othello a paper.*⌝
OTHELLO
I kiss the instrument of their pleasures.   240
DESDEMONA
And what's the news, good cousin Lodovico?
IAGO
I am very glad to see you, signior.
Welcome to Cyprus.
LODOVICO
I thank you. How does Lieutenant Cassio?
IAGO   Lives, sir.   245
DESDEMONA
Cousin, there's fall'n between him and my lord
An unkind breach, but you shall make all well.
OTHELLO   Are you sure of that?
DESDEMONA   My lord?
OTHELLO, ⌜*reading*⌝ "This fail you not to do, as you   250
   will"—
LODOVICO
He did not call; he's busy in the paper.
Is there division 'twixt my lord and Cassio?
DESDEMONA
A most unhappy one. I would do much
T' atone them, for the love I bear to Cassio.   255
OTHELLO   Fire and brimstone!
DESDEMONA   My lord?
OTHELLO   Are you wise?
DESDEMONA
What, is he angry?
LODOVICO   May be the letter moved him.   260
For, as I think, they do command him home,
Deputing Cassio in his government.
DESDEMONA   ⟨By my troth,⟩ I am glad on 't.

266. **mad:** Editors and critics have been hard-pressed to explain why Othello should call Desdemona mad.

274. **teem with:** prolifically spawn

275. **falls:** lets fall; **crocodile:** a creature thought to shed hypocritical tears

284. **turn:** i.e., turn back

285, 286. **turn:** (1) return; (2) change (i.e., become unfaithful)

289. **painted:** i.e., counterfeited, faked; **passion:** emotion

291. **anon:** i.e., soon

293. **place:** official position

Crocodile tears. (4.1.275)
From Jacob Typot, *Symbola diuina . . .* (1652).

OTHELLO   Indeed?
DESDEMONA   My lord?   265
OTHELLO   I am glad to see you mad.
DESDEMONA   Why, sweet Othello!
OTHELLO, ⌜*striking her*⌝ Devil!
DESDEMONA   I have not deserved this.
LODOVICO
My lord, this would not be believed in Venice,   270
Though I should swear I saw 't. 'Tis very much.
Make her amends. She weeps.
OTHELLO   O, devil, devil!
If that the earth could teem with woman's tears,
Each drop she falls would prove a crocodile.   275
Out of my sight!
DESDEMONA   I will not stay to offend you.
                             ⌜*She begins to leave.*⌝
LODOVICO   Truly ⟨an⟩ obedient lady.
I do beseech your Lordship call her back.
OTHELLO   Mistress.   280
DESDEMONA, ⌜*turning back*⌝ My lord?
OTHELLO   What would you with her, sir?
LODOVICO   Who, I, my lord?
OTHELLO
Ay, you did wish that I would make her turn.
Sir, she can turn, and turn, and yet go on,   285
And turn again. And she can weep, sir, weep.
And she's obedient, as you say, obedient.
Very obedient.—Proceed you in your tears.—
Concerning this, sir—O, well-painted passion!—
I am commanded home.—Get you away.   290
I'll send for you anon.—Sir, I obey the mandate
And will return to Venice.—Hence, avaunt!
                             ⌜*Desdemona exits.*⌝
Cassio shall have my place. And, sir, tonight
I do entreat that we may sup together.

295–96. **Goats and monkeys:** These are animals reputed to be very active sexually.
298. **all in all sufficient:** i.e., capable in all respects
299. **virtue:** (1) manliness; (2) integrity
304. **safe:** sound, sane
305. **that:** i.e., that which; **censure:** judgment, perhaps condemnation, of
307. **would:** wish
311. **use:** habit
312. **blood:** emotions
318. **courses will denote:** i.e., conduct will reveal

You are welcome, sir, to Cyprus. Goats and   295
  monkeys!   *He exits.*
LODOVICO
Is this the noble Moor, whom our full senate
Call all in all sufficient? Is this the nature
Whom passion could not shake, whose solid virtue
The shot of accident nor dart of chance   300
Could neither graze nor pierce?
IAGO   He is much
  changed.
LODOVICO
Are his wits safe? Is he not light of brain?
IAGO
He's that he is. I may not breathe my censure   305
What he might be. If what he might he is not,
I would to heaven he were.
LODOVICO   What? Strike his wife?
IAGO
'Faith, that was not so well. Yet would I knew
That stroke would prove the worst.   310
LODOVICO   Is it his use?
Or did the letters work upon his blood
And new-create ⟨this⟩ fault?
IAGO   Alas, alas!
It is not honesty in me to speak   315
What I have seen and known. You shall observe
  him,
And his own courses will denote him so
That I may save my speech. Do but go after
And mark how he continues.   320
LODOVICO
I am sorry that I am deceived in him.
                                        They exit.

4.2 Othello questions Emilia about Cassio and Desdemona's relationship, acting as if Emilia is the mistress of a brothel and Desdemona one of her prostitutes. Othello denounces Desdemona to her face as a whore. Desdemona turns for help to Iago, who reassures her.

Roderigo, protesting to Iago that his gifts to Desdemona have won him no favor from her, threatens to ask for the return of the gifts. Iago counters this threat by telling Roderigo that Desdemona will leave for Mauritania with Othello unless Roderigo can delay them. The best way to do this, says Iago, is by killing Cassio.

---

  5. **made up:** formed
  10. **mask:** conventional public attire for women of the time
  13. **durst:** dare; **honest:** chaste, faithful
  14. **at stake:** i.e., as my bet; **other:** i.e., otherwise
  15. **abuse:** deceive; wrong
  17. **Let . . . curse:** i.e., may God punish him with the curse he laid on the serpent in Genesis (". . . upon thy belly shalt thou go, and dust shalt thou eat all the days of thy life.")
  19. **happy:** fortunate (in his wife)
  22. **She:** i.e., Emilia
  22–23. **she's . . . much:** i.e., the simplest brothel-keeper can tell the same kind of story
  23. **whore:** perhaps Emilia; perhaps Desdemona
  24. **closet:** private room; or, cabinet, chest

Scene 2
Enter Othello and Emilia.

OTHELLO   You have seen nothing then?
EMILIA
Nor ever heard, nor ever did suspect.
OTHELLO
Yes, you have seen Cassio and she together.
EMILIA
But then I saw no harm, and then I heard
Each syllable that breath made up between them.   5
OTHELLO
What, did they never whisper?
EMILIA   Never, my lord.
OTHELLO   Nor send you out o' th' way?
EMILIA   Never.
OTHELLO
To fetch her fan, her gloves, her mask, nor nothing?   10
EMILIA   Never, my lord.
OTHELLO   That's strange.
EMILIA
I durst, my lord, to wager she is honest,
Lay down my soul at stake. If you think other,
Remove your thought. It doth abuse your bosom.   15
If any wretch have put this in your head,
Let heaven requite it with the serpent's curse,
For if she be not honest, chaste, and true,
There's no man happy. The purest of their wives
Is foul as slander.   20
OTHELLO   Bid her come hither. Go.
                                   Emilia exits.
She says enough. Yet she's a simple bawd
That cannot say as much. This is a subtle whore,
A closet lock and key of villainous secrets.
And yet she'll kneel and pray. I have seen her do 't.   25

32. Some . . . function: i.e., do your job (as a brothel-keeper)

34. procreants: i.e., those who procreate, copulate

36. mystery: trade; **dispatch:** hurry

43. Lest: for fear that

51. heavy: sorrowful

Enter Desdemona and Emilia.

DESDEMONA   My lord, what is your will?
OTHELLO
Pray you, chuck, come hither.
DESDEMONA   What is your
  pleasure?
OTHELLO
Let me see your eyes. Look in my face.   30
DESDEMONA   What horrible fancy's this?
OTHELLO, ⌜*to Emilia*⌝ Some of your function,
  mistress.
Leave procreants alone, and shut the door.
Cough, or cry "hem," if anybody come.   35
Your mystery, your mystery! ⟨Nay,⟩ dispatch.
                                         Emilia exits.
DESDEMONA, ⌜*kneeling*⌝
Upon my ⟨knees,⟩ what doth your speech import?
I understand a fury in your words,
⟨But not the words.⟩
OTHELLO   Why? What art thou?   40
DESDEMONA
Your wife, my lord, your true and loyal wife.
OTHELLO   Come, swear it. Damn thyself,
Lest, being like one of heaven, the devils themselves
Should fear to seize thee. Therefore be double
  damned.   45
Swear thou art honest.
DESDEMONA   Heaven doth truly know it.
OTHELLO
Heaven truly knows that thou art false as hell.
DESDEMONA, ⌜*standing*⌝
To whom, my lord? With whom? How am I false?
OTHELLO
Ah, Desdemon, away, away, away!   50
DESDEMONA
Alas the heavy day, why do you weep?

52. **motive:** cause
53. **haply:** perhaps
54. **calling back:** i.e., being called back to Venice
58. **try:** test
64–65. **A fixèd . . . finger at:** The image may be that of Othello as like a number on the dial of a clock, with the hand that points to him moving so slowly that it does not seem to move at all. He seems forever to be an object of scorn to the world. **time of scorn:** i.e., scornful time, or scornful world
67. **there:** i.e., his love for Desdemona; **garnered up:** stored
69. **fountain:** fountainhead, spring
71. **cistern:** i.e., pool of foul standing water (cesspool)
72. **knot and gender:** i.e., couple and engender
72–74. **turn . . . hell:** i.e., let even rose-lipped Patience change to pale grimness **cherubin:** angel (These were often depicted as rosy-faced, smiling infants with wings.)
76–77. **summer flies . . . blowing:** The picture drawn here is of the most terrible sexual promiscuity. **shambles:** slaughterhouse **quicken:** become "quick," i.e., pregnant **even with blowing:** as soon as they are themselves deposited as eggs
81. **ignorant:** unknown (to me)
82. **fair paper:** i.e., Desdemona
84. **commoner:** prostitute

Am I the motive of these tears, my lord?
If haply you my father do suspect
An instrument of this your calling back,
Lay not your blame on me. If you have lost him,   55
I have lost him too.
OTHELLO   Had it pleased heaven
To try me with affliction, had they rained
All kind of sores and shames on my bare head,
Steeped me in poverty to the very lips,   60
Given to captivity me and my utmost hopes,
I should have found in some place of my soul
A drop of patience. But alas, to make me
⟨A⟩ fixèd figure for the time of scorn
To point his slow ⟨unmoving⟩ finger at—   65
Yet could I bear that too, well, very well.
But there where I have garnered up my heart,
Where either I must live or bear no life,
The fountain from the which my current runs
Or else dries up—to be discarded thence,   70
Or keep it as a cistern for foul toads
To knot and gender in—turn thy complexion there,
Patience, thou young and rose-lipped cherubin,
Ay, ⌈there⌉ look grim as hell.
DESDEMONA
I hope my noble lord esteems me honest.   75
OTHELLO
O, ay, as summer flies are in the shambles,
That quicken even with blowing! O thou weed,
Who art so lovely fair, and smell'st so sweet
That the sense aches at thee, would thou hadst
⟨ne'er⟩ been born!   80
DESDEMONA
Alas, what ignorant sin have I committed?
OTHELLO
Was this fair paper, this most goodly book,
Made to write "whore" upon? What committed?
[Committed? O thou public commoner,

88. it: i.e., what you committed; **moon winks:** The moon is associated with Cynthia or Diana, goddess of chastity, who is here said to be closing her eyes in the face of Desdemona's activities.

90. mine: subterranean passage (In mythology the winds were said to retire into caves within the earth.)

96. vessel: body (a biblical term)

103. cry you mercy: i.e., beg your pardon

107. keeps the gate of hell: Compare Proverbs 7.27: "Her [the harlot's] house is the way to hell."

108. done our course: i.e., finished our business

111. conceive: think

Diana. (3.3.442)
From Robert Whitcombe, *Janua diuorum* . . . (1678).

I should make very forges of my cheeks   85
That would to cinders burn up modesty,
Did I but speak thy deeds. What committed?]
Heaven stops the nose at it, and the moon winks;
The bawdy wind that kisses all it meets
Is hushed within the hollow mine of earth   90
And will not hear 't. What committed?
⟨Impudent strumpet!⟩
DESDEMONA   By heaven, you do me wrong!
OTHELLO   Are not you a strumpet?
DESDEMONA   No, as I am a Christian!   95
If to preserve this vessel for my lord
From any other foul unlawful touch
Be not to be a strumpet, I am none.
OTHELLO   What, not a whore?
DESDEMONA   No, as I shall be saved.   100
OTHELLO   Is 't possible?
DESDEMONA
O, heaven forgive us!
OTHELLO   I cry you mercy, then.
I took you for that cunning whore of Venice
That married with Othello.—You, mistress,   105

Enter Emilia.

That have the office opposite to Saint Peter
And keeps the gate of hell—you, you, ay, you!
We have done our course. There's money for your
   pains.   ⌜*He gives her money.*⌝
I pray you turn the key and keep our counsel.   110
                                        He exits.
EMILIA
Alas, what does this gentleman conceive?
How do you, madam? How do you, my good lady?
DESDEMONA   Faith, half asleep.
EMILIA
Good madam, what's the matter with my lord?

121. **go by water:** i.e., be said with tears
125. **meet:** proper
126. **stick:** fasten
127. **opinion:** i.e., criticism; **least misuse:** smallest misbehavior
134. **bewhored:** i.e., called her whore
135. **despite:** contempt, spite; **heavy:** (1) grievous; (2) violent
141. **in his drink:** i.e., drunken
142. **callet:** female companion (**Callet,** like "hussy," "strumpet," "minx," "harlot," "harlotry," and "whore," is a term of abuse attached to women accused of having sex outside of marriage. Some of these names, along with "prostitute," "commoner," and "customer," are also applied to women who have sex in exchange for money.)

DESDEMONA With who?   115
EMILIA Why, with my lord, madam.
[DESDEMONA Who is thy lord?
EMILIA He that is yours, sweet lady.]
DESDEMONA
  I have none. Do not talk to me, Emilia.
  I cannot weep, nor answers have I none   120
  But what should go by water. Prithee, tonight
  Lay on my bed my wedding sheets. Remember.
  And call thy husband hither.
EMILIA Here's a change indeed.   *She exits.*
DESDEMONA
  'Tis meet I should be used so, very meet.   125
  How have I been behaved that he might stick
  The small'st opinion on my least misuse?

Enter Iago and Emilia.

IAGO
  What is your pleasure, madam? How is 't with you?
DESDEMONA
  I cannot tell. Those that do teach young babes
  Do it with gentle means and easy tasks.   130
  He might have chid me so, for, in good faith,
  I am a child to chiding.
IAGO What is the matter, lady?
EMILIA
  Alas, Iago, my lord hath so bewhored her,
  Thrown such despite and heavy terms upon her   135
  ⟨As⟩ true hearts cannot bear.
DESDEMONA Am I that name, Iago?
IAGO   What name, fair
  lady?
DESDEMONA
  Such as she said my lord did say I was.   140
EMILIA
  He called her "whore." A beggar in his drink
  Could not have laid such terms upon his callet.

151. **Beshrew:** curse; **trick:** foolishness, whim
153. **I will be hanged if:** i.e., I will bet my life that; **eternal:** infernal, damned
154. **busy:** meddlesome
155. **cogging:** fraudulent; **cozening:** deceiving
159. **halter:** hangman's noose
162. **What form?:** i.e., in what way
162–63. **What likelihood?:** i.e., what indications are there
164. **abused:** deceived; injured
165. **scurvy:** vile
166. **that:** i.e., I pray that; **companions:** fellows (a contemptuous term); **unfold:** disclose
170. **Speak within door:** i.e., speak more temperately

IAGO Why did he so?

DESDEMONA
I do not know. I am sure I am none such.

IAGO
Do not weep, do not weep! Alas the day!   145

EMILIA
Hath she forsook so many noble matches,
Her father and her country and her friends,
To be called "whore"? Would it not make one
   weep?

DESDEMONA It is my wretched fortune.   150

IAGO
Beshrew him for 't! How comes this trick upon him?

DESDEMONA Nay, heaven doth know.

EMILIA
I will be hanged if some eternal villain,
Some busy and insinuating rogue,
Some cogging, cozening slave, to get some office,   155
Have not devised this slander. I will be hanged else.

IAGO
Fie, there is no such man. It is impossible.

DESDEMONA
If any such there be, heaven pardon him.

EMILIA
A halter pardon him, and hell gnaw his bones!
Why should he call her "whore"? Who keeps her   160
   company?
What place? What time? What form? What
   likelihood?
The Moor's abused by some most villainous knave,
Some base notorious knave, some scurvy fellow.   165
O ⟨heaven,⟩ that such companions thou 'dst unfold,
And put in every honest hand a whip
To lash the rascals naked through the world,
Even from the east to th' west!

IAGO   Speak within door.   170

171. **squire:** fellow
172. **the seamy side without:** i.e., inside out (referring to the seams in a piece of clothing), the ugly side out
181. **discourse:** course
182, 184. **that:** i.e., if
184. **yet:** still
187. **Comfort forswear:** i.e., may comfort forsake
189. **defeat:** destroy
192. **addition:** title, name
193. **world's mass of vanity:** i.e., every pleasure in the world
194. **humor:** mood
195. **does him offense:** i.e., annoys him
200. **stays the meat:** i.e., are waiting for supper

EMILIA
  O, fie upon them! Some such squire he was
  That turned your wit the seamy side without
  And made you to suspect me with the Moor.
IAGO
  You are a fool. Go to!
DESDEMONA   Alas, Iago,   175
  What shall I do to win my lord again?
  Good friend, go to him. For by this light of heaven,
  I know not how I lost him. ⌜*She kneels.*⌝ [Here I
    kneel.
  If e'er my will did trespass 'gainst his love,   180
  Either in discourse of thought or actual deed,
  Or that mine eyes, mine ears, or any sense
  Delighted them ⌜in⌝ any other form,
  Or that I do not yet, and ever did,
  And ever will—though he do shake me off   185
  To beggarly divorcement—love him dearly,
  Comfort forswear me! ⌜*She stands.*⌝ Unkindness may
    do much,
  And his unkindness may defeat my life,
  But never taint my love. I cannot say "whore"—   190
  It does abhor me now I speak the word.
  To do the act that might the addition earn,
  Not the world's mass of vanity could make me.]
IAGO
  I pray you be content. 'Tis but his humor.
  The business of the state does him offense,   195
  ⟨And he does chide with you.⟩
DESDEMONA
  If 'twere no other—
IAGO   It is but so, I warrant.
                      ⌜*Trumpets sound.*⌝
  Hark how these instruments summon to supper.
  The messengers of Venice stays the meat.   200
  Go in and weep not. All things shall be well.
          Desdemona and Emilia exit.

206-7. **daff'st me ... device:** put me off with some trick

208. **conveniency:** convenient occasion (to court Desdemona)

209. **of hope:** i.e., for increasing my hopes

210. **put up:** i.e., accept, put up with

216. **naught:** nothing

219. **votaress:** nun

221. **comforts:** encouragement; **sudden respect:** immediate regard

226. **fopped:** cheated, deceived

232. **satisfaction:** i.e., in a duel

233. **have said:** i.e., have spoken, said what you have to say

235. **intendment of doing:** i.e., I intend to do

Enter Roderigo.

How now, Roderigo?
RODERIGO   I do not find
That thou deal'st justly with me.
IAGO   What in the contrary?   205
RODERIGO   Every day thou daff'st me with some de-
vice, Iago, and rather, as it seems to me now,
keep'st from me all conveniency than suppliest me
with the least advantage of hope. I will indeed no
longer endure it. Nor am I yet persuaded to put up   210
in peace what already I have foolishly suffered.
IAGO   Will you hear me, Roderigo?
RODERIGO   ⟨Faith,⟩ I have heard too much, and your
words and performances are no kin together.
IAGO   You charge me most unjustly.   215
RODERIGO   With naught but truth. I have wasted my-
self out of my means. The jewels you have had
from me to deliver ⟨to⟩ Desdemona would half have
corrupted a votaress. You have told me she hath
received them, and returned me expectations and   220
comforts of sudden respect and acquaintance, but I
find none.
IAGO   Well, go to! Very well.
RODERIGO   "Very well." "Go to!" I cannot go to, man,
nor 'tis not very well! ⟨By this hand, I say 'tis very⟩   225
scurvy, and begin to find myself fopped in it.
IAGO   Very well.
RODERIGO   I tell you 'tis not very well! I will make
myself known to Desdemona. If she will return me
my jewels, I will give over my suit and repent my   230
unlawful solicitation. If not, assure yourself I will
seek satisfaction of you.
IAGO   You have said now.
RODERIGO   Ay, and said nothing but what I protest
intendment of doing.   235

240. **directly:** honestly

250. **engines for:** plots against

251-52. **within reason and compass:** i.e., reasonably possible **compass:** bounds, scope

254. **depute:** i.e., appoint

258-59. **abode be lingered:** his stay be extended

259-60. **wherein . . . determinate:** i.e., and no accident can be so conclusive in extending his stay

261. **How:** i.e., what

262. **uncapable of:** i.e., incapable of taking

265. **profit:** benefit

266. **harlotry:** See note to line 142.

269. **fall out:** happen

"Mauritania." (4.2.257)
From Lucan, *Lucan's Pharsalia . . .* (1718).

IAGO Why, now I see there's mettle in thee, and even
from this instant do build on thee a better opinion
than ever before. Give me thy hand, Roderigo.
Thou hast taken against me a most just exception,
but yet I protest I have dealt most directly in thy   240
affair.
RODERIGO It hath not appeared.
IAGO I grant indeed it hath not appeared, and your
suspicion is not without wit and judgment. But,
Roderigo, if thou hast that in thee indeed which I   245
have greater reason to believe now than ever—I
mean purpose, courage, and valor—this night show
it. If thou the next night following enjoy not Desdemona, take me from this world with treachery and
devise engines for my life.   250
RODERIGO Well, what is it? Is it within reason and
compass?
IAGO Sir, there is especial commission come from
Venice to depute Cassio in Othello's place.
RODERIGO Is that true? Why, then, Othello and Desde- 255
mona return again to Venice.
IAGO O, no. He goes into Mauritania and ⟨takes⟩ away
with him the fair Desdemona, unless his abode be
lingered here by some accident—wherein none
can be so determinate as the removing of Cassio.   260
RODERIGO How do you mean, removing him?
IAGO Why, by making him uncapable of Othello's
place: knocking out his brains.
RODERIGO And that you would have me to do?
IAGO Ay, if you dare do yourself a profit and a right. He   265
sups tonight with a harlotry, and thither will I go to
him. He knows not yet of his honorable fortune. If
you will watch his going thence (which I will
fashion to fall out between twelve and one), you may
take him at your pleasure. I will be near to second 270
your attempt, and he shall fall between us. Come,

272. **amazed:** astounded
274. **high:** i.e., fully, quite
275. **grows to waste:** i.e., is already wasting away, or, perhaps, being wasted by our inactivity
276. **further reason:** i.e., more justification

4.3 Othello, walking with Lodovico, orders Desdemona to go to bed and to dismiss Emilia. As Emilia helps Desdemona prepare for bed, they discuss marital infidelity, with Desdemona arguing that no woman would be unfaithful to her husband and Emilia arguing that women have the same desires as men do.

7-8. **be returned:** i.e., return
12. **incontinent:** immediately

stand not amazed at it, but go along with me. I will
show you such a necessity in his death that you shall
think yourself bound to put it on him. It is now high
supper time, and the night grows to waste. About it!   275
RODERIGO   I will hear further reason for this.
IAGO   And you shall be satisfied.
                                            They exit.

                        Scene 3
        Enter Othello, Lodovico, Desdemona, Emilia, and
                        Attendants.

LODOVICO
   I do beseech you, sir, trouble yourself no further.
OTHELLO
   O, pardon me, 'twill do me good to walk.
LODOVICO
   Madam, good night. I humbly thank your Ladyship.
DESDEMONA   Your Honor is most welcome.
OTHELLO
   Will you walk, sir?—O, Desdemona—   5
DESDEMONA   My lord?
OTHELLO   Get you to bed on th' instant. I will be
   returned forthwith. Dismiss your attendant there.
   Look 't be done.
DESDEMONA   I will, my lord.   10
                ⌜*All but Desdemona and Emilia*⌝ *exit.*
EMILIA
   How goes it now? He looks gentler than he did.
DESDEMONA
   He says he will return incontinent,
   And hath commanded me to go to bed,
   And ⟨bade⟩ me to dismiss you.
EMILIA   Dismiss me?   15
DESDEMONA
   It was his bidding. Therefore, good Emilia,

19. **would:** wish
20. **approve:** commend, praise
21. **stubbornness:** harshness; **checks:** reprimands
22. **have grace and favor in them:** i.e., are attractive to me
24. **All's one:** all right; or, it doesn't matter
31. **fortune:** i.e., what happened to her
33–34. **I have . . . hang:** i.e., I can barely restrain myself from hanging
38. **proper:** good-looking
41. **would:** i.e., who would
42. **nether:** lower

Give me my nightly wearing, and adieu.
We must not now displease him.
EMILIA   I would you had never seen him.
DESDEMONA
So would not I. My love doth so approve him   20
That even his stubbornness, his checks, his frowns—
Prithee, unpin me—have grace and favor ⟨in them.⟩
EMILIA
I have laid those sheets you bade me on the bed.
DESDEMONA
All's one. Good ⟨faith,⟩ how foolish are our minds!
If I do die before ⟨thee,⟩ prithee, shroud me   25
In one of ⟨those⟩ same sheets.
EMILIA   Come, come, you talk!
DESDEMONA
My mother had a maid called Barbary.
She was in love, and he she loved proved mad
And did forsake her. She had a song of willow,   30
An old thing 'twas, but it expressed her fortune,
And she died singing it. That song tonight
Will not go from my mind. [I have much to do
But to go hang my head all at one side
And sing it like poor Barbary. Prithee, dispatch.   35
EMILIA   Shall I go fetch your nightgown?
DESDEMONA   No, unpin me here.
This Lodovico is a proper man.
EMILIA   A very handsome man.
DESDEMONA   He speaks well.   40
EMILIA   I know a lady in Venice would have walked
   barefoot to Palestine for a touch of his nether lip.
DESDEMONA, ⌜*singing*⌝
   The poor soul sat ⌜*sighing*⌝ *by a sycamore tree,*
      Sing all a green willow.
   Her hand on her bosom, her head on her knee,   45
      Sing willow, willow, willow.

52. **Lay by these:** i.e., put these things aside
54. **hie thee:** i.e., hurry; **anon:** right away
56. **approve:** commend
64. **bode:** forebode, portend
68. **abuse:** deceive; ill-use
69. **In such gross kind:** i.e., in such an obscene way (by committing adultery)
74. **by this heavenly light:** a mild oath (which Emilia treats as if it means "in the daylight")

The fresh streams ran by her and murmured her
   moans,
  Sing willow, willow, willow;
Her salt tears fell from her, and softened the   50
   stones—
Lay by these.
  Sing willow, willow, willow.
Prithee hie thee! He'll come anon.
  Sing all a green willow must be my garland.   55
  Let nobody blame him, his scorn I approve.
Nay, that's not next.] Hark, who is 't that knocks?
EMILIA It's the wind.
DESDEMONA
  [*I called my love false love, but what said he then?*
   Sing willow, willow, willow.   60
  If I court more women, you'll couch with more
   men.]—
So, get thee gone. Good night. Mine eyes do itch;
Doth that bode weeping?
EMILIA   'Tis neither here nor there.   65
[DESDEMONA
I have heard it said so. O these men, these men!
Dost thou in conscience think—tell me, Emilia—
That there be women do abuse their husbands
In such gross kind?
EMILIA   There be some such, no   70
  question.]
DESDEMONA
Wouldst thou do such a deed for all the world?
EMILIA
Why, would not you?
DESDEMONA   No, by this heavenly light!
EMILIA
Nor I neither, by this heavenly light.   75
I might do 't as well i' th' dark.
DESDEMONA
Wouldst thou do such a deed for all the world?

78. **price:** prize
79. **vice:** fault
82. **Marry:** i.e., indeed
83. **joint ring:** puzzle ring, made up of two or three rings that fit together; a love token; **measures of lawn:** i.e., lengths of fine linen
84–85. **petty exhibition:** trivial gift
85. **'Uds:** i.e., God's
91. **having:** possessing; **for:** i.e., in exchange for
92. **might:** i.e., could
95. **to th' vantage:** i.e., in addition
96. **store:** populate; **played:** wagered (with, perhaps, a pun on "played" as "engaged in sexual sport")
98. **they:** i.e., husbands; **slack:** neglect; **duties:** obligations to their wives (perhaps sexual)
101. **Throwing:** i.e., imposing
102. **scant:** cut back; **having:** allowance; **in despite:** i.e., out of spite or malice
103. **galls:** i.e., capacities for resentment; **grace:** goodness, forgiveness
104. **revenge:** i.e., appetite for revenge
105. **sense:** i.e., the five senses; **They:** i.e., wives
108. **they:** i.e., husbands
109. **change:** i.e., exchange; **sport:** (1) fun; (2) amorous play
110. **affection:** passion, lust
111. **frailty:** human weakness

EMILIA The world's a huge thing. It is a great price
for a small vice.
DESDEMONA In troth, I think thou wouldst not.   80
EMILIA In troth, I think I should, and undo 't when I
had done ⟨it.⟩ Marry, I would not do such a thing for
a joint ring, nor for measures of lawn, nor for
gowns, petticoats, nor caps, nor any petty exhibition. But for the whole world—⟨'Uds pity!⟩ Who   85
would not make her husband a cuckold to make
him a monarch? I should venture purgatory for 't.
DESDEMONA Beshrew me if I would do such a wrong
for the whole world!
EMILIA Why, the wrong is but a wrong i' th' world;   90
and, having the world for your labor, 'tis a wrong in
your own world, and you might quickly make it
right.
DESDEMONA I do not think there is any such woman.
EMILIA Yes, a dozen; and as many to th' vantage as   95
would store the world they played for.
[But I do think it is their husbands' faults
If wives do fall. Say that they slack their duties,
And pour our treasures into foreign laps;
Or else break out in peevish jealousies,   100
Throwing restraint upon us. Or say they strike us,
Or scant our former having in despite.
Why, we have galls, and though we have some grace,
Yet have we some revenge. Let husbands know
Their wives have sense like them. They see, and   105
smell,
And have their palates both for sweet and sour,
As husbands have. What is it that they do
When they change us for others? Is it sport?
I think it is. And doth affection breed it?   110
I think it doth. Is 't frailty that thus errs?
It is so too. And have not we affections,
Desires for sport, and frailty, as men have?

114. **use:** treat; **Else:** otherwise

116–17. **God . . . mend:** i.e., may God enable me to find ways, not of learning to do wrong from imitating wrongdoers, but of learning to improve myself by departing from their example (Instead of learning adultery from wayward husbands, Desdemona prays to learn chastity instead.) **uses:** ways, habits

Then let them use us well. Else let them know,
The ills we do, their ills instruct us so.]   115
DESDEMONA
Good night, good night. ⟨God⟩ me such uses send,
Not to pick bad from bad, but by bad mend.

They exit.

The Tragedy of

OTHELLO,
The Moor of Venice

ACT 5

5.1 In the dark streets of Cyprus, Roderigo attacks Cassio, who, uninjured, stabs Roderigo. Iago then wounds Cassio in the leg. Othello, hearing Cassio cry out, thinks that Iago has killed him, and departs to murder Desdemona. Iago then kills the wounded Roderigo. While Iago, joined by Lodovico and Gratiano, tends to Cassio, Bianca arrives. Iago accuses her of being a whore and of engineering the plot against Cassio that led to his injury.

---

1. **bulk:** something projecting out from a building, perhaps a stall; **straight:** immediately
3. **bare:** unsheathed
7. **miscarry:** fail
12. **quat:** contemptuous term for a youngster (literally, pimple or small boil); **to the sense:** to the quick
15. **Live Roderigo:** i.e., if Roderigo lives
17. **bobbed:** took by deception

ACT 5

Scene 1
Enter Iago and Roderigo.

IAGO
Here, stand behind this ⟨bulk.⟩ Straight will he
  come.
Wear thy good rapier bare, and put it home.
Quick, quick! Fear nothing. I'll be at thy elbow.
It makes us or it mars us—think on that,   5
And fix most firm thy resolution.

RODERIGO
Be near at hand. I may miscarry in 't.

IAGO
Here, at thy hand. Be bold and take thy stand.
                     ⌈*He moves aside.*⌉

RODERIGO
I have no great devotion to the deed,
And yet he hath given me satisfying reasons.   10
'Tis but a man gone. Forth, my sword! He dies.
                 ⌈*He draws his sword.*⌉

IAGO, ⌈*aside*⌉
I have rubbed this young quat almost to the sense,
And he grows angry. Now, whether he kill Cassio,
Or Cassio him, or each do kill the other,
Every way makes my gain. Live Roderigo,   15
He calls me to a restitution large
Of gold and jewels that I bobbed from him

223

22. **unfold me:** i.e., disclose my lies

26. **But:** i.e., except; **my coat is better:** Perhaps Cassio simply means his coat is thicker or tougher, but perhaps he means that he wears leather or metal armor under his coat.

27. **make proof of:** test

32. **even:** just

34. **he:** i.e., Cassio; **brave:** fine, worthy

36. **Minion:** This term, here addressed to Desdemona, could mean both "darling" and "hussy."

37. **unblest fate:** i.e., damnation; **hies:** hurries onward

38. **Forth of:** i.e., out from

As gifts to Desdemona.
It must not be. If Cassio do remain,
He hath a daily beauty in his life   20
That makes me ugly. And besides, the Moor
May unfold me to him. There stand I in much peril.
No, he must die. ⟨Be 't⟩ so. I ⟨hear⟩ him coming.

Enter Cassio.

RODERIGO
I know his gait. 'Tis he!—Villain, thou diest!
                ⌜*He thrusts at Cassio.*⌝

CASSIO
That thrust had been mine enemy indeed   25
But that my coat is better than thou know'st.
I will make proof of thine.
            ⌜*He draws, and stabs Roderigo.*⌝

RODERIGO   O, I am slain!
                  ⌜*Roderigo falls.*
      Iago stabs Cassio in the leg, and exits.⌝

CASSIO
I am maimed forever! Help, ho! Murder, murder!

Enter Othello.

OTHELLO
The voice of Cassio! Iago keeps his word.   30
RODERIGO   O, villain that I am!
OTHELLO, ⌜*aside*⌝ It is even so.
CASSIO   O, help ho! Light! A surgeon!
OTHELLO, ⌜*aside*⌝
'Tis he! O brave Iago, honest and just,
That hast such noble sense of thy friend's wrong!   35
Thou teachest me.—Minion, your dear lies dead,
And your unblest fate hies. Strumpet, I come.
⟨Forth⟩ of my heart those charms, thine eyes, are
    blotted.

42. **passage:** i.e., people passing
43. **'Tis some mischance:** i.e., there's something wrong
47. **heavy:** gloomy, overcast
49. **in to:** i.e., near
52. **one:** i.e., one who; **in his shirt:** i.e., perhaps, in his night attire; or, without his outer garments
54. **cries on:** shouts
62. **What:** i.e., who

Thy bed, lust-stained, shall with lust's blood be   40
    spotted.   *Othello exits.*

          Enter Lodovico and Gratiano.

CASSIO
    What ho! No watch? No passage? Murder, murder!
GRATIANO
    'Tis some mischance. The voice is very direful.
CASSIO   O, help!
LODOVICO   Hark!   45
RODERIGO   O wretched villain!
LODOVICO
    Two or three groan. 'Tis heavy night.
    These may be counterfeits. Let's think 't unsafe
    To come in to the cry without more help.
RODERIGO
    Nobody come? Then shall I bleed to death.   50

          Enter Iago ⟨with a light.⟩

LODOVICO   Hark!
GRATIANO
    Here's one comes in his shirt, with light and
        weapons.
IAGO
    Who's there? Whose noise is this that cries on
        murder?   55
LODOVICO
    We do not know.
IAGO   ⟨Did⟩ not you hear a cry?
CASSIO   Here, here! For ⟨heaven's⟩ sake, help me!
IAGO   What's the matter?
GRATIANO, ⌜*to Lodovico*⌝
    This is Othello's ancient, as I take it.   60
LODOVICO
    The same indeed, a very valiant fellow.
IAGO, ⌜*to Cassio*⌝
    What are you here that cry so grievously?

63. **spoiled, undone:** seriously injured, destroyed
67. **make:** i.e., get
79. **prove us:** find us to be by experience; **praise:** appraise, value
82. **I cry you mercy:** i.e., I beg your pardon

CASSIO
  Iago? O, I am spoiled, undone by villains.
  Give me some help!
IAGO
  O me, lieutenant! What villains have done this?   65
CASSIO
  I think that one of them is hereabout
  And cannot make away.
IAGO   O treacherous villains!
  ⌜*To Lodovico and Gratiano.*⌝ What are you there?
  Come in, and give some help.   70
RODERIGO   O, help me ⟨here!⟩
CASSIO
  That's one of them.
IAGO, ⌜*to Roderigo*⌝   O murd'rous slave! O villain!
                           ⌜*He stabs Roderigo.*⌝
RODERIGO
  O damned Iago! O inhuman dog!
IAGO
  Kill men i' th' dark?—Where be these bloody   75
    thieves?
  How silent is this town! Ho, murder, murder!—
  What may you be? Are you of good or evil?
LODOVICO
  As you shall prove us, praise us.
IAGO   Signior Lodovico?   80
LODOVICO   He, sir.
IAGO
  I cry you mercy. Here's Cassio hurt by villains.
GRATIANO   Cassio?
IAGO
  How is 't, brother?
CASSIO   My leg is cut in two.   85
IAGO   Marry, heaven forbid!
  Light, gentlemen. I'll bind it with my shirt.

92. **notable:** notorious
92–93. **may . . . should be:** i.e., do you know who they are
99. **trash:** i.e., Bianca
110. **accidents:** events

Enter Bianca.

BIANCA
  What is the matter, ho? Who is 't that cried?
IAGO
  Who is 't that cried?
BIANCA   O, my dear Cassio,   90
  My sweet Cassio! O Cassio, Cassio, Cassio!
IAGO
  O notable strumpet! Cassio, may you suspect
  Who they should be that have thus mangled you?
CASSIO No.
GRATIANO
  I am sorry to find you thus; I have been to seek you.   95
[IAGO
  Lend me a garter. So.—O for a chair
  To bear him easily hence!]
BIANCA
  Alas, he faints. O, Cassio, Cassio, Cassio!
IAGO
  Gentlemen all, I do suspect this trash
  To be a party in this injury.—   100
  Patience awhile, good Cassio.—Come, come;
  Lend me a light. ⌈*Peering at Roderigo.*⌉ Know we this
    face or no?
  Alas, my friend and my dear countryman
  Roderigo? No! Yes, sure. ⟨O heaven,⟩ Roderigo!   105
GRATIANO What, of Venice?
IAGO Even he, sir. Did you know him?
GRATIANO Know him? Ay.
IAGO
  Signior Gratiano? I cry your gentle pardon.
  These bloody accidents must excuse my manners   110
  That so neglected you.
GRATIANO   I am glad to see you.
IAGO
  How do you, Cassio?—O, a chair, a chair!

116. **said:** i.e., done

118. **For:** i.e., as for

119. **Save you your labor:** i.e., do not take the trouble (Perhaps Bianca is tending to Cassio; or, perhaps, Iago is suggesting that Bianca is feigning sorrow for Cassio's injury.)

126. **gastness:** dread, terror

138. **know of:** i.e., find out from

A chair. (5.1.113)
From Pietro Bertelli, *Diuersarum nationum habitus* . . . (1594–96).

GRATIANO   Roderigo?

IAGO

   He, he, 'tis he! ⌜*A chair is brought in.*⌝ O, that's well   115
     said; the chair.—
   Some good man bear him carefully from hence.
   I'll fetch the General's surgeon.—For you, mistress,
   Save you your labor.—He that lies slain here,
     Cassio,   120
   Was my dear friend. What malice was between you?

CASSIO

   None in the world. Nor do I know the man.

IAGO, ⌜*to Bianca*⌝

   What, look you pale?—O, bear him ⟨out⟩ o' th' air.
     ⌜*Cassio, in the chair, and Roderigo are carried off.*⌝
   ⌜*To Gratiano and Lodovico.*⌝ Stay you, good
     gentlemen.—Look you pale, mistress?—   125
   Do you perceive the gastness of her eye?—
   Nay, if you stare, we shall hear more anon.—
   Bchold her well. I pray you, look upon her.
   Do you see, gentlemen? Nay, guiltiness will speak
   Though tongues were out of use.   130

         ⟨*Enter Emilia.*⟩

EMILIA

   Alas, what is the matter? What is the matter,
     husband?

IAGO

   Cassio hath here been set on in the dark
   By Roderigo and fellows that are scaped.
   He's almost slain, and Roderigo dead.   135

EMILIA

   Alas, good gentleman! Alas, good Cassio!

IAGO

   This is the fruits of whoring. Prithee, Emilia,
   Go know of Cassio where he supped tonight.
   ⌜*To Bianca.*⌝ What, do you shake at that?

141. **charge:** command
143. **honest:** chaste
146. **see . . . dressed:** i.e., see that (he) gets his wounds dressed
147. **tell 's:** i.e., tell us
151. **fordoes:** undoes, destroys

5.2 Desdemona is asleep in bed when Othello enters. He kisses her and wakes her and once again charges her with infidelity. Over her protests of innocence, he smothers her. When Emilia comes to tell Othello about the violence in the streets, he acknowledges the killing, telling her that Iago had informed him of Desdemona's infidelity. Emilia's cries of "Murder" bring Iago, Montano, and Gratiano. Iago, under pressure, admits accusing Desdemona. When Emilia discloses the truth about the handkerchief, Othello tries, unsuccessfully, to kill Iago, and Iago kills Emilia. Othello, aware of his enormous error in regarding Desdemona as unfaithful, stabs himself, falling dead on the bed beside Emilia and Desdemona. Iago is taken away to be tortured and killed.

---

5. **monumental:** i.e., used in making monuments
6. **else:** otherwise
8. **flaming minister:** i.e., the torch that serves me
10. **Should I:** i.e., if I should; **But once:** i.e., but if I once
11. **cunning'st:** most artfully created; **excelling:** superior, surpassing

(continued)

BIANCA
  He supped at my house, but I therefore shake not.   140
IAGO
  O, did he so? I charge you go with me.
EMILIA O fie upon thee, strumpet!
BIANCA
  I am no strumpet, but of life as honest
  As you that thus abuse me.
EMILIA As I? ⟨Faugh!⟩ Fie upon thee!   145
IAGO
  Kind gentlemen, let's go see poor Cassio dressed.—
  Come, mistress, you must tell 's another tale.—
  Emilia, run you to the citadel
  And tell my lord and lady what hath happed.—
  Will you go on afore? ⌜*Aside.*⌝ This is the night   150
  That either makes me or fordoes me quite.
           They exit ⌜in different directions.⌝

Scene 2

Enter Othello ⟨with a light,⟩ and Desdemona in her bed.

OTHELLO
  It is the cause, it is the cause, my soul.
  Let me not name it to you, you chaste stars.
  It is the cause. Yet I'll not shed her blood,
  Nor scar that whiter skin of hers than snow,
  And smooth as monumental alabaster.   5
  Yet she must die, else she'll betray more men.
  Put out the light, and then put out the light.
  If I quench thee, thou flaming minister,
  I can again thy former light restore
  Should I repent me. But once put out thy light,   10
  Thou cunning'st pattern of excelling nature,
  I know not where is that Promethean heat
  That can thy light relume. When I have plucked ⟨the⟩
    rose,

12. **Promethean heat:** Shakespeare seems to be combining two separate Greek myths about Prometheus, one in which Prometheus gave fire to humankind and one in which he was the creator of humankind. **heat:** fire; spark of life

13. **relume:** relight

18. **Justice:** Justice is often depicted as a woman in a blindfold with a set of scales in one hand and a sword in the other.

22. **fatal:** deadly

23. **cruel tears:** i.e., tears that show no pity

30. **bethink yourself:** i.e., think; **crime:** sin

32. **Solicit for it straight:** i.e., pray for heavenly grace at once

33. **Alack:** i.e., alas

35. **walk by:** i.e., stand aside

36, 37. **would not:** do not wish to

37. **forfend:** forbid

I cannot give it vital growth again.   15
It needs must wither. I'll smell ⟨it⟩ on the tree.
O balmy breath, that dost almost persuade
Justice to break her sword! ⌜*He kisses her.*⌝ One
    more, one more.
Be thus when thou art dead, and I will kill thee   20
And love thee after. One more, and ⟨this⟩ the last.
                                        ⟨*He kisses her.*⟩
So sweet was ne'er so fatal. I must weep,
But they are cruel tears. This sorrow's heavenly:
It strikes where it doth love. She wakes.

DESDEMONA
Who's there? Othello?   25

OTHELLO   Ay, Desdemona.

DESDEMONA   Will you come to bed, my lord?

OTHELLO
Have you prayed tonight, Desdemon?

DESDEMONA   Ay, my lord.

OTHELLO
If you bethink yourself of any crime   30
Unreconciled as yet to heaven and grace,
Solicit for it straight.

DESDEMONA   Alack, my lord,
What may you mean by that?

OTHELLO
Well, do it, and be brief. I will walk by.   35
I would not kill thy unprepcrèd spirit.
No, ⟨heaven⟩ forfend! I would not kill thy soul.

DESDEMONA   Talk you of killing?

OTHELLO
Ay, I do.

DESDEMONA   Then heaven have mercy on me.   40

OTHELLO   Amen, with all my heart.

DESDEMONA
If you say ⟨so,⟩ I hope you will not kill me.

OTHELLO   Humh.

54. **portents:** omens
55. **point on me:** i.e., predict my future
66. **presently:** immediately
68. **each article:** each item or count in the charge against you (a legal term)
69. **conception:** idea, thought
70. **groan withal:** i.e., groan with (Coupled with the use of **conception** a line earlier, **groan** suggests a woman in labor to deliver a child she has conceived.)

DESDEMONA
And yet I fear you, for you're fatal then
When your eyes roll so. Why I should fear I know   45
  not,
Since guiltiness I know not, but yet I feel I fear.
OTHELLO
Think on thy sins.
DESDEMONA   They are loves I bear to you.
OTHELLO Ay, and for that thou diest.   50
DESDEMONA
That death's unnatural that kills for loving.
Alas, why gnaw you so your nether lip?
Some bloody passion shakes your very frame.
These are portents, but yet I hope, I hope
They do not point on me.   55
OTHELLO   Peace, and be still.
DESDEMONA
I will so. What's the matter?
OTHELLO   That handkerchief
Which I so loved, and gave thee, thou gav'st to
  Cassio.   60
DESDEMONA
No, by my life and soul! Send for the man
And ask him.
OTHELLO
Sweet soul, take heed, take heed of perjury.
Thou art on thy deathbed.
DESDEMONA
Ay, but not yet to die.   65
OTHELLO   ⟨Yes,⟩ presently.
Therefore confess thee freely of thy sin.
For to deny each article with oath
Cannot remove nor choke the strong conception
That I do groan withal. Thou art to die.   70
DESDEMONA
⟨Then Lord⟩ have mercy on me!

74. **Offend:** wrong
75-76. **with such . . . love:** i.e., in terms of the love that heaven authorizes us to feel for all humankind
76. **token:** i.e., love token
77. **in 's:** i.e., in his
78. **stone my heart:** turn my heart to stone
84. **confess:** testify to
85. **confessed:** i.e., owned up
87. **used:** i.e., sexually
92. **ta'en order:** i.e., made arrangements
95. **stomach:** appetite
96. **undone:** destroyed

OTHELLO   I say "Amen."
DESDEMONA
And have you mercy, too. I never did
Offend you in my life, never loved Cassio
But with such general warranty of heaven   75
As I might love. I never gave him token.
OTHELLO
By heaven, I saw my handkerchief in 's hand!
O perjured woman, thou dost stone my heart
And ⟨mak'st⟩ me call what I intend to do
A murder, which I thought a sacrifice!   80
I saw the handkerchief!
DESDEMONA   He found it, then.
I never gave it him. Send for him hither.
Let him confess a truth.
OTHELLO   He hath confessed.   85
DESDEMONA   What, my lord?
OTHELLO
That he hath used thee.
DESDEMONA   How? Unlawfully?
OTHELLO   Ay.
DESDEMONA
He will not say so.   90
OTHELLO   No. His mouth is stopped.
Honest Iago hath ta'en order for 't.
DESDEMONA
O, my fear interprets. What, is he dead?
OTHELLO
Had all his hairs been lives, my great revenge
Had stomach for them all.   95
DESDEMONA
Alas, he is betrayed, and I undone.   ⌜*She weeps.*⌝
OTHELLO
Out, strumpet! Weep'st thou for him to my face?
DESDEMONA
O banish me, my lord, but kill me not!

106. **within:** i.e., offstage
115. **By and by:** soon
116. **'Tis like:** i.e., probably
118, 120. **she:** i.e., Emilia
119. **she:** i.e., Desdemona
125. **yawn:** i.e., open up with an earthquake; **alteration:** i.e., this important change in the world, namely, Desdemona's death

OTHELLO   Down, strumpet!

DESDEMONA
   Kill me tomorrow, let me live tonight.   100
OTHELLO   Nay, if you strive—
DESDEMONA
   But half an hour!
[OTHELLO   Being done, there is no pause.]
DESDEMONA
   But while I say one prayer!
OTHELLO   It is too late.   105
                           ⟨He⟩ smothers her.
EMILIA, ⌈within⌉
   My lord, my lord? What ho! My lord, my lord!
OTHELLO
   What noise is this?—Not dead? Not yet quite dead?
   I that am cruel am yet merciful.
   I would not have thee linger in thy pain.
   So, so.   110
EMILIA, within   What, ho! My lord, my lord!
OTHELLO   Who's
      there?
EMILIA, ⌈within⌉
   O, good my lord, I would speak a word with you.
OTHELLO
   Yes. 'Tis Emilia.—By and by.—She's dead.   115
   'Tis like she comes to speak of Cassio's death.
   The noise was ⟨here.⟩ Ha, no more moving?
   Still as the grave. Shall she come in? Were 't good?
   I think she stirs again. No. What's best to do?
   If she come in, she'll sure speak to my wife.   120
   My wife, my wife! What wife? I have no wife.
   O insupportable! O heavy hour!
   Methinks it should be now a huge eclipse
   Of sun and moon, and that th' affrighted globe
   ⟨Should⟩ yawn at alteration.   125
EMILIA, ⌈within⌉   I do beseech you
   That I may speak with you. O, good my lord—

129. **Soft, by and by:** i.e., wait a moment; **curtains:** i.e., bed curtains
135. **error:** i.e., wandering out of the sphere in which it was thought to travel around the earth
136. **wont:** accustomed to
137. **mad:** lunatic (*luna:* moon, in Latin)
147. **Out:** an interjection of dismay or lamentation

OTHELLO
I had forgot thee. O, come in, Emilia.—
Soft, by and by, let me the curtains draw.—
Where art thou?   130

Enter Emilia.

                    What's the matter with thee now?
EMILIA
O, my good lord, yonder's foul murders done.
OTHELLO   What? Now?
EMILIA   But now, my lord.
OTHELLO
It is the very error of the moon.   135
She comes more nearer earth than she was wont
And makes men mad.
EMILIA   Cassio, my lord, hath killed
A young Venetian called Roderigo.
OTHELLO
Roderigo killed? And Cassio killed?   140
EMILIA   No, Cassio is not killed.
OTHELLO
Not Cassio killed? Then murder's out of tune,
And sweet revenge grows harsh.
DESDEMONA   O falsely, falsely murdered.
EMILIA
⟨O Lord,⟩ what cry is that?   145
OTHELLO   That? What?
EMILIA
Out, and alas, that was my lady's voice!
Help! Help ho! Help! O lady, speak again!
Sweet Desdemona, O sweet mistress, speak!
DESDEMONA   A guiltless death I die.   150
EMILIA   O, who hath done this deed?
DESDEMONA   Nobody. I myself. Farewell.
Commend me to my kind lord. O, farewell.
                                        ⟨*She dies.*⟩

162. **folly:** unchasteness

163. **belie:** tell lies about her

164. **false as water:** Proverbial: as unstable (**false**) as water

167. **top:** cover in coition (a term used for animals); **else:** i.e., if you doubt me

168. **were:** i.e., would be

169. **But:** i.e., except

176. **chrysolite:** In Shakespeare's day, this precious stone was thought to be the same as topaz. It was famous as the huge gem out of which an Egyptian king had a statue of his wife carved.

"Burning hell." (5.2.159)
From Jan David, *Veridicus Christianus* . . . (1601).

OTHELLO
  Why, how should she be murdered?
EMILIA   Alas, who   155
  knows?
OTHELLO
  You ⟨heard⟩ her say herself, it was not I.
EMILIA
  She said so. I must needs report the truth.
OTHELLO
  She's like a liar gone to burning hell!
  'Twas I that killed her.   160
EMILIA
  O, the more angel she, and you the blacker devil!
OTHELLO
  She turned to folly, and she was a whore.
EMILIA
  Thou dost belie her, and thou art a devil!
OTHELLO   She was false as water.
EMILIA   Thou art rash as fire to say   165
  That she was false. O, she was heavenly true!
OTHELLO
  Cassio did top her. Ask thy husband else.
  O, I were damned beneath all depth in hell
  But that I did proceed upon just grounds
  To this extremity. Thy husband knew it all.   170
EMILIA   My husband?
OTHELLO   Thy husband.
EMILIA   That she was false to wedlock?
OTHELLO
  Ay, with Cassio. Had she been true,
  If heaven would make me such another world   175
  Of one entire and perfect chrysolite,
  I'd not have sold her for it.
EMILIA   My husband?
OTHELLO
  Ay, 'twas he that told me on her first.

183. **iterance:** repetition
185. **made mocks with:** i.e., made a mockery of
192. **bargain:** contract, purchase (i.e., her marriage)
197. **Peace, you were best:** i.e., you'd better be silent
199. **gull:** dupe, gullible person

An honest man he is, and hates the slime   180
That sticks on filthy deeds.
EMILIA   My husband?
OTHELLO
What needs this iterance, woman? I say, thy
   husband.
[EMILIA
O mistress, villainy hath made mocks with love!—   185
My husband say she was false?
OTHELLO   He, woman.
I say thy husband. Dost understand the word?
My friend, thy husband; honest, honest Iago.]
EMILIA
If he say so, may his pernicious soul   190
Rot half a grain a day! He lies to th' heart!
She was too fond of her most filthy bargain.
                        ⌜*He draws his sword.*⌝
OTHELLO   Hah?
EMILIA   Do thy worst!
This deed of thine is no more worthy heaven   195
Than thou wast worthy her.
OTHELLO   Peace, you were best!
EMILIA
Thou hast not half that power to do me harm
As I have to be hurt. O gull! O dolt,
As ignorant as dirt! Thou hast done a deed—   200
I care not for thy sword. I'll make thee known,
Though I lost twenty lives. Help! Help, ho! Help!
The Moor hath killed my mistress! Murder, murder!

        Enter Montano, Gratiano, and Iago.

MONTANO
What is the matter? How now, general?
EMILIA
O, are you come, Iago? You have done well,   205
That men must lay their murders on your neck.

213. **apt:** plausible, credible
219. **Charm:** i.e., silence
220. **bound:** compelled, morally obligated
222. **forfend:** forbid
223. **set . . . on:** incited
229. **then:** Emilia is probably referring to her speech at 4.2.153.
231. **charge:** order

GRATIANO What is the matter?

EMILIA, ⌜*to Iago*⌝
Disprove this villain, if thou be'st a man.
He says thou told'st him that his wife was false.
I know thou didst not. Thou 'rt not such a villain.   210
Speak, for my heart is full.

IAGO
I told him what I thought, and told no more
Than what he found himself was apt and true.

EMILIA
But did you ever tell him she was false?

IAGO I did.   215

EMILIA
You told a lie, an odious, damnèd lie!
Upon my soul, a lie, a wicked lie!
She false with Cassio? Did you say with Cassio?

IAGO
With Cassio, mistress. Go to! Charm your tongue.

EMILIA
I will not charm my tongue. I am bound to speak.   220
[My mistress here lies murdered in her bed.

ALL O heavens forfend!

EMILIA, ⌜*to Iago*⌝
And your reports have set the murder on!

OTHELLO
Nay, stare not, masters; it is true indeed.

GRATIANO 'Tis a strange truth.   225

MONTANO
O monstrous act!

EMILIA   Villainy, villainy, villainy!
I think upon 't, I think! I smell 't! O villainy!
I thought so then. I'll kill myself for grief!
O villainy! Villainy!]   230

IAGO
What, are you mad? I charge you get you home.

232. **leave:** permission
240. **uncle:** i.e., Gratiano, brother to Brabantio
243. **shows:** looks, seems
246. **Shore his old thread in twain:** cut in two the thread of his life (In classical mythology, life is represented as a thread spun by Clotho, measured out by Lachesis, and cut by Atropos. These three are the Fates.)
247. **turn:** deed
248. **better angel:** i.e., guardian angel
249. **reprobance:** reprobation, damnation
253. **gratify:** reward
254. **recognizance:** token, emblem
261. **liberal as the north:** i.e., as freely as the blowing of the north wind

EMILIA
Good gentlemen, let me have leave to speak.
'Tis proper I obey him, but not now.
Perchance, Iago, I will ne'er go home.
OTHELLO O, O, O! ⟨*Othello falls on the bed.*⟩ 235
EMILIA Nay, lay thee down, and roar!
For thou hast killed the sweetest innocent
That e'er did lift up eye.
OTHELLO, ⌜*standing*⌝ O, she was foul!—
I scarce did know you, uncle. There lies your niece, 240
Whose breath indeed these hands have newly
  stopped.
I know this act shows horrible and grim.
GRATIANO
Poor Desdemon, I am glad thy father's dead.
Thy match was mortal to him, and pure grief 245
Shore his old thread in twain. Did he live now,
This sight would make him do a desperate turn,
Yea, curse his better angel from his side,
And fall to reprobance.
OTHELLO
'Tis pitiful. But yet Iago knows 250
That she with Cassio hath the act of shame
A thousand times committed. Cassio confessed it,
And she did gratify his amorous works
With that recognizance and pledge of love
Which I first gave her. I saw it in his hand. 255
It was a handkerchief, an antique token
My father gave my mother.
EMILIA O ⟨God!⟩ O heavenly ⟨God!⟩
IAGO ⟨Zounds,⟩ hold your peace!
EMILIA 'Twill out, 'twill out. I peace? 260
No, I will speak as liberal as the north.
Let heaven and men and devils, let them all,
All, all, cry shame against me, yet I'll speak.
IAGO Be wise, and get you home.
⌜*He draws his sword.*⌝

269. **fortune:** chance
278. **coxcomb:** i.e., fool (literally, a fool's cap)
281–82. **Are . . . thunder?:** i.e., has Jove, the mythological thundergod, no stones to use to strike down Iago? Does Jove need them all for thunder? (Jove is sometimes portrayed as attacking people with thunderbolts.)
287. **recovered:** got hold of
288. **without:** from the outside

EMILIA
  I will not.   265
GRATIANO   Fie, your sword upon a woman!
EMILIA
  O thou dull Moor, that handkerchief thou speak'st
    of
  I found by fortune, and did give my husband—
  For often, with a solemn earnestness   270
  (More than indeed belonged to such a trifle),
  He begged of me to steal 't.
IAGO   Villainous whore!
EMILIA
  She give it Cassio? No, alas, I found it,
  And I did give 't my husband.   275
IAGO   Filth, thou liest!
EMILIA
  By heaven, I do not, I do not, gentlemen!
  ⌈*To Othello.*⌉ O murd'rous coxcomb, what should
    such a fool
  Do with so good a wife?   280
OTHELLO   Are there no stones in heaven
  But what serves for the thunder?—Precious villain!
        ⟨*The Moor runs at Iago* ⌈*but is disarmed.*⌉
                 Iago kills his wife.⟩
GRATIANO
  The woman falls! Sure he hath killed his wife.
EMILIA
  Ay, ay! O, lay me by my mistress' side.   ⟨*Iago exits.*⟩
GRATIANO   He's gone, but his wife's killed.   285
MONTANO
  'Tis a notorious villain. Take you this weapon
  Which I have ⟨here⟩ recovered from the Moor.
  Come, guard the door without. Let him not pass,
  But kill him rather. I'll after that same villain,
  For 'tis a damnèd slave.   290
              ⟨*Montano and Gratiano*⟩ *exit.*
OTHELLO   I am not valiant neither,

292. **whipster:** slight, contemptible person

293. **honor outlive honesty:** i.e., the reputation of being honorable outlast honor itself

295. **bode:** forebode, portend

296–97. **play . . . music:** Proverbially, swans were said to sing at their deaths.

303. **the ice brook's temper:** i.e., tempered or hardened in ice-cold water

305. **dear:** i.e., dearly

308. **naked:** i.e., weaponless

315. **your stop:** the obstruction you are capable of providing

318. **butt:** terminal point, boundary

319. **sea-mark:** the boundary or limit of the flow of the sea (This word could also refer to a landmark or a beacon.); **utmost:** furthermost

320. **go back:** i.e., move away from me; **lost:** groundless

321. **Man but a rush:** i.e., wield no more than a bulrush

But every puny whipster gets my sword.
But why should honor outlive honesty?
Let it go all.
[EMILIA   What did thy song bode, lady?   295
Hark, canst thou hear me? I will play the swan
And die in music.
⌜*She sings.*⌝ *Willow, willow, willow.*]
Moor, she was chaste. She loved thee, cruel Moor.
So come my soul to bliss, as I speak true.   300
So speaking as I think, alas, I die.   ⟨*She dies.*⟩
OTHELLO
I have another weapon in this chamber.
It ⟨is⟩ a sword of Spain, the ice brook's temper.
O, here it is.—Uncle, I must come forth.
GRATIANO, ⟨*within*⟩
If thou attempt it, it will cost thee dear;   305
Thou hast no weapon and perforce must suffer.
OTHELLO
Look in upon me, then, and speak with me,
Or naked as I am I will assault thee.

⌜*Enter Gratiano.*⌝

GRATIANO
What is the matter?
OTHELLO   Behold, I have a weapon.   310
A better never did itself sustain
Upon a soldier's thigh. I have seen the day
That with this little arm and this good sword
I have made my way through more impediments
Than twenty times your stop. But—O vain boast!—   315
Who can control his fate? 'Tis not so now.
[Be not afraid, though you do see me weaponed.
Here is my journey's end, here is my butt
And very sea-mark of my utmost sail.
Do you go back dismayed? 'Tis a lost fear.   320
Man but a rush against Othello's breast,

324. at compt: i.e., at the Last Judgment

326–27. Cold . . . like thy chastity: Shakespeare often links chastity with coldness, sometimes setting it in opposition to the heat of lust, sometimes connecting it with Diana, goddess of chastity and of "the cold fruitless moon" (as he calls it in *A Midsummer Night's Dream*).

331. steep-down: precipitous

336. I look . . . feet: i.e., to see if he has the cloven feet reputed to mark a devil

343. practice: deception, machinations

The Last Judgment, or "compt." (5.2.324)
From *A Series of Antient . . . Paintings . . . on the Walls of the Chapel . . . at Stratford upon Avon* (etched and published in 1807 by Thomas Fisher).

And he retires. Where should Othello go?
                    ⌜*He looks toward the bed.*⌝
Now, how dost thou look now? O ill-starred wench,]
Pale as thy smock, when we shall meet at compt,
This look of thine will hurl my soul from heaven,   325
And fiends will snatch at it. Cold, cold, my girl?
Even like thy chastity.—O cursèd, cursèd slave!—
Whip me, you devils,
From the possession of this heavenly sight!
Blow me about in winds, roast me in sulfur,   330
Wash me in steep-down gulfs of liquid fire!
O Desdemon! Dead, Desdemon! Dead! O, O!

Enter Lodovico, Cassio ⟨in a chair,⟩ Montano, and Iago,
                    with Officers.

LODOVICO
Where is this rash and most unfortunate man?
OTHELLO
That's he that was Othello. Here I am.
LODOVICO
Where is that viper? Bring the villain forth.   335
                    ⌜*Iago is brought forward.*⌝
OTHELLO
I look down towards his feet; but that's a fable.—
If that thou be'st a devil, I cannot kill thee.
                    ⌜*He stabs Iago.*⌝
LODOVICO   Wrench his sword from him.
                    ⌜*Othello is disarmed.*⌝
IAGO   I bleed, sir, but not killed.
OTHELLO
I am not sorry neither. I'd have thee live,   340
For in my sense 'tis happiness to die.
LODOVICO
O thou Othello, that ⟨wert⟩ once so good,
Fall'n in the practice of a ⟨damnèd⟩ slave,
What shall be said to thee?

347. **naught:** nothing
348. **part:** partly
353. **demi-devil:** i.e., half-human, half-devil
361. **befall'n:** happened
365. **imports:** concerns
369. **gross:** glaring, flagrant
370. **discontented paper:** i.e., letter expressing discontent
373. **belike:** probably
375. **caitiff:** wretch

OTHELLO   Why, anything.   345
  An honorable murderer, if you will,
  For naught I did in hate, but all in honor.
LODOVICO
  This wretch hath part confessed his villainy.
  Did you and he consent in Cassio's death?
OTHELLO   Ay.   350
CASSIO
  Dear general, I never gave you cause.
OTHELLO
  I do believe it, and I ask your pardon.
  Will you, I pray, demand that demi-devil
  Why he hath thus ensnared my soul and body?
IAGO
  Demand me nothing. What you know, you know.   355
  From this time forth I never will speak word.
LODOVICO   What? Not to pray?
GRATIANO   Torments will ope your lips.
OTHELLO   Well, thou dost best.
LODOVICO   Sir,   360
  You shall understand what hath befall'n,
  Which, as I think, you know not. Here is a letter
  Found in the pocket of the slain Roderigo,
  And here another. ⌐*He shows papers.*¬ The one of
    them imports   365
  The death of Cassio, to be undertook
  By Roderigo.
OTHELLO   O villain!
CASSIO   Most heathenish and most gross.
LODOVICO
  Now here's another discontented paper   370
  Found in his pocket, too; and this it seems
  Roderigo meant t' have sent this damnèd villain,
  But that, belike, Iago in the interim
  Came in and satisfied him.
OTHELLO   O, thou pernicious caitiff!—   375

379. **even:** just
381. **wrought to his desire:** i.e., worked out in accord with his wishes
385. **Brave:** challenge, defy; **whereon:** i.e., for which cause
386. **cast:** cashiered; **he:** i.e., Roderigo
388. **set . . . on:** incited
391. **For:** i.e., as for
393. **hold him:** i.e., keep him alive
394. **close prisoner rest:** i.e., remain a closely guarded prisoner
395. **Till that:** i.e., until
397. **Soft you:** i.e., wait a minute
401. **unlucky:** unfortunate
403. **aught:** i.e., anything
405. **being wrought:** i.e., having been stirred up or worked up
406. **Perplexed:** confused, tormented
407. **base:** vile; **Judean:** This is the reading of the First Folio, where it is spelled *Iudean;* the First Quarto reads *Indian.* Very probably one of these readings is a printing or scribal error, since the spellings differ, essentially, only in the second letter (*u/n*). It is impossible to be certain which is the error, which the correct reading.
408. **Richer:** i.e., worth more; **subdued:** i.e., subdued by tears

How came you, Cassio, by that handkerchief
That was my wife's?
CASSIO   I found it in my chamber.
And he himself confessed it but even now,
That there he dropped it for a special purpose   380
Which wrought to his desire.
OTHELLO   O fool, fool, fool!
CASSIO
There is besides, in Roderigo's letter,
How he upbraids Iago, that he made him
Brave me upon the watch, whereon it came   385
That I was cast. And even but now he spake,
After long seeming dead: Iago hurt him,
Iago set him on.
LODOVICO, ⌜to Othello⌝
You must forsake this room and go with us.
Your power and your command is taken off,   390
And Cassio rules in Cyprus. For this slave,
If there be any cunning cruelty
That can torment him much and hold him long,
It shall be his. You shall close prisoner rest,
Till that the nature of your fault be known   395
To the Venetian state. — Come, bring away.
OTHELLO
Soft you. A word or two before you go.
I have done the state some service, and they
     know 't.
No more of that. I pray you in your letters,   400
When you shall these unlucky deeds relate,
Speak of me as I am. Nothing extenuate,
Nor set down aught in malice. Then must you speak
Of one that loved not wisely, but too well;
Of one not easily jealous, but being wrought,   405
Perplexed in the extreme; of one whose hand,
Like the base Judean, threw a pearl away
Richer than all his tribe; of one whose subdued
     eyes,

411. **Arabian trees:** i.e., myrrh trees
412. **medicinable:** i.e., medicinal
414. **malignant:** evil
418. **period:** end (of his speech and of his life)
The conclusion of a speech is called a **period.**
420. **ere:** before
424. **Spartan:** i.e., cruel
425. **fell:** fierce, cruel
427. **object:** spectacle
428. **keep:** guard
430. **succeed on:** i.e., fall to
432. **censure:** judgment and/or sentence
434. **straight:** i.e., straightway, immediately
435. **heavy:** woeful, sorrowful

Albeit unused to the melting mood, 410
Drops tears as fast as the Arabian trees
Their medicinable gum. Set you down this.
And say besides, that in Aleppo once,
Where a malignant and a turbanned Turk
Beat a Venetian and traduced the state, 415
I took by th' throat the circumcisèd dog,
And smote him, thus. ⟨*He stabs himself.*⟩
LODOVICO O bloody period!
GRATIANO All that is spoke is marred.
OTHELLO, ⌈*to Desdemona*⌉
  I kissed thee ere I killed thee. No way but this, 420
  Killing myself, to die upon a kiss. ⟨*He*⟩ *dies.*
CASSIO
  This did I fear, but thought he had no weapon,
  For he was great of heart.
LODOVICO, ⌈*to Iago*⌉   O Spartan dog,
  More fell than anguish, hunger, or the sea, 425
  Look on the tragic loading of this bed.
  This is thy work.—The object poisons sight.
  Let it be hid.—Gratiano, keep the house,
  And seize upon the fortunes of the Moor,
  For they succeed on you. ⌈*To Cassio.*⌉ To you, lord 430
    governor,
  Remains the censure of this hellish villain.
  The time, the place, the torture, O, enforce it.
  Myself will straight aboard, and to the state
  This heavy act with heavy heart relate. 435
                          They exit.

Textual Notes

The reading of the present text appears to the left of the bracket. Unless otherwise stated, this reading is from the First Folio (**F**). The earliest sources of readings not in **F** are indicated as follows: **Q** is the First Quarto of 1622; **Q2** is the Second Quarto of 1630; **Ed.** is an earlier editor of Shakespeare, beginning with the anonymous editor of the Second Folio of 1632. No sources are given for emendations of punctuation or for corrections of obvious typographical errors, like turned letters, that produce no known word. Other symbols: **SD** means stage direction; **SP** means speech prefix; *uncorr.* means the first or uncorrected state of **F** or **Q**; *corr.* means the second or corrected state of **F** or **Q**; ~ stands in place of a word already quoted before the bracket; ⌃ indicates the omission of a punctuation mark.

1.1   1. Tush] Q; *omit* F   2. thou] you Q   2. hast] has Q   4. 'Sblood] Q; *omit* F   11. Off-capped] Oft capt Q   16. And in conclusion] Q; *omit* F   18. chose] chosen Q   26. togèd] Q; Tongued F   30. other] Q; others F   31. Christened] Christian Q   31. beleed] led Q   33. creditor.] ~, Q   35. God] Q; *omit* F   35. Moorship's] Worships Q   37. Why] But Q   39. And] *omit* Q   39. by old] by the olde Q   41. affined] assign'd Q   46. all be] be all Q   59. These] Those Q   71. daws] Doues Q   72. full] Q; fall F   72. thick-lips] Q (thicklips); Thicks-lips F   73. carry 't] carry'et Q   76. streets,] streete Q   79. chances] changes Q   79. on 't] out Q   85. Signior] Siginor F   86. Thieves, thieves] Theeues, theeues, theeues Q   87. your daughter] you Daughter Q   88. SD *Enter Brabantio, above*] "*Bra. Aboue.*" *as SP* F; Brabantio *at a window.* Q   92. your doors] all doore Q   94. Zounds]

Q; *omit* F   97. now, now, very] now, very Q   106. worser] worse Q   109. thee.] ~, Q   111. bravery] Q; knauerie F   115. spirit] Q; spirits F   115. them] Q; their F   122. Zounds] Q; *omit* F   124. and]; *omit* Q   129. comes] come Q   130. now] Q; *omit* F   136–52. If 't . . . yourself] *omit* Q   155. thus deluding you] this delusion Q   162. place] F *corr.;* dlace F *uncorr.;* pate Q   163. producted] produc'd Q   165. However] F, Q *uncorr.:* Now euer Q *corr.*   169. none] not Q   171. hell] hells Q   171. pains] Q; apines F   177. SD *with Servants and Torches*] *and seruants with Torches* Q   184. she deceives] thou deceiuest Q   194. maidhood] manhood Q   197. Yes, sir, I have indeed] I haue sir Q   198. would] that Q   199. you] yon Q   203. Pray you lead on] Pray leade me on Q   205. night] Q; might F   206. SD *Exeunt.* Q

1.2   0. SD *Iago, Attendants*] Iago, *and attendants* Q   2. stuff] stuft Q   2. o' th'] of Q   2. conscience] ~. Q   4. Sometimes] Q; Sometime F   12. you] *omit* Q   13. Be assured] For be sure Q   17. restraint or] restraint and Q   18. The] That Q   19. Will] Weele Q   23. Which, when I know] *omit* Q   24. promulgate) ^] promulgate. F; provulgate, Q   25. siege] height Q   32. yond] yonder Q   33. Those] These Q   37. Is it] it is Q   38. SD *Six lines earlier in* F; *six and a half lines earlier in* Q *as* "Cassio *with lights, Officers, and torches.*"   39. Duke] Q; Dukes F   40. you] your Q   44. Even] Q; Enen F   48. sequent] frequent Q   54. hath] *omit* Q   54. about] aboue Q   57. but] *omit* Q   67. Have with you] Ha, with who? Q   68. comes another] F *corr.* (come sanother), Q; come another F *uncorr.*   68. SD *3 lines earlier in* Q *as* "*Enters* Brabantio, Roderigo, *and others with lights and weapons.*"   75. Roderigo! Come] Ed.; *Rodorigo,* come F *uncorr.,* Q; *Rodorigoc? Cme* F *corr.*   83. things] thing Q   84. If . . . bound] *omit* Q   87. darlings] Q; Deareling F   91–96. Judge . . . thee] *omit* Q   97. For] Such Q

104. Whither] where Q   105. To] And Q   109. I] Q; *omit*
F   113. bring] beare Q   119. not an idle] F *corr.*, Q;
nota n idle F *uncorr.*   **1.3**   0. SD F; *Enter Duke and Senators, set at a Table
with lights and Attendants.* Q   1. these] Q; this F   5.
hundred forty] hundred and forty Q   8. the aim] they
aym'd Q   12. in] to Q   13. article] articles Q   15. SP
SAILOR] *One* Q   15. SD *1 line earlier in* Q *as "Enter a
Messenger."*   16. SP OFFICER] *Sailor* Q   16. galleys]
Galley Q   17. what's] *omit* Q   20. By . . . Angelo] *omit*
Q   25. Turk,] Q; ~; F   29–36. For . . . profitless] *omit*
Q   37. Nay] And Q   38. SD *a Messenger*] *a* 2. Messenger
Q   41. them] *omit* Q   42. FIRST SENATOR Ay . . . guess]
omit Q   43. restem] resterine Q   51. he] here Q   53.
to] wish Q   55. SD *1 line earlier in* Q *as "Enter* Braban-
tio, Othello, Roderigo, Iago, Cassio, Desdemona, *and
Officers."*   60. lacked] lacke Q   62. nor] Q; hor F   65.
hold on] any hold of Q   65. grief] griefes Q   67. and]
snd F   71. SP FIRST SENATOR] *Sen.* F; *All* Q   76. Being
. . . sense] *omit* Q   77. Sans] F, Q *corr.* (Saunce); Since
Q *uncorr.*   82. your] its Q   82. yea] *omit* Q   89. your]
yonr F   97. soft] set Q   102. feats] feate Q   102. broil]
Q; Broiles F   106. unvarnished tale] vn-varnish'd u Tale
F   110. proceeding I am] proceedings am I Q   114.
herself.] ~ ^ F   117. maimed] F (main'd)   117. imper-
fect^] ~. F   118. could] would Q   124. wrought upon]
wtought vp on F   125. SP DUKE] Q; *omit* F   125. vouch]
youth Q   126. wider] certaine Q   126. overt] Q; over
F   127. Than these] These are Q   128. seeming do]
seemings, you Q   129. SP FIRST SENATOR] Q; *Sen.*
F   138. The trust . . . you] *omit* Q   142. SD *Iago and
Attendants exit.*] Ed.; *Exit two or three.* Q *1 line earlier*
143. till] Q; tell F   143. truly] faithful Q   144. I do . . .
blood] *omit* Q   151. battles] Q; Battaile F   151. for-
tunes] Q; fortune F   155. spoke] spake Q   156. accidents by] accident of Q   160. of] and Q   161. portance

in] with it all Q　161. traveler's] trauells Q　163. and]
Q; *omit* F　163. heads] Q; head F　165. my process] the
process Q　166. other] Q; others F　168. Do grow] Q;
Grew F　168. These things] this Q　171. thence] Q;
hence F　172. Which] And Q　178. parcels] parcell
Q　179. intentively] Q; instinctiuely F　181. distressful]
distressed Q　183. sighs] Q; kisses F　184. in] I Q　192.
hint] heate Q　196. SD *Attendants*] *and the rest* Q　204.
on my head] lite on me Q　212. the lord of] Lord of all
my Q　224. Which . . . heart] *omit* Q　230. grise] greefe
Q　231. Into your favor] Q; *omit* F　235. new] more
Q　236. preserved] presern'd F　250. piercèd] Q;
pierc'd F　251. ear] Q; eares F　252. I humbly beseech
you, proceed] Beseech you now, Q　252–53. of state] of
the state Q　254. a] *omit* Q　257–58. a sovereign] Q; a
more souereigne F　262. grave] great Q　263. couch]
Ed.; Coach F, Cooch Q　265. alacrity] Alacartie F　266.
do] would Q　270. reference] reuerence Q　271. With]
Which Q　273. Why] If you please, bee't Q　276. would
I] I, I would not Q　276. reside] recide F　278. gra-
cious] Grcaious F　279. your prosperous] a gracious
Q　281. T' assist] And if Q　282. Desdemona] speake
Q　283. did] Q; *omit* F　284. storm] scorne Q　286.
very quality] vtmost pleasure Q　292. why] which Q
295–96. Let her have your voice. / Vouch with me,
heaven] Your voyces Lords: beseech you let her will /
Haue a free way Q　298. heat ( ] Ed.; ~ ˄ F; ~, Q　299.
me] Ed.; my F, Q　300. to her] of her Q　302. great]
good Q　303. For] Q; When F　304. Of] And Q　304.
seel] foyles Q　305. officed] actiue Q　305. instru-
ments] Q; Instrument F　309. estimation] reputation
Q　311. her] *omit* Q　311. affair cries] affaires cry
Q　312. it] *omit* Q　313–14. tonight. OTHELLO With]
tonight. *Desd.* To night my Lord? *Du.* This night. *Oth*
With Q　313. SP FIRST SENATOR] Ed.; *Sen.* F　313. away]
hence Q　316. nine] ten Q　319. With] Q; And F　319.

and] or Q   320. import] concerne Q   321. So] *omit*
Q   332. SP FIRST] Q; *omit* F   333. if thou hast eyes]
haue a quicke eye Q   334. and may] may doe Q   334.
SD *He exits.*] *Exeunt.* Q   339. them] her Q   341. worldly
matters] Q; wordly matter F   342. the] the the F   342.
SD *Othello*] *Moore* Q; *omit* F   348. If] Well, if Q   348.
after. Why] after it. Why Q   350. is torment] is a
torment Q   351. have we] we haue Q   353. O, villainous!] *omit* Q   355. betwixt] betweene Q   355–56.
found man] found a man Q   362. are our gardens] are
gardens Q   368. balance] Q; braine F   373. our] Q; or
F   379. have professed] professe Q   383. thou the]
these Q   385. be that] Q; be long that F   385. long] Q;
omit F   386. to] unto Q   387. his] *omit* Q   387–88. in
her] *omit* Q   392. bitter as] acerbe as the Q   393.
She . . . youth.] *omit* Q   394. error] Q; errors F   394–
95. choice. Therefore] choyce; shee must haue change,
shee must. Therefore Q   399. a] Q; *omit* F   401. thyself]
omit Q   405–6. if . . . issue] *omit* Q   408. retell] tell
Q   410. conjunctive] communicative Q   412. pleasure,
me] pleasure and me Q   420–24. RODERIGO What say
you . . . purse.] Q; *omit* F   425. RODERIGO I'll . . . land]
omit Q   425. SD *2 lines earlier in* Q (*Roderigo exits.*)
428. a] Q; *omit* F   428. snipe] Snpe F   431. 'Has] Q;
She ha's F   432. But] Yet Q   436. his] this Q   436.
plume] make Q   437. Let's] let me Q   438. ear] Q;
eares F   442. is of] *omit* Q   442. nature] nature too
Q   443. seem] seemes Q
   2.1 0. SD *Enter . . . Gentlemen.*] *Enter* Montanio,
Gouernor of Cypres, *with two other Gentlemen.*] Q   3.
heaven] hauen Q   5. hath spoke] does speake Q   8.
mountains melt on them] the huge mountaine meslt
Q   11. foaming] banning Q   12. chidden] chiding Q 16.
ever-fixèd] euer fired Q   21. to] they Q   21. SD *third*] Q;
omit F   22. lads! Our] Lords, your Q   23. Turks] *Turke*
Q   24. A noble] Another Q   26. their] the Q   28–29. in,

Othello

/ A Veronesa.] Ed.;~: ~~, F, Q   31. on shore] ashore
Q   36. prays] Q; praye F   38. heaven] Q; Heauens
F   43–44. Even . . . regard.] *omit* Q   43. aerial] Ed.;
Eriall F   45. SP THIRD GENTLEMAN] Q; *Gent.* F   47.
arrivance] Q; Arriuancie F   48. you] to Q   48. this] Q;
the F   48. warlike] worthy Q   49. O] and Q   50. the]
their Q   56. SD *within.*] *Mess.* Q   56. SD *Enter* . . .] Q
(1 line earlier); *omit* F   58. SP MESSENGER] Q; *Gent.*
F   60. Governor] guernement Q   60. SD *2 lines later in*
Q; *omit* F   61, 65, 73. SP SECOND GENTLEMAN] Q; *Gent.*
F   61. their] the Q   62. friends] friend Q   69. quirks
of] *omit* Q   71. tire the ingener] Ed.; tyre the Ingeniuer
F; beare all excellency Q   72. How] *omit* Q   74. SP
CASSIO] *omit* Q   74. 'Has] He has Q   75. high] by Q   77.
ensteeped] enscerped Q   77. clog] Q; enclogge F   79.
mortal] common Q   82. spake] spoke Q   88. Make
love's quick pants in] And swiftly come to Q   90.
And . . . comfort!] Q; *omit* F   90. SD *3 lines earlier in*
Q   92. on shore] ashore Q   98. tell of] tell me of
Q   102. of sea] of the sea Q   103. SD *Within* . . . sail]
one-half line later in F; *2 lines earlier in* Q   105. SP
SECOND GENTLEMAN] Q; *Gent.* F   105. their] Q; this
F   107. See . . . news.] So speakes this voyce Q   112.
Sir,] For Q   113. oft bestows] has bestowed Q   116. In
faith] I know Q   117. still] I; for Q   117. list] Q; leaue
F   119. her tongue] het tongue F   122. of door] adores
Q   126. SP *omit* Q   127. true, . . . Turk.] Ed. ~:~, F
131. wouldst write] wouldst thou write Q   133. to 't]
too, t F   142. brains] braine Q   145. *useth*] vsing Q
148. *hit*] Q; *fit* F   152. *an heir*] a haire Q   153. fond]
omit Q   158. Thou praisest] that praises Q   160–61.
authority] Q; authorithy F   161. merit] merrits Q   172.
See . . . behind] *omit* Q   173. *wight*] Q; wightes F   183.
With] *omit* Q   183. I] *omit* Q   184. fly] Flee Q   185.
gyve] Ed.; give F; catch Q   185. thee] you Q   185. thine]
your Q   185. courtship] courtesies Q   189. Very] *omit*

Q   190. an] Q; and F   191. to] at Q   192. clyster] Q
(Clister); Cluster F   192. SD *1 line later in* Q; *omit*
F   196. SD *3 lines earlier in* Q   201. calms] calmenesse
Q   213. powers] power Q   215. SD *1 line later in* Q; *omit*
F   216. discords] discord Q   224. does my] doe our
Q   224. this] the Q   228. own] one Q   233. SD *All . . .*
exit.] *Exit Othello and Desdemona.* F; *Exit.* Q   235.
harbor] Habour Q   235. hither] Q; thither F   239.
must] will Q   239–40. thee this:] ~,~ Q   245. And will
she] Q; To F   246. thy] the Q   246. it] so Q   249. again]
Q; a game F   249. to give] giue Q   250. appetite,] Ed.;
~. F, Q   250. loveliness] Loue lines Q   255. in] to Q
258. eminent] eminently Q   259. fortune] Forune F
260. further] farder Q   261. humane seeming] hand-
seeming Q   262. compassing] Q; compass F   262. most]
omit Q   262. loose] *omit* Q   263. affection] affections
Q   263. Why . . . none] *omit* Q   263–64. slipper and
subtle] subtle slippery Q   264. finder-out of occasions]
Q; a finder of occasion F   264. has] Q; he's F   265–66.
advantages, though true advantage] the true aduantages
Q   266. itself] themselues Q   266. a devilish knave]
omit Q   275. Blessed pudding!] *omit* Q   276–77. Didst
not mark that?] *omit* Q   278. that I did] *omit* Q   279.
obscure] *omit* Q   282. Villainous thoughts, Roderigo]
omit Q   283. mutualities] Q; mutabilities F   283–84.
hard at] hand at Q   284. master and] *omit* Q   285.
Pish!] *omit* Q   287. the] your Q   291. course] cause
Q   295. haply may] haply with his Trunchen may Q
298. taste again] trust again't Q   301. the] *omit* Q   303.
you] I Q   311. loving, noble] noble, louing Q   317.
lusty] lustfull Q   320. or] nor Q   321. evened] euen
Q   321. for wife] for wift F   325. trace] crush Q   328.
rank] Q; right F   329. nightcap] Q; Night-Cape F
    2.2   0. SD *Othello's Herald with*] F (*Othello's, Herald*);
a Gentleman reading Q   1. SP HERALD] *omit* Q   2.
general,] Q; ~. F   3–4. fleet, every] Fleete; that euery

Q 5. to make] make Q 5. bonfires] bonefires Q 6.
addition] minde Q 8. nuptial] Nuptialls Q 10. of
feasting] *omit* Q 10. present] presenr F 11. have] hath
Q 11. Heaven] Q; *omit* F 12. SD *He exits.*] *omit* Q
2.3 0. SD *Enter . . . Attendants.*] *Enter* Othello,
Cassio, *and* Desdemona Q 2. that] the Q 4. direction]
directed Q 12. That . . . 'tween] The . . . twixt Q 15–
16. o' th' clock] aclock Q 25. to] of Q 28. is it not] tis
Q 28. alarum] alarme Q 29. She] It Q 33. black] the
black Q 42. unfortunate] Q; infortunate F 54. out]
outward Q 55. caroused] ~. F 57. else] lads Q 58.
honors] honour Q 61. they] the Q 63. Am I] I am
Q 63. to put] Q; put to F 66. SD *2 lines earlier in* F *and*
3 in Q (*Enter* Montanio, Cassio, *and others.*) 67. God]
Q; heauen F 73. *clink*] clinke, clinke Q 75. *O, man's*] *a*
Q 78. God] Q; Heauen F 83. Englishman] Q (*English*
man); Englishmen F 83. exquisite] expert Q 93.
and-a] a Q 100. *Then*] Q; *And* F 102. 'Fore God] Q;
Why F 105. to be] *omit* Q 106. God's] Q; heau'ns
F 107. souls must] soules that must Q 107–8. and . . .
saved] *omit* Q 112. too] *omit* Q 115. God] Q; *omit*
F 119. left] left hand Q 120. I speak] speake Q 121.
SP GENTLEMEN] *All* Q 122. Why] *omit* Q 122–23.
think then that] think that Q 130. puts] put Q 134.
the] Q; his F 140. Prizes] Praises Q 140. virtue]
vertues Q 141. looks] looke Q 149. Not] Nor Q 151.
SD *"Help, help!" within.*] Q 152. SD *pursuing*] *driuing in*
Q 153. Zounds] Q; *omit* F 155. duty? I'll] duty: but I'le
Q 156. twiggen] wicker Q 159. Nay] *omit* Q 159. I
pray you, sir] pray sir Q 166. God's will] Q; Alas
F 167. sir—Montano—sir] Ed.; Sir Montano: F; Sir
Montanio, sir, Q 168. SD *A bell is rung.*] Q (*A bell rung.*)
3 lines earlier in Q 169. that which] that that Q 170.
God's will] Q; Fie, fie F 170. hold] Q; *omit* F 171. You
will be shamed] Q; You'le be asham'd F 171. SD
Attendants] *Gentlemen with weapons* Q 173. Zounds]

Q; *omit* F   175. He dies!] *omit* Q   177. Hold, ho!] Hold,
hold Q   177. sir—Montano] Ed.; Sir Montano F; sir
Montanio Q   179. sense of place] Ed.; place of sense F,
Q   180. Hold, for] hold, hold, for Q   185. for] forth
Q   193. for] to Q   195. breast] Q; breastes F   199.
Those] These Q   200. comes] came Q   200. are] were
Q   202. wont be] Q; wont to be F   205. mouths] men
Q   212. me,] Q; ~. F   215. sometimes] sometime Q
220. collied] coold Q   221. Zounds, if I] Q; If I once
F   229. quarrel] quarrels Q   231. began 't] began Q
232. partially] partiality Q   232. leagued] Ed.; league F,
Q   236. cut] out Q   239. Thus] Q; This F   248. the] Q;
then F   250. oath] oaths Q   251. say] see Q   255.
cannot I] can I not Q   256. forget.] Q (~;); ~, F   265.
SD *attended*] *with others* Q   268. dear] *omit* Q   269.
now] Q; *omit* F   277. SD *Exit.* F; *Exit Moore,* Desdemona, *and attendants.* Q, *1 line later*   280. God] Q; Heauen
F   281. Reputation, reputation, reputation! O, I] Reputation, reputation, I Q   282. part of] part sir of Q   285. I
thought] Q; I had thought F   286. sense] offence Q
291. are ways] Q; are more ways F   294. to affright] ro
affright F   297. slight] light Q   298. and so indiscreet]
and indiscreete Q   298–300. Drunk . . . shadow?] *omit*
Q   309. God] Q; *omit* F   311. pleasance, revel] Reuell,
pleasure Q   319. and] *omit* Q   320. so] Q; *omit* F   326.
O, strange!] *omit* Q   327. ingredient] ingredience Q
328. familiar] famillar F   332–33. at a time, man] at
some time Q   333. I'll] Q; I F   336–37. denotement]
Ed.; deuotement F, Q   338. her help] her, shee'll helpe
Q   339. of] *omit* Q   340. disposition she] disposition
that shee Q   342. broken joint] braule Q   345. strong-
er] Q; stonger F   349–50. I will] will I Q   352. here] Q;
omit F   355. SD *Cassio*] *omit* Q   363. were 't] Q; were F
369. course↗] Ed.; ~, F; ~. Q   371. the] their Q   373.
whiles] while Q   374. fortune] fortunes Q   382. SD
one-half line later in F   387. and] *omit* Q   388–89.

pains, and so, with no] paines, as that comes to, and no
Q 389. a little more] with that Q 390. again] *omit*
Q 396. hast] Q; hath F 398. Yet] But Q 399. By th'
Mass] Q; Introth F 403. SD *omit* Q 404. Two] Some
Q 406. on.] Q; ~ ‸ F 407. the while] Ed.; a while F,
Q 410. SD *He exits.*] *Exeunt.* Q
3.1 0. SD *with Musicians*] Q2; *Musitians, and Clowne*
F; *with Musitians and the Clowne* Q 3. SD] Q2 (*They
play and enter the Clown*) 4. in] at Q 6, 8, 10, 15, 19.
SP MUSICIAN] F (*Mus.*); *Boy* Q 7. you] cald Q 13–14.
for love's sake] of all loues Q 20. up] *omit* Q 21. into
air] *omit* Q 21. SD *omit* Q 22. hear] Q; heare me
F 26. General's wife] Q (Cenerals wife); Generall F
31. CASSIO Do . . . friend.] Q; *omit* F 31. 1st SD *omit*
Q 31. 2nd SD *one line earlier in* Q 43. SD *one line
earlier in* F *and* Q 47. sure] soone Q 55. To . . . front]
Q; *omit* F 64. CASSIO I . . . you.] *omit* Q 64. SD] Q;
omit F
3.2 0. SD *Iago, and Gentlemen*] Iago, *and other
Centlemen* Q 2. Senate] State Q 7. SP GENTLEMEN]
Ed.; *Gent.* F, Q 7. We] Q; Well F
3.3 3. warrant] know Q 4. cause] case Q 5. fellow!] ~:— Q; ~, F 11. I know 't] O sir Q 13. strange-
ness] strangest Q 16. That] The Q 18. circumstance]
Q; Circumstances F 30. thy cause away] thee cause:
away Q 30. SD *and Iago*] Iago, *and Gentlemen* Q 35.
purposes] purpose Q 42. steal] sneake Q 43. your]
you Q 57. Yes, faith] Q; I sooth F 58. grief] griefes
Q 59. To] I Q 68. or] Q; on F 69. noon] morne
Q 69. on Wednesday] or Wensday Q 71. In faith]
Ifaith Q 73. example] examples Q 77. would] could
Q 78. mamm'ring] muttering Q 79. with] Q; wirh
F 82. By'r Lady] Q (Birlady); Trust me F 91. difficult
weight] difficulty Q 98. Be as] be it as Q 106. you] Q;
he F 108. thought] thoughts Q 112. oft] often Q 114.
Ay] *omit* Q 121. By heaven] Q; Alas F 121. thou

echo'st] he ecchoes Q 121. me ⌃] ~; F 122. thy] his
Q 123. dost] didst Q 125. even] but Q 128. In] Q; Of
F 132. conceit] counsell Q 137. giv'st them] giue em
Q 139. fright] affright Q 142. dilations] denotements
Q 145. be sworn] presume Q 147. what] that Q 152.
as] *omit* Q 153-54. thy worst of thoughts] the worst of
thought Q 155. words] word Q 158. that all slaves are
free to] Q; that: All Slaues are free F 162. that] a
Q 164. But some] Q; Wherein F 165. sessions] Session Q 173. oft] Q; of F 174. that your wisdom] I
intreate you then Q 175. conceits] coniects Q 176.
Would] You'd Q 177. his] my Q 179. and] or Q 181.
What . . . mean?] Zouns Q 182. woman] woman's Q
183. their] our Q 191. By heaven] Q; *omit* F 191.
thoughts] thought Q 194. SP OTHELLO] *omit* Q 194.
Ha?] *omit* Q 195. SP IAGO] *omit* Q 195. beware, my
lord, of] beware Q 197. The] That Q 200. strongly] Q;
soundly F 205. God] Q; Heauen F 211. oncc] Q; *omit*
F 213. blown] Q; blow'd F 216. well] Q; *omit* F 224.
this] it Q 229. eyes] eie Q 233. God] Q; Heauen
F 234. not] *omit* Q 236. leave 't] leaue Q 236. keep
't] Q2; kept F, keepe Q 252. I' faith] Q; Trust me
F 254. my] Q; your F 261. As my thoughts aim not at]
Q; Which my Thoughts aym'd not F 261. worthy] trusty
Q 272. Foh! One] Fie we Q 273. disproportion] Q;
disproportions F 279. Farewell, farewell] Farewell Q
285. SP IAGO] *omit* Q 286. To] F, Q *uncorr.*; *Iag.* To Q
corr. 287. Although 'tis] Tho it be Q 289. hold] Q;
omit F 291. his] her Q 298. SD *He exits.*] F, Q *corr.*;
omit Q *uncorr.* 300. qualities] Q; Quantities F 301.
dealings] dealing Q 307. vale] valt Q 312. of] in
Q 313. keep] F, Q *corr.*; leepe Q *uncorr.* 313. the] a
Q 314. of] Q; to F 318. Look where she] Desdemona
Q 318. SD *2 lines later in* Q 319. false, heaven] false, O
then heauen Q 319. mocks] Q; mock'd F 322. island-
ers] Ilander Q 325. do . . . faintly] is your speech so

faint Q   327. Faith] Q; Why F   328. it hard] your head
Q   329. well] well againe Q   333. SD Q (*1 line later*);
Exit F (*1 line earlier*)   343. but to please] know, but for
Q   343. SD *1 line earlier in* Q   346. You have] *omit*
Q   348. wife] thing Q   350. handkerchief] handkercher
Q (*throughout*)   355. stol'n] stole Q   356. faith] Q; but
F   365. Give 't me] Give mee 't Q   367. acknown] you
knowne Q   368. SD *1 line later in* Q   373. The Moor . . .
poison] *omit* Q   376. act] art Q   377. mines] mindes
Q   377. SD *one-half line later in* F; *1 line earlier in*
Q   383. me] me, to me Q   387. know 't] know Q   389.
of] Q; in F   391. fed well] *omit* Q   401. troops] troope
Q   407. rude] wide Q   408. dread clamors] great clam-
or Q   411. thou] F, Q *corr.;* you Q *uncorr.*   413. mine]
mans Q   414. better] better [first t inverted] F   427.
forgive] defend Q   429. God b' wi' you! Take] F (God
buy you: take); God buy you, take Q   429–30. mine . . .
thine] F, Q *corr.;* thine . . . mine Q *uncorr.*   430. liv'st]
Q (liuest); lou'st F   434. sith] since Q   438–45. OTHELLO
By . . . satisfied!] *omit* Q   441. Her] Q2; My F   446. SP]
omit Q   446. see you] see sir, you Q   449. and] *omit*
Q   451. supervisor] Q; super-vision F   456. do] did
Q   465. might] may Q   466. reason] reason, that Q
468. in] into Q   476. wary] merry Q   478. O] out
Q   478. creature!" then] F (Creature: then); creature,
and then Q   480. then] Q; *omit* F   481. sighed] Q; sigh
F   481. kissed] Q; kisse F   482. Cried] Q; cry F   486.
denoted] deuoted Q   487. 'Tis] *Iago* Tis Q   488. SP
IAGO] *omit* Q   491. but] Q; yet F   494, 497. wife's] F, Q
(wiues)   500. any that was] Ed.; any, it was F, Q   500.
hers,] Q; ~. F   504. true] time Q   507. the . . . hell]
thy . . . Cell Q   511. Yet] Pray Q   512. blood, blood,
blood] blood, *Iago*, blood Q   513. perhaps] Q; *omit*
F   514–22. Iago . . . heaven] *omit* Q   516. feels] Q2;
keepes F   521. SD *He kneels.*] Q (*placed after* "be
content," *line 511*)   525. SD *Iago kneels.*] Q (*2 lines*

later) 529. execution] excellency Q   529. hands] hand
Q   531. in me] *omit* Q   532. business] worke so Q
540. at your] as you Q   541–42. damn her, damn her]
dam her Q
3.4 0. SD *Clown*] *the Clowne* Q   1. where Lieuten-
ant] where the Leiutenant Q   5. SP *omit* Q   5. me] one
Q   6. 'tis] is Q   8–10. CLOWN To tell . . . this?] *omit*
Q   12. here, or he lies] *omit* Q   13. mine own] my
Q   19. on] in Q   21. man's wit] a man Q   22. doing it]
doing of it Q   23. that] Q; the F   25. have lost] loose Q
34. SD *1 line earlier in* Q   35. till] Tis Q *uncorr.;* Let Q
corr. 43. yet has] Q; hath F   45. Hot, hot] Not hot
Q   46. prayer] praying Q   55. Come now] come, come
Q   58. sorry] sullen Q   64. faith] Q; indeed F   71.
repeated in Q   73. loathèd] lothely Q   75. wived] wiue
Q   78. lose 't] loose Q   83. course] make Q   86.
which] with Q   87. Conserved] Conserues Q   88. I'
faith] Q; Indeed F   90. God] Q; Heauen F   92. rash]
rashly Q   94. Heaven] Q; *omit* F   97. How] Ha Q   100.
can. But] can sir, but Q   102. Pray you] I pray Q   103.
the] that Q   108–9. DESDEMONA. I pray . . . the handker-
chief] Q; *omit* F   114. I' faith] Q; In sooth F   115.
Zounds!] Q; Away F   118. handkerchief] Handerker-
chikfe F   119. the] F, Q *corr.;* this Q *uncorr.*   119. of it]
omit Q   123. SD *4 lines earlier in* Q   131. office] duty
Q   132. honor.] ~, F, Q   134. nor my] neither Q   139.
shut] shoote Q   157. is he] can he be Q   160. SD
one-half line earlier in F; *omit* Q   166. their] the Q   168.
a] that Q   170. observancy] obseruances Q   184. that]
Q; the F   189. 1st SD *one-half line earlier in* F; *2 lines
earlier in* Q   194. I' faith] Q; Indeed F   199. O] No
Q   201. leaden] laden Q   202. continuate] conuenient
Q   207. absence ʌ]~: F; ~, Q   208. Well, well] *omit*
Q   214. by my faith] Q; in good troth F   216. neither]
sweete Q   224–25. BIANCA Why . . . not.] *omit* Q   224.
pray] ptay F   231. SD *They exit*] Q; *Exeunt omnes* F

4.1 5, 7. in bed] abed Q   12. If] So Q   24. infectious] infected Q   31. Or voluntary] or by the voluntaty Q   32. Convincèd] F, Q *corr.*; Coniured Q *uncorr.*   38. Faith] Q; Why F   39. What? What?] But what? Q   44. Zounds] Q; *omit* F   45–46. Handkerchief—confessions —handkerchief] handkerchers, Confession, handkerchers Q   46–52. To confess . . . devil!] *omit* Q   49. instruction] Iustruction F   52. SD *He . . . trance.*] F (*Falls in a Traunce.*); *He fals downe.* Q *corr.*; *omit* Q *uncorr.* 54. medicine, work] Q; Medicine workes F   58. SD *one line later in* Q   59. Cassio] *Cassio* [a inverted] F   64. No, forbear] Q; *omit* F   73. you not] you? no Q   74. fortune] fortunes Q   78. it] *omit* Q   79. Good] F, Q *corr.*; God Q *uncorr.*   82. lie] lyes Q   85. couch] Coach Q   91. o'erwhelmèd] ere while, mad Q   92. unsuiting] Q *corr.*; vnfitting Q *uncorr.*; resulting F   94. 'scuses] scuse Q 95. Bade] Bid Q   95. return] retire Q   96. Do] *omit* Q   97. fleers] Ieeres Q   112. clothes] Q; Cloath F   114. one).] ~)‸F   115. restrain] refraine Q   116. SD *2 lines earlier in* Q   118. construe] Q (conster); conserue F 119. behaviors] behauiour Q   120. you, lieutenant] you now Leiutenant Q   124. power] Q; dowre F   128. knew woman] knew a woman Q   129. i' faith] Q; indeed F   133. o'er] on Q   133. well said, well said] well said Q   138. her] Q; *omit* F   138. What, a customer] *omit* Q   138. Prithee] I prethee Q   141. They] *omit* Q   142. Faith] Q; Why F   142. that you] you shall Q   145. scored] stor'd Q   145. me? Well] ~ ‸ ~ Q   149. beckons] Q; becomes F   151. the] F *corr.*, Q; the the F *uncorr.* 153. the] this Q   153. By . . . falls] Q; and falls me F   158. shakes] hales Q   160. O] *omit* Q   163. SD *1 line earlier in* Q   164. SP CASSIO] *omit* Q (*speech continues to Iago*)   164. fitchew] ficho Q   170. the work] the whole worke Q   171. know not] not know Q   173. your] the Q   177. If . . . If] An . . . an Q   178. not, come] F *corr.*, Q; ~ ‸ ~F *uncorr.*   181. Faith] Q; *omit* F   181. streets]

streete Q   183. Faith] Q; Yes F   187. SD Q; *omit* F   194
–96. IAGO Yours . . . whore] *omit* Q (*The catchword*
"Iag." in Q *at the bottom of the page preceding this missing*
speech indicates that a speech by Iago was dropped.)
199. that] *omit* Q   200. Ay] And Q   209. so] F *corr.*, Q; fo
F *uncorr.*   211. O . . . times] A thousand thousand
times Q   214. Nay] I Q   215. O . . . Iago] the pitty
Q   216. are] be Q   217. touch] touches Q   223. night.]
~, Q   228. pleases. Very] F (~:~); ~ ˄ ~ Q   232. SD *A*
trumpet sounds.] Q (*A Trumpet*) *one-half line earlier in*
Q   234. I warrant] *omit* Q   234. SD *Enter Lodovico* . . .]
Two lines earlier in F *and* Q   235. Lodovico. This comes]
F (*Lodouico,* this, comes); *Lodouico* / Come Q   236.
See . . . wife's] and see . . . wife is Q   237. God] Q; *omit*
F   237. you] the Q   239. the Senators] Senators Q
253. 'twixt my] betweene thy Q   255. atone them] F
corr., Q (attone them); attone, them F *uncorr.*   260. the
letter] Q; thLe etter F *uncorr.*; thLetter F *corr.*   262.
government] F *corr.* (Gouernment), Q; Gouerment F
uncorr.   263. By my troth] Q; Trust me F   267. Why]
How Q   274. woman's] womens Q   278. an] Q; *omit*
F   290. home] here Q   296. SD *He exits.*] F, Q *corr.*;
omit Q *uncorr.*   298. Is . . . nature] This the noble nature Q   305. censure ˄] Ed.; ~. F; ~, Q 306. If what] if as
Q   313. this] Q; his F   318. denote] F *corr.* (deonte), Q;
deuote F *uncorr.*   320. And] F *corr.*, Q; An d F *uncorr.*
    4.2 3. Yes, you] Yes, and you Q   10. gloves, her
mask] mask, her gloves Q   17. heaven] heauens Q   19.
their wives] her Sex Q   21. SD *one line earlier in* Q   23.
cannot] F *corr.*, Q; cannt F *uncorr.*   27. you] *omit*
Q   36. Nay] Q; May F   37. knees] Q; knee F   38.
words,] Q; ~. F   39. But . . . words] Q; *omit* F   44.
seize] F (ceaze); cease Q   52. motive] occasion Q   52.
these] those Q   55, 56. lost] left Q   56. I] Why I Q   58.
they rained] he ram'd Q   59. kind] kindes Q   60.
Steeped me] F *corr.*, Q (Steep'd me); Steed'dme F

uncorr.   61. utmost] *omit* Q   62 place] part Q   64. A]
Q; The F   65. unmoving] Q; and mouing F   65. finger]
fingers Q   65. at—] at—oh, oh, Q   73. thou] thy Q   74.
Ay, there] Ed.; I heere F, Q   76. as summer] F *corr.*; as a
Sommer F *uncorr.*; as summers Q   77. thou weed] thou
blacke weede Q   78. Who] why Q   78. and] Thou
Q   80. ne'er] Q; never F   82. paper,] Q; ~? F   83.
upon] on Q   84–87. Committed . . . committed] *omit*
Q   90. hollow] hallow Q   92. Impudent strumpet] Q;
omit F   97. other] hated Q   102. forgive us] forgiue-
nesse Q   103. then] *omit* Q   105. SD *5 lines earlier in*
Q   107. gate of] gates in Q   107. you, you, ay, you] I,
you, you, you Q   117–18. DESDEMONA Who . . . lady]
omit Q   120. answers] answer Q 121. But] Bnt F   122.
my] our Q   125. very meet] very well Q   127. least
misuse] F *corr.*; least mise vse F *uncorr.* m svse F
uncorr.; greatest abuse Q   132. to] at Q   134. be-
whored] F *corr.*, Q (bewhor'd); be whor'd F *uncorr.*
136. As] Q; That F   136. hearts] F *corr.*, Q; heart F
uncorr.   136. bear] Q beare it F   140. said] sayes Q
141. "whore." A] F *corr.* (whore: a), Q; ~ ^ ~ F *uncorr.*
147. country and] Countrey, all Q   164. most villain-
ous] outragious Q   166. heaven] Q; Heauens F 168.
rascals] rascall Q   170. door] dores Q   171. them] him
Q   171. them! Some] F *corr.* (them:some), Q; the m
some F *uncorr.*   175. Alas] O Good Q   178–93. Here
. . . me] *omit* Q   183. them in] Q2; them: or F   183.
form,] Q2; ~. F   195. offense,] Q; ~. F   196. And . . .
you] Q; *omit* F   198. warrant] warrant you Q   199.
summon to] summon you to Q   200. The messengers
. . . stays the meat] And the great Messengers . . . stay
Q   201. SD] *Exit women* Q   207–8. now, keep'st] thou
keepest Q   213–14. RODERIGO Faith, I have heard too
much, and your words and] *Rodori.* I haue heard too
much: and your words and F *corr.*; A nd hell gnaw his
bones, F *uncorr.*; *Rod.* Faith I haue heard too much, for

your words Q   214. performances] performance Q
216. With . . . truth] *omit* Q   217. my] *omit* Q   218.
deliver to Desdemona] Q; deliver *Desdemona* F   220.
expectations] expectation Q   221. acquaintance] ac-
quittance Q   223. well] good Q   225. nor 'tis] it is
Q   225. By this hand, I say 'tis very] Q; Nay I think it is
F   228. I . . . 'tis] I say it is Q   234. and said] and I haue
said Q   237. instant] time Q   239. exception] conception Q   241. affair] affaires Q   245. in] within Q   248.
the] rhe F   248. enjoy] enioyest Q   251. what is it] *omit*
Q   251. within reason] Q; ~,~ F   253. commission]
command Q   257. takes] Q; taketh F   261. removing
him] remouing of him Q   265. Ay, if] I, and if Q   265. a
right] right Q   266. harlotry] harlot Q
   4.3   0. SD *Two lines earlier in* Q (*after* "About it")   2.
'twill] it shall Q   8. Dismiss] dispatch Q   10. SD *one-
half line earlier in* F *and* Q   13. And] He Q   14. bade] Q;
bid F   19. I would] Q; ~, ~ F   21. his frowns] and
frownes Q   22. in them] Q; *omit* F   23. have laid] F
corr., Q; ~,~ F *uncorr.*   23. those] these Q   24. faith] Q;
Father F   25. thee] Q; *omit* F   26. those] Q; these F   30.
had] has Q   33–57. I . . . next] *omit* Q   35. Barbary]
Brabarie F   42. nether] F *corr.*; neither F *uncorr.*   43.
soul sat sighing] Q2; soul sat singing F *corr.*; *Sonle set
sining* F *uncorr.*   46. *willow* 3] *Wtllough* F   49, 60. *Sing
willow, willow, willow*] F (*Sing Willough, &c*)   52–53.
Lay . . . *willow.*] F (*Sing Willough, &c.* (Lay by these)
Willough, Willough.)   57. who is 't] who's Q   59–62.
I . . . men] *omit* Q   59. then] F *corr.*; theu F *uncorr.*   63.
So] Now Q   66–71. DESDEMONA . . . question] *omit* Q
77. Wouldst . . . deed] Would . . . thing Q   80. In] Good
Q   81. In] By my Q   82. it] Q; *omit* F   83. ring, nor]
ring; or Q   84. petticoats] or Petticotes Q   84. petty]
such Q   85. for the] Q; for all the F   85. 'Uds pity] Q;
why F   97–115. But . . . so] *omit* Q   116. God] Q;
Heauen F   116. uses] vsage Q

5.1 1. bulk] Q Barke F   5. on] of Q   8. stand] sword Q   9. deed] dead Q   10. hath] has Q   12. quat] gnat Q   13. angry. Now] ~ ʌ ~: Q   15. gain] game Q   17. Of] For Q   19. be.] ~, Q   22. much] *omit* Q   23. Be 't . . . hear] Q; But . . . heard F   26. know'st] think'st Q   29. Help] light Q   32. It is] Harke tis Q   37. unblest . . . hies] fate . . . hies apace Q   38. Forth] Q; For F   43. voice] cry Q   47. groan] grones Q   47. 'Tis] it is a Q   49. in to] Ed.; into F, Q   52. light] lights Q   56. We] I Q   57. Did] Q; Do F   58. heaven's] Q; heauen F   65. me] my Q   66. that] the Q   71. here] Q; there F   74. dog!] dog,—o, o, o. Q   75. men] him Q   75. these] those Q   91. My sweet] O my sweete Q   91. O Cassio, Cassio, Cassio!] *Cassio, Cassio* Q   93. have thus] thus haue Q   96–97. IAGO Lend . . . hence!] *omit* Q   100. be a party] beare a part Q   100. injury] *omit* Q   101. Come, come] *omit* Q   105. O heaven] Q; Yes, 'tis F   109. your] you Q   115. He, he] He Q   116. the] a Q   123. out] Q; *omit* F   125. gentlemen] Gentlewoman Q   126. gastness] ieastures Q   127. if . . . stare] an . . . stirre Q   127. hear] haue Q   130. SD Q; *omit* F   135. Roderigo dead] Q; *Rodorigo* quite dead F   137. fruits] fruite Q   137. Prithee] pray Q   142. O, fie] Fie, fie Q   145. Faugh] Q; *omit* F   150. afore] I pray Q   151. makes] markes Q

5.2 0. SD *Enter Othello, and Desdemona in her bed*] *Enter* Othello *with a light* Q   10. thy light] thine Q   11. cunning'st] cunning Q   13. relume] returne Q   13. the] Q; thy F   16. needs must] must needes Q   16. it] Q; thee F   17. O] A Q   17. dost] doth Q   18. Justice to] Iustice her selfe to Q   18–19. sword! One more, one more] sword once more Q   21. One] once Q   21. this] Q; that's F   21. SD Q; *omit* F   24. where] when Q   33. Alack] Alas Q   37. heaven] Q; Heauens F   42. so] Q; *omit* F   50. Ay] *omit* Q   54. I hope, I hope] I hope Q   66. Yes] Q; *omit* F   69. conception] conceit Q   71.

Then Lord] Q; O Heauen F   78. my] thy Q   79. mak'st]
Q (makest); makes F   84. Let] And let Q   87. used thee]
—vds death Q   93. O] *omit* Q   93. interprets. What]
interprets then, —what Q   97. Out] O Q   101. if] an
Q   103. OTHELLO Being . . . pause] *omit* Q   104. SP
omit Q   105. SD F; *he stifles her* Q   105–6. *her.* EMILIA]
Ed.; *her. Æmilia at the door. Æmil.* F; *her. Des.* O Lord,
Lord, Lord. Emillia *calls within. Em.* Q   107. noise]
voyce Q   108. that am] F *corr.*, Q; am that F *uncorr.*
111. *within*] *omit* Q   117. here] Q; high F   119. best to
do] the best Q   121. What] my Q   125. Should] Q; Did
F   127. That] *omit* Q   127. O] *omit* Q   130. SD *1 line
earlier in* Q   136. nearer] neere the Q   145. O Lord] Q;
Alas F   147. that was] it is Q   153. SD *omit* F   157.
heard] Q; heare F   158. the] a Q   165. art] as Q   174.
Cassio. Had] *Cassio:* nay, had Q   179. on her] *omit* Q
183. iterance] iteration Q   185–89. EMILIA O . . . Iago]
omit Q   194. worst] wotst F   198. that] the Q   201.
known] know Q   203. SD *Iago.*] Iago, *and others.* Q
206. murders] murder Q   207. SP GRATIANO] *All* Q
221–30. My mistress . . . Villainy!] *omit* Q   235. SD Q;
omit F   243. horrible] terrible Q   246. in twain] at
wane Q   249. reprobance] reprobation Q   254. that]
the Q   258. God] Q; Heauen F   258. God] Q; Powres
F   259. Zounds] Q; Come F   260. 'twill out. I peace?]
'twill: I hold my peace sir, no Q   261. No . . . liberal]
no, I'le be in speaking, liberall Q   261. north] ayre
Q   268. of] on Q   274. give] gaue Q   280. wife] woman
Q   282. SD *2 lines earlier in* Q; *omit* F   284. SD Q; *omit*
F   286. you this] your Q   287. here] Q; *omit* F   290. SD
Q; *Exit* F   295–98. What . . . *willow*] *omit* Q   301. alas,
I die] I die, I die Q   301. SD Q; *omit* F   303. is] Q; was
F   307. with] to Q   315. your] you Q   317–23. Be . . .
wench] *omit* Q   327. cursèd, cursèd] cursed Q   332.
Desdemon! Dead, Desdemon] *Desdemona, Desdemona*
Q   332. O, O] O, o, o Q   332. SD Enter *Lodvico, Cassio,*

Montano and Iago with Officers] *Enter* Lodouico, Montano, Iago, *and Officers,* Cassio *in a Chaire* Q   333. unfortunate] infortunate Q   335. that] this Q   337. that] *omit* Q   338. Wrench] Wring Q   340. live] F, Q *corr.*; loue Q *uncorr.* 342. wert] Q; was F   343. damnèd] Q (damued); cursed F   344. shall] should Q   347. I did] did I Q   351. never gave] did never give Q   352. your] you Q   353. you, I pray] you pray Q   362. know not.] Q; ~~) F   373. interim] nicke Q   375. thou] the Q   376. that] a Q   379. but] *omit* Q   396. bring away] bring him away Q   397. before you go] *omit* Q   402. me as I am] them as they are Q   407. Judean] F (Iudean); *Indian* Q   412. medicinable] medicinall Q   417. SD Q; *omit* F   426. loading] lodging Q   430. on] to Q   435. SD *They exit*] F (*Exeunt*); *Exeunt omnes* Q

Othello:
A Modern Perspective

Susan Snyder

Early in Act 2 of *Othello,* the newly married Othello and Desdemona are reunited in Cyprus, having survived a storm at sea that threatened their separate ships. The meeting is rapturous, almost beyond words:

> OTHELLO
> I cannot speak enough of this content.
> It stops me here; it is too much of joy.
> > *They kiss.*
> And this, and this, the greatest discords be
> That e'er our hearts shall make!
>
> > (2.1.214–17)

In a film, the background music would swell at this point. These lovers, a dark-skinned Moorish general and a white Venetian lady, have triumphed over daunting obstacles: racial difference and the attendant cultural taboos, disparities of culture and of age, the angry opposition of Desdemona's father, Brabantio, urged on by Othello's malicious subordinate, Iago, the threat of the attacking Turkish fleet, and finally the raging storm that scattered the Turks and might well have swamped the Venetian ships as well. On this high note of joy, with the forces against their happiness destroyed or rendered powerless, the married life of Desdemona and Othello begins.

But less than two days later, the marriage is utterly destroyed and with it Othello and Desdemona themselves. Discords arise between them that cannot be

287

resolved with kisses. Indeed, when we next see Othello kissing his wife (5.2.18, 21), it is as a nostalgic gesture before he executes her as an unfaithful wife. Even allowing for the conventional economy and foreshortening of drama, this is a precipitous breakdown of love and trust. What goes so quickly and terribly wrong with the marriage of Othello and Desdemona? In what follows, I suggest various approaches to this question; some overlap, some point in opposing directions. Neither separately nor in conjunction can they offer anything like "the whole truth."

The most obvious and immediate answer is Iago. It is he who plots to poison Othello's happiness, and to bring down Cassio as well by getting him first stripped of his military position and then suspected by the Moor as Desdemona's lover. It is Iago whom everyone onstage condemns at the play's conclusion: in the space of the last 130 lines or so, various appalled characters call him viper, devil, wretch, pernicious caitiff, Spartan dog, and (repeatedly) slave and villain. At the Cyprus reunion in 2.1, Iago's malevolence already adds a jarring note to the triumphant background music. Directly after the speech quoted above—Othello's wish that kisses be their greatest discords—Iago says, in an aside,

> O, you are well tuned now,
> But I'll set down the pegs that make this music,
> As honest as I am.

The question of what drives Iago to ruin the Othello music is one that has long been debated. To his pawn, Roderigo, and to the audience in soliloquy, Iago speaks at one time or another of many grievances: Othello has made Cassio his lieutenant rather than Iago, who wanted, and claims to have deserved, the post; Iago suspects that his wife, Emilia, has betrayed him with the Moor;

Iago wants revenge, whether by possessing Desdemona (to be "even with him, wife for wife") or by shattering Othello's marital happiness; Cassio is his chosen instrument because Cassio is attractive to women and an additional threat to Iago's husbandly rights of ownership over Emilia. In spite of this wealth of inciting causes, critics have felt a disparity between the magnitude of Iago's malevolent work and the motives he gives for it. There are too many of them, for one thing. The fears of being cuckolded, mentioned only once or twice, don't seem to go very deep. And when Iago, after engineering Cassio's downfall, does get the lieutenancy at the end of Act 3, scene 3, he expresses no satisfaction either then or later.

Deeper insight comes from a few glimpses Iago affords us into his feelings, apart from the occasions he cites. "I hate the Moor" is his obsessive litany: "I have told thee often, and I retell thee again and again . . ." (1.3.407–8). This may well be suspect, like anything else he says to Roderigo, but even when alone he reiterates it:

> I hate the Moor,
> And it is thought abroad that 'twixt my sheets
> 'Has done my office.   (1.3.429–31)

The phrasing—"*And* it is thought," not "*Because* it is thought"—detaches the hatred from any immediate cause, gives it a dark life of its own. Bernard Spivack pointed out this unexpected *And* and the resulting detachment. He concluded that Iago was a descendant of the Vice character in medieval allegorical drama.[1] At times, certainly, Iago's malevolence seems too absolute for ordinary motivation, presenting rather what Melville called (in the Iago-like Claggart he created for *Billy Budd*) "the mystery of iniquity." But the reader or viewer, as well as the actor assigned to play Iago, may nevertheless find enlightenment of various kinds in human psychology. It is possible, for example, to see Iago not as an inhuman embodiment of evil but as a man who habitually feels the fine qualities and good fortunes of others as injuries to himself. He seems to point to that characteristic in himself later in the play when he tells us why Cassio has to die. As one who can expose Iago's deception to Othello, Cassio is a practical danger, but that is just an afterthought to Iago's more basic resentment of Cassio: "He hath a daily beauty in his life / That makes me ugly" (5.1.20–21).

If Iago feels himself a have-not, the graces of Cassio and Desdemona and the glamorous life and language of Othello must rankle in maddening contrast. Probing the subtext further, we may see recurring through his real and imagined grievances the anxiety of displacement. The fantasies of being dislodged from his sole rights as a husband by Othello or Cassio are problematic; more firmly based in reality, and more galling, is his displacement by Cassio as Othello's lieutenant—and intimate friend. The Moor has passed over his ensign, Iago, with all his experience in the battlefield, to choose the well-bred Cassio, courtly in behavior and schooled in "bookish theoric" (1.1.25). Iago himself is of the lower class: "honest," the label he constantly receives from others, is complimentary but also patronizing, used to pat inferiors on the head. Insecurity about his "place" in the social hierarchy blends into the specific obsession about the military position he has failed to attain. Complaining, he sounds rather like an NCO jeering angrily at the advancement of a West Point graduate:

> 'Tis the curse of service.
> Preferment goes by letter and affection,
> And not by old gradation, where each second
> Stood heir to th' first.   (1.1.37–40)

Promotion by seniority (*gradation*) would presumably have rewarded Iago for his long service in the field, but now it is *letter and affection* that count: letters of recommendation from influential people,[2] and Othello's own partiality for Cassio, stronger than any regard he had for Iago. In spite of the experience he and his general shared in several campaigns, Iago is shut out from this affection, the closeness that draws Othello naturally to make his (well-born) friend his lieu-tenant, the one who will act in his stead and represent him. The rejection can be seen as a double one: as Cassio appropriates Othello on the one hand, Desdemona draws him on the other, away from the bond of fellow soldiers into a new intimacy of marriage.

Iago might thus say with Hamlet, "How all occasions do inform against me": each event stirs his general sense of being put down, discounted, and excluded. His shrewd intelligence makes him all the more resentful at being subordinate to both Othello and Cassio in the army hierarchy. He exults in manipulating them, in being the one truly in command. Manipulating Cassio is easy, for the lieutenant has a defined weakness, susceptibility to drink. With Roderigo's help it is not difficult for Iago to lead Cassio on to brawling on the watch and quick demotion. Does Othello also show signs of vulnerability? For some critics, narcissism and self-dramatization are all too apparent in the "noble Moor," enough to destroy his marriage even without much help from Iago.[3] Without so thoroughly discounting Othello's greatness, we may well recognize in him a social insecurity that renders him open to Iago's insinuations.

IAGO
   I know our country disposition well.
   In Venice they do let God see the pranks

> They dare not show their husbands. Their best
>   conscience
> Is not to leave 't undone, but keep 't unknown.
> OTHELLO   Dost thou say so?   (3.3.232–37)

Othello has no knowledge of his own to counter this insider's generalizations about Venetian wives. He knows nothing of Venice apart from the few months' residence during which his courtship took place. A soldier since boyhood, he is unused to *any* peacetime society. Although he is a Venetian by association and allegiance, whatever he knows of the customs and assumptions of Venice is learned, not instinctive. If Iago, a native, says Venetian women are habitually unfaithful, it must be so ("Dost *thou* say so?"). Paul Robeson, whose second New York *Othello* production opened soon after the end of World War II, compared the Moor's insecurity to what an American soldier in the occupying army in Japan might feel in courting a Japanese woman, totally ignorant of the culture and its customs and having no basis on which to disbelieve the advice offered him.

Besides denying him cultural experience, Othello's warrior-past unfits him for his present dilemma in another way. He is decisive, as a good commander must be. He does not hesitate in doubt, and when resolved must act:

>   To be once in doubt
> Is once to be resolved. . . .
> I'll see before I doubt; when I doubt, prove;
> And on the proof, there is no more but this:
> Away at once with love or jealousy.
>   (3.3.210–23)

What works for the soldier is tragic for the husband; it pushes him past the doubt he cannot tolerate to an act of closure that is irrevocable.

Between Othello's years of exclusively masculine experience in the "tented field" and Desdemona's sheltered Venetian girlhood stretches a gap that even the most loving marriage can hardly bridge. He is black, she is white. He is middle-aged, she is young. That neither this disparity in age nor Othello's unfamiliarity with Venice is in the story on which Shakespeare based his play (in that story, for example, the Moor is a longtime resident) suggests that the playwright was deliberately accentuating this marriage as a union of opposites. The source story also has the bride and groom live together in Venice for several months after the marriage; Shakespeare, keeping his own emphasis, sends his newlyweds off immediately to the challenges of Cyprus, allowing no time to foster personal or social familiarity. Othello and Desdemona are so thoroughly deprived of common ground as to constitute a paradigm of difference in marriage. It is as if Shakespeare were directing our attention to the tragic vulnerability of love itself. Desdemona's devotion is total; and while Othello's love may be based in part on her mirroring back to him his best self ("She loved me for the dangers I had passed, / And I loved her that she did pity them" [1.3.193–94]), he has clearly invested his life in their new relationship. Each is dependent on the other, yet each is necessarily separated in isolated selfhood. Beyond Othello's personal deficiencies, then, we may focus on this unresolvable contradiction and the cross-purposes and misunderstandings it breeds, inherent in any love relation but in *Othello* dramatically accented and thematized.

The play's hero as well as its villain may thus be implicated in the disaster that befalls the marriage. From a different perspective, one may see additional psychological dimensions to this tragedy, a tragedy in which social forces have determining power beyond merely individual drives and deficiencies. It is, of course, Venetian *society* that labels Othello and Iago inferior, Iago for being far down in the social hierarchy and Othello for being foreign and dark-skinned.[4] Yet while neither Othello nor Iago is at home in the prevailing social system, they are both deeply embedded in it, like all the other characters, and are shaped by it. The play's title, as Michael Long notes, is not just *Othello* or *The Moor* but *Othello, The Moor of Venice.*[5] The tragedy evolves from and reacts to a particular society, which is dramatized for us first in Venice itself and then, precariously maintained, in its fortified outpost, Cyprus. Venetian society is in many ways attractive, embellished by graceful accomplishments like Desdemona's singing, playing, and dancing (3.3.216), sustained by a civil order one can take for granted. Brabantio disbelieves those who claim he has been robbed: "This is Venice. My house is not a grange [i.e., a farmhouse]" (1.1.119). Act 1, scene 3 shows us a rational government whose officers deliberate carefully under pressure, hear evidence judiciously.

But if the senators do justice to the alien Moor who has married a senator's daughter, they are motivated less by fairness than by their desperate need for General Othello to stop the Turkish "theft" of their possession, Cyprus. Brabantio charges Othello with a similar theft on a personal level (1.2.80), and even when it is plain that Desdemona married of her own accord, her father still addresses her as "jewel," a precious possession whose "escape" is galling (1.3.225). The Venetian value system of acquiring and possessing is clear in the frequency of commercial images in the play's language, including other literal and metaphoric "jewels" that implicate Iago and even Othello. When Iago repeatedly advises "put money in thy purse," Roderigo is persuaded he can win Desdemona with jewels. Good name is a jewel, Iago assures Othello—and therefore can be stolen. Iago is in fact the thief of Desdemona's good name, just as he pockets Roderigo's real jewels. Othello, too, shows the shaping power of this preoccupation with buying and selling, manipulating and increasing wealth, fearing theft. "Had she been true," he says of his beautiful wife,

> If heaven would make me such another world
> Of one entire and perfect chrysolite [i.e., topaz],
> I'd not have sold her for it.   (5.2.175–77)

The pervasive notion of woman as property, prized indeed but more as object than as person, indicates one aspect of a deep-seated sexual pathology in Venice. Othello admires Desdemona's skin as she sleeps, "whiter . . . than snow, / And smooth as monumental alabaster" (5.2.4–5). Besides the beauty of alabaster—yet another precious substance—its coldness and stillness are the keynotes. Earlier he had been troubled to feel her hand, "Hot, hot, and moist," and sense there "a young and sweating devil . . . That commonly rebels" (3.4.45–49). What he wants, it seems, is a beautiful form with no wayward life at all. "Be thus when thou art dead, and I will kill thee / And love thee after" (5.2.20–21).

Fear of women's sexuality is omnipresent in *Othello.* Iago fans to flames the coals of socially induced unease in Othello, fantasizes on his own about being cuckolded by Othello and Cassio. In an ideology that can value only cloistered, desireless women, any woman who departs from this passivity will cause intense anxiety. One result is a version of the familiar "virgin/whore syndrome," which Cassio actually enacts in the play with the two women who concern him most. He exalts "the divine Desdemona," commanding the Cypriots to kneel to her as if to a goddess (2.1.93). He resists strongly when Iago's conversation puts her in a sexual context, refusing to speculate about the wedding night, insisting on her modesty (2.3.26–27). The woman with whom he *is* sexually involved, Bianca, is a strumpet—or is she? Bianca denies it, and we have no evidence from the text that she sells her favors as Iago says. The 1623 Folio list of characters which labels her "a courtesan" is most likely the work of someone in the printing house, the label being derived from the accusations of Iago, Cassio, and Emilia; but perhaps we should separate Shakespeare's characterization of Bianca from that of these characters. Perhaps what we ought to register is not that Bianca is a slut but that Cassio treats her like a slut. If she has desired him and slept with him, she has, in his eyes, become a slut. Desdemona's own frankly expressed desire for her husband in Act 1, scene 3 contrasts significantly with his denial of such feelings for her, and after he has possessed her there are suggestions that the revulsion he feels is for his sexual bond with her as well as for her purported adultery with Cassio.[6]

This is perhaps the most insidious tragic design in *Othello*, a psychosocial web that ensnares men and women alike. It is never named. In the last scene, Emilia vows to speak out in spite of men—"Let heaven and men and devils, let them all, / All, all, cry shame against me, yet I'll speak" (5.2.262–63). But before she can, Iago stabs her into silence. Othello tries to sum up his life before ending it, but his moving picture of "one that loved not wisely, but too well" is incomplete. In that same speech he likens Desdemona to "a pearl . . . richer than all his tribe," still caught in the Venetian economy of worth. Othello stops his own groping self-analysis with his sword, and Iago, still alive, refuses explanation: "What you know, you know. / From this time forth I never will speak word." And the onlookers cannot contemplate the marriage of opposites so disastrously concluded, Desdemona and Othello dead on their marriage bed. "The object poisons sight," shudders Lodovico; "Let it be hid."

---

1. *Shakespeare and the Allegory of Evil* (New York: Columbia University Press, 1958), p. 448 and more generally chs. 1 and 12.
2. Iago himself has in fact tried to wield influence of this kind, employing "three great ones of the city" to plead his case with Othello (1.1.9).
3. This view was most strongly argued by F. R. Leavis in "Diabolic Intellect and the Noble Hero: A Note on *Othello*," *Scrutiny* 6 (1937–38): 259–83. The National Theatre production of 1964, with Laurence Olivier as Othello, was based on Leavis's interpretation.
4. This shared status as outsiders may well draw Othello, when his confidence is shaken, to rely all the more on Iago. Director Joe Dowling took this approach in his 1991 production in New York's Shakespeare in the Park series: Richard Bernstein, "Looking Inside that Outsider, Othello the Moor," *New York Times*, June 16, 1991, pp. 5, 34.
5. *The Unnatural Scene: A Study in Shakespearean Tragedy* (London: Methuen, 1976), p. 39.
6. Desdemona, not Othello, begs that they may pursue their married life in Cyprus: "That I did love the Moor to live with him / My downright violence and storm of fortunes / May trumpet to the world. My heart's subdued / Even to the very quality of my lord . . . if I be left behind, / A moth of peace, and he go to the war, / The rites [of lovemaking] for why I love him are bereft me." She was also the initiator in their courtship. Othello in supporting her plea disclaims the urgency of desire: "I . . . beg it not / To please the palate of my appetite, / Nor to comply with heat (the young affects /

In me defunct)." In the last scene, commanded to remember her sins, Desdemona replies, "They are loves I bear to you" (5.2.49). "Ay, and for that thou diest," responds Othello, seeming to find that loving desire for her own husband as sinful as that he imagines she has for Cassio.

Further Reading

Othello

Altman, Joel B. " 'Preposterous Conclusions': Eros, *Enargeia*, and the Composition of *Othello*." *Representations* 18 (1987): 129–57.

Shakespeare's inquiry into the nature of probability and improbability provides the focus of Altman's essay. While *Othello* may be "fraught . . . with improbabilities," in the words of seventeenth-century critic Thomas Rymer, the very process of understanding that makes it seem so is, in Altman's estimation, the subject of Shakespeare's questioning throughout the canon. Shakespeare resists the seventeenth century's tendency to ground both thought and action in a "scientific or moral or aesthetic certainty." It is in *Othello*, however, where Shakespeare most strenuously attempts to reveal that the "probable is really nothing more than the contingent."

Burke, Kenneth. "*Othello*: An Essay to Illustrate a Method." In *Othello: Critical Essays*, ed. Susan Snyder, pp. 127–68. New York and London: Garland, 1988.

Othello performs a "conspiracy," to use Burke's term, in which Desdemona, Othello, and Iago are partners. They represent a trinity of ownership: Othello as the possessor, Desdemona as what he possesses, and Iago as the threat to Othello's miserliness. The loss of the handkerchief is related to the conspiracy, for it is the privacy of Desdemona made public. In his belief that she has bestowed the handkerchief upon another, Othello feels a sense of "universal loss." The play reveals that "ownership" projected into realms where there is no

299

unquestionable security invites, ultimately, estrangement and profound loneliness.

Cavell, Stanley. *"Othello* and the Stake of the Other." In *Disowning Knowledge in Six Plays by Shakespeare,* pp. 125–42. Cambridge: Cambridge University Press, 1987.

Building on the initial premise that "the pivot of *Othello*'s interpretation of skepticism is Othello's placing of a finite woman in the place of God," Cavell suggests that the tragedy of the play lies in Othello's refusal to acknowledge Desdemona's imperfection. Cavell concludes that the consequences of this refusal of knowledge are not only the denial and death of Desdemona but also the failure of Othello's own capacity to acknowledge, that is, his "imagination of stone."

Donaldson, Peter. "Liz White's *Othello.*" *Shakespeare Quarterly* 38 (1987): 482–95.

Liz White's 1980 film of *Othello* is entirely the work of African-Americans, both the cast and the technical crew. Othello is played as a young, emotionally sensitive African in the midst of lighter-skinned urban African-Americans. The text's vivid black/white polarities are muted in the film. Because Othello is ethnically akin to the "Venetians," the tragedy of the last act is especially viable. In rejecting Othello, "the 'Venetians' are rejecting a part of themselves."

Greenblatt, Stephen. "The Improvisation of Power." In *Renaissance Self-Fashioning: From More to Shakespeare,* pp. 222–54. Chicago: University of Chicago Press, 1980.

Greenblatt maintains that, in the sixteenth century, there was an increased self-consciousness about the fashioning of a human identity as a manipulable, artful process. In *Othello,* Greenblatt perceives a pattern of "submission to narrative self-fashioning." It is Othello's own subscription to a carefully constructed narrative self that allows his identity to be subverted (if unintentionally) by Desdemona's submission to it and, in a more sinister vein, by Iago's role as an improviser in this ceaseless narrative invention.

Grennan, Eamon. "The Women's Voices in *Othello:* Speech, Song, Silence." *Shakespeare Quarterly* 38 (1987): 275–92.
    For Grennan, *Othello* is not only a play of voices but also a play about voices. He cites the myriad and diverse voices of the play but focuses specifically on the speech of the women, arguing that an understanding of the play's "moral experience" follows an understanding of the women's speech. The women, in their speech, songs, and, finally, silence, provide a "moral measure" as a thematic subtext that illuminates the meaning of the tragic action.

Jones, Eldred. *Othello's Countrymen: The African in English Renaissance Drama.* London: Oxford University Press, 1965.
    Jones undertakes a study of the dramatic representation of Africans on the English Renaissance stage. He finds *Othello* to make a significant departure from the Renaissance's traditional dramatic treatment of Moors in that Shakespeare endows Othello with noble qualities. For Jones, the racial prejudice of Iago and Brabantio is invoked specifically so that it can be rejected.

Murray, Timothy. "*Othello's* Foul Generic Thoughts and Methods." In *Persons in Groups: Social Behavior as Identity Formation in Medieval and Renaissance Europe,* ed. Richard C. Trexler, pp. 67–77. Binghamton, N.Y.: Medieval and Renaissance Texts and Studies, 1985.
    Murray shows that patriarchal Elizabethan society

feared the theater, for, given the prevailing assumption that women were inclined to imitate, dangerous female identities could be forged if women were exposed to staged vice. The lucidity and logical discourse of Desdemona, then, worked to demystify the exclusive authority of men. Desdemona's ability to read signs and interpret events implies that maxims about women's inferiority are "impotent and archaic." Her self-fashioning and sexual frankness, however, open her up to suspicion within the cultural codes of men and ultimately spell her doom.

Neely, Carol Thomas. "Women and Men in *Othello:* 'what should such a fool / Do with so good a woman'." *Shakespeare Studies* 10 (1977): 133–58.
    Refuting the arguments of "Othello critics" and "Iago critics," Neely reads the central theme in the play as love and the central conflict of the play as between the men and the women. The women inherit their roles from the heroines of Shakespeare's comedies, yet despite their lack of competitiveness, jealousy, and class consciousness, they are constrained in the tragedies by the male characters from exercising their traditional roles as mediators. Neely argues that it is Emilia, recognizing and responding to this conflict, who most dramatically and symbolically represents the balance of the play.

Neill, Michael. "Unproper Beds: Race, Adultery, and the Hideous in *Othello.*" *Shakespeare Quarterly* 40 (1989): 383–412.
    Neill proposes that *Othello*'s most potent theatrical image is the bed. The play repeatedly gestures toward it in its absence and, at the end, the bed becomes the "place" where the action is centered. As such, it becomes the "imaginative center of the play"—the focus of Iago's fantasies, Othello's speculations, and the audi-

ence's voyeuristic imagination. Because of the conventional symbolic importance attached to the marriage bed, the emphasis on the bed and on its violation in *Othello* forms the basis for a whole set of ideas about racial adulteration and sexual transgression.

Newman, Karen. " 'And wash the Ethiop white': Femininity and the Monstrous in *Othello*." In *Shakespeare Reproduced*, ed. Jean E. Howard and Marion O'Connor, pp. 143–62. London: Methuen, 1987.

Newman investigates the production of race and gender difference throughout *Othello* and examines the way the black man and the desiring woman are linked as representatives of the monstrous. Connecting *Othello* with other Elizabethan representations of blackness and femininity, Newman reads *Othello* as contesting the conventional ideologies of race and gender in early modern England. In general Newman urges a resistant reading of Shakespeare that contests the "hegemonic forces the plays at the same time affirm."

Orkin, Martin. "*Othello* and the 'Plain Face' of Racism." *Shakespeare Quarterly* 38 (1987): 166–88.

Orkin begins by discussing Renaissance attitudes to people of color in Shakespeare's England. He moves on to detail instances where racist mythologies inscribed critical responses to the play and ends with a focused examination of how, in South Africa, silence about the racist tendencies of some *Othello* criticism actually lends support to prevailing racist doctrines. For Orkin, in its scrutiny of Iago's use of racism and its rejection of pigmentation as an indication of human worth, the play "continues to oppose racism."

Rosenberg, Marvin. *The Masks of Othello: The Search for the Identity of Othello, Iago, and Desdemona by Three*

Centuries of Actors and Critics. Berkeley and Los Angeles: University of California Press, 1961.

Rosenberg charts the development of character images of Othello, Iago, and Desdemona on the stage and page during the last three centuries, providing an overview of approaches. He further demonstrates how both actors and critics have reshaped the text for performance. He argues against symbolic or skeptical interpretations of the play, claiming its complex humanity can be fully realized only on the stage.

Siemon, James R. " 'Nay, that's not next': *Othello*, V.ii in Performance, 1760–1900." *Shakespeare Quarterly* 37 (1986): 38–51.

Focusing on the final scene of the play, Siemon uses annotated promptbooks and performance records to explore how variations in staging and performance in the later eighteenth and nineteenth centuries suggest "a coherence of interpretation based on particular notions of both tragedy and femininity." The constant alterations of and deviations from the Quarto and Folio texts reveal how many implicit and explicit directions had to be ignored to make the final scene conform to the "particular tragic mold" favored by the eighteenth and nineteenth centuries.

Snyder, Susan. *The Comic Matrix of Shakespeare's Tragedies*. Princeton: Princeton University Press, 1979.

Snyder proposes that the tragedy of *Othello* develops from a questioning of comic assumptions about love, nature, and reasoning. By posing Iago against Othello and Desdemona, Shakespeare explores the strains and contradictions within the comic convention and uncovers their deeply tragic implications.

Spivack, Bernard. *Shakespeare and the Allegory of Evil*. New York: Columbia University Press, 1958.

Focusing on popular dramatic conventions that preceded Elizabethan drama, Spivack traces the figure of Iago and other major villains in the "family of Iago" back to late medieval dramatic traditions. Spivack shows Iago to be a descendant of the late morality figure of Vice. Iago's malignity is curiously without motive because he is not fully human, but an allegorical representation of evil.

Stallybrass, Peter. "Patriarchal Territories: The Body Enclosed." In *Rewriting the Renaissance: The Discourses of Sexual Difference in Early Modern Europe*, eds. Margaret W. Ferguson, Maureen Quilligan, and Nancy J. Vickers, pp. 123–42. Chicago and London: University of Chicago Press, 1986.

Within the dominant discourse of early modern England, women were formulated under contradictory categories: gender or class. As a gender, they were postulated as a single set. As a class, however, inequalities of wealth and birth divided them into distinct social groups. In this context, Othello's marriage to Desdemona is significant only when differentiations of class are recognized, for Othello marries "above his station" in terms of class. In "acquiring" Desdemona, Othello is a success, but in possessing her he lives with the fear of imminent loss. The openness of Desdemona that allowed Othello successfully to woo her must be, for him, closed off; after marriage, he linguistically moves her from the category of class to the category of gender, making her a figure of inconstancy. Thus the play constructs two Desdemonas and reveals the "antithetical thinking of the developing Renaissance state."

Shakespeare's Language

Abbott, E. A. *A Shakespearian Grammar.* New York: Haskell House, 1972.
This compact reference book, first published in 1870, helps with many difficulties in Shakespeare's language. It systematically accounts for a host of differences between Shakespeare's usage and sentence structure and our own.

Blake, Norman. *Shakespeare's Language: An Introduction.* New York: St. Martin's Press, 1983.
This general introduction to Elizabethan English discusses various aspects of the language of Shakespeare and his contemporaries, offering possible meanings for hundreds of ambiguous constructions.

Dobson, E. J. *English Pronunciation, 1500–1700.* 2 vols. Oxford: Clarendon Press, 1968.
This long and technical work includes chapters on spelling (and its reformation), phonetics, stressed vowels, and consonants in early modern English.

Houston, John. *Shakespearean Sentences: A Study in Style and Syntax.* Baton Rouge: Louisiana State University Press, 1988.
Houston studies Shakespeare's stylistic choices, considering matters such as sentence length and the relative positions of subject, verb, and direct object. Examining plays throughout the canon in a roughly chronological, developmental order, he analyzes how sentence structure is used in setting tone, in characterization, and for other dramatic purposes.

Onions, C. T. *A Shakespeare Glossary.* Oxford: Clarendon Press, 1986.

This revised edition updates Onions's standard, selective glossary of words and phrases in Shakespeare's plays that are now obsolete, archaic, or obscure.

Partridge, Eric. *Shakespeare's Bawdy.* London: Routledge & Kegan Paul, 1955.
After an introductory essay, "The Sexual, the Homosexual, and Non-Sexual Bawdy in Shakespeare," Partridge provides a comprehensive glossary of "bawdy" phrases and words from the plays.

Robinson, Randal. *Unlocking Shakespeare's Language: Help for the Teacher and Student.* Urbana, Ill.: National Council of Teachers of English and the ERIC Clearinghouse on Reading and Communication Skills, 1989.
Specifically designed for the high-school and undergraduate college teacher and student, Robinson's book addresses the problems that most often hinder present-day readers of Shakespeare. Through work with his own students, Robinson found that many readers today are particularly puzzled by such stylistic characteristics as subject-verb inversion, interrupted structures, and compression. He shows how our own colloquial language contains comparable structures, and thus helps students recognize such structures when they find them in Shakespeare's plays. This book supplies worksheets—with examples from major plays—to illuminate and remedy such problems as unusual sequences of words and the separation of related parts of sentences.

Shakespeare's Life

Baldwin, T. W. *William Shakspere's Petty School.* Urbana: University of Illinois Press, 1943.
Baldwin here investigates the theory and practice of

the petty school, the first level of education in Elizabethan England. He focuses on that educational system primarily as it is reflected in Shakespeare's art.

Baldwin, T. W. *William Shakspere's Small Latine and Lesse Greeke.* 2 vols. Urbana: University of Illinois Press, 1944.

Baldwin attacks the view that Shakespeare was an uneducated genius—a view that had been dominant among Shakespeareans since the eighteenth century. Instead, Baldwin shows, the educational system of Shakespeare's time would have given the playwright a strong background in the classics, and there is much in the plays that shows how Shakespeare benefited from such an education.

Beier, A. L., and Roger Finlay, eds. *London 1500–1700: The Making of the Metropolis.* New York: Longman, 1986.

Focusing on the economic and social history of early modern London, these collected essays probe aspects of metropolitan life, including "Population and Disease," "Commerce and Manufacture," and "Society and Change."

Bentley, G. E. *Shakespeare's Life: A Biographical Handbook.* New Haven: Yale University Press, 1961.

This "just-the-facts" account presents the surviving documents of Shakespeare's life against an Elizabethan background.

Chambers, E. K. *William Shakespeare: A Study of Facts and Problems.* 2 vols. Oxford: Clarendon Press, 1930.

Analyzing in great detail the scant historical data, Chambers's complex, scholarly study considers the nature of the texts in which Shakespeare's work is preserved.

Cressy, David. *Education in Tudor and Stuart England.* London: Edward Arnold, 1975.

This volume collects sixteenth-, seventeenth-, and early-eighteenth-century documents detailing aspects of formal education in England, such as the curriculum, the control and organization of education, and the education of women.

Dutton, Richard. *William Shakespeare: A Literary Life.* New York: St. Martin's Press, 1989.

Not a biography in the traditional sense, Dutton's very readable work nevertheless "follows the contours of Shakespeare's life" as he examines Shakespeare's career as playwright and poet, with consideration of his patrons, theatrical associations, and audience.

Fraser, Russell. *Young Shakespeare.* New York: Columbia University Press, 1988.

Fraser focuses on Shakespeare's first thirty years, paying attention simultaneously to his life and art.

De Grazia, Margreta. *Shakespeare Verbatim: The Reproduction of Authenticity and the Apparatus of 1790.* Oxford: Clarendon Press, 1991.

De Grazia traces and discusses the development of such editorial criteria as authenticity, historical periodization, factual biography, chronological developments, and close reading, locating as the point of origin Edmond Malone's 1790 edition of Shakespeare's works. There are interesting chapters on the First Folio and on the "legendary" versus the "documented" Shakespeare.

Schoenbaum, S. *William Shakespeare: A Compact Documentary Life.* New York: Oxford University Press, 1977.

This standard biography economically presents the essential documents from Shakespeare's time in an accessible narrative account of the playwright's life.

Shakespeare's Theater

Bentley, G. E. *The Profession of Player in Shakespeare's Time, 1590–1642.* Princeton: Princeton University Press, 1984.

Bentley readably sets forth a wealth of evidence about performance in Shakespeare's time, with special attention to the relations between player and company, and the business of casting, managing, and touring.

Berry, Herbert. *Shakespeare's Playhouses.* New York: AMS Press, 1987.

Berry's six essays collected here discuss (with illustrations) varying aspects of the four playhouses in which Shakespeare had a financial stake: the Theatre in Shoreditch, the Blackfriars, and the first and second Globe.

Cook, Ann Jennalie. *The Privileged Playgoers of Shakespeare's London.* Princeton: Princeton University Press, 1981.

Cook's work argues, on the basis of sociological, economic, and documentary evidence, that Shakespeare's audience—and the audience for English Renaissance drama generally—consisted mainly of the "privileged."

Greg, W. W. *Dramatic Documents from the Elizabethan Playhouses.* 2 vols. Oxford: Clarendon Press, 1931.

Greg itemizes and briefly describes almost all the play manuscripts that survive from the period 1590 to around 1660, including, among other things, players' parts. His second volume offers facsimiles of selected manuscripts.

Gurr, Andrew. *Playgoing in Shakespeare's London.* Cambridge: Cambridge University Press, 1987.

Gurr charts how the theatrical enterprise developed from its modest beginnings in the late 1560s to become a thriving institution in the 1600s. He argues that there were important changes over the period 1567–1644 in the playhouses, the audience, and the plays.

Harbage, Alfred. *Shakespeare's Audience.* New York: Columbia University Press, 1941.
Harbage investigates the fragmentary surviving evidence to interpret the size, composition, and behavior of Shakespeare's audience.

Hattaway, Michael. *Elizabethan Popular Theatre: Plays in Performance.* London: Routledge & Kegan Paul, 1982.
Beginning with a study of the popular drama of the late Elizabethan age—a description of the stages, performance conditions, and acting of the period—this volume concludes with an analysis of five well-known plays of the 1590s, one of them (*Titus Andronicus*) by Shakespeare.

Shapiro, Michael. *Children of the Revels: The Boy Companies of Shakespeare's Time and Their Plays.* New York: Columbia University Press, 1977.
Shapiro chronicles the history of the amateur and quasi-professional child companies that flourished in London at the end of Elizabeth's reign and the beginning of James's.

The Publication of Shakespeare's Plays

Blayney, Peter. *The First Folio of Shakespeare.* Hanover, Md.: Folger, 1991.
Blayney's accessible account of the printing and later life of the First Folio—an amply illustrated catalogue to

a 1991 Folger Shakespeare Library exhibition—analyzes the mechanical production of the First Folio, describing how the Folio was made, by whom and for whom, how much it cost, and its ups and downs (or, rather, downs and ups) since its printing in 1623.

Hinman, Charlton. *The Printing and Proof-Reading of the First Folio of Shakespeare.* 2 vols. Oxford: Clarendon Press, 1963.
In the most arduous study of a single book ever undertaken, Hinman attempts to reconstruct how the Shakespeare First Folio of 1623 was set into type and run off the press, sheet by sheet. He also provides almost all the known variations in readings from copy to copy.

Hinman, Charlton. *The Norton Facsimile: The First Folio of Shakespeare.* New York: W. W. Norton, 1968.
This facsimile presents a photographic reproduction of an "ideal" copy of the First Folio of Shakespeare; Hinman attempts to represent each page in its most fully corrected state.

Key to
Famous Lines and Phrases

A fellow almost damned in a fair wife   [Iago—1.1.22]

. . . I will wear my heart upon my sleeve
                                [Iago—1.1.70]

. . . one of those that will not serve God if the devil
    bid you.   [Iago—1.1.122-23]

She swore . . . 'twas strange, 'twas passing strange
                            [Othello—1.3.184-85]

. . . as tenderly be led by th' nose
As asses are.   [Iago—1.3.444-45]

. . . I am nothing if not critical.   [Iago—2.1.134]

To suckle fools and chronicle small beer.
                                [Iago—2.1.175]

When devils will the blackest sins put on,
They do suggest at first with heavenly shows
                            [Iago—2.3.371-72]

Good name in man and woman, dear my lord,
Is the immediate jewel of their souls.
                            [Iago—3.3.182-83]

O, beware, my lord, of jealousy!
It is the green-eyed monster . . .   [Iago—3.3.195-96]

Trifles light as air
Are to the jealous confirmations strong
As proofs of holy writ.   [Iago—3.3.370–72]

Not poppy nor mandragora
Nor all the drowsy syrups of the world
Shall ever medicine thee to that sweet sleep
Which thou owedst yesterday.   [Iago—3.3.379–82]

O, now, forever
Farewell the tranquil mind . . .
Othello's occupation's gone!   [Othello—3.3.399–409]

Heaven truly knows that thou art false as hell.
                                [Othello—4.2.48]

It is the cause, it is the cause, my soul.
                                [Othello—5.2.1]

She was false as water.   [Othello—5.2.164]

As ignorant as dirt!   [Emilia—5.2.200]

Here is my journey's end, here is my butt
And very sea-mark of my utmost sail.
                                [Othello—5.2.318–19]

. . . one that loved not wisely, but too well
                                [Othello—5.2.404]